Love Walks on Wounded Feet

Love Walks on Wounded Feet

More Sermons for the Lectionary, Year A,
Advent through Eastertide

Bruce L. Taylor

WIPF & STOCK · Eugene, Oregon

LOVE WALKS ON WOUNDED FEET
More Sermons for the Lectionary, Year A, Advent through Eastertide

Copyright © 2022 Bruce L. Taylor. All rights reserved. Except for brief quotations in critical publications or reviews, no part of this book may be reproduced in any manner without prior written permission from the publisher. Write: Permissions, Wipf and Stock Publishers, 199 W. 8th Ave., Suite 3, Eugene, OR 97401.

Wipf & Stock
An Imprint of Wipf and Stock Publishers
199 W. 8th Ave., Suite 3
Eugene, OR 97401

www.wipfandstock.com

PAPERBACK ISBN: 978-1-6667-3728-8
HARDCOVER ISBN: 978-1-6667-9651-3
EBOOK ISBN: 978-1-6667-9655-1

Unless otherwise noted, scripture quotations are from Common Bible: New Revised Standard Version Bible, copyright © 1989 National Council of the Churches of Christ in the United States of America. Used by permission. All rights reserved worldwide. Emphasis added.

Scripture quotations marked (RSV) are from Revised Standard Version of the Bible, copyright © 1946, 1952, and 1971 National Council of the Churches of Christ in the United States of America. Used by permission. All rights reserved. Emphasis added.

Scripture quotations marked (NIV) are from THE HOLY BIBLE, NEW INTERNATIONAL VERSION®, NIV® Copyright © 1973, 1978, 1984, 2011 by Biblica, Inc.® Used by permission. All rights reserved worldwide. Emphasis added.

In memory of Roger and Grace Davis

Table of Contents

Introduction | xi

First Sunday of Advent—"Empire of Peace" | 1
Isaiah 2:1–5; Romans 13:11–14; Matthew 24:36–44

Second Sunday of Advent—"Broaden Your Hope" | 7
Isaiah 11:1–10; Romans 15:4–13; Matthew 3:1–12

Third Sunday of Advent—"What We Hear and See" | 12
Isaiah 35:1–10; James 5:7–10; Matthew 11:2–11

Fourth Sunday of Advent—"A Promise Kept" | 17
Isaiah 7:10–16; Romans 1:1–7; Matthew 1:18–25

Christmas Eve (Early Evening)—"A Lamb's Tale" | 22
Isaiah 9:2–7; Titus 2:11–14; Luke 2:1–20

Christmas Eve—"Insiders Now" | 28
Isaiah 9:2–7; Titus 2:11–14; Luke 2:1–20

Nativity of Jesus Christ / Christmas Day—
    "A Christmas Carol—Epilogue" | 33
Isaiah 57:7–10; Hebrews 1:1–4; John 1:1–14

First Sunday after Christmas—"Not Ashamed of Us" | 39
Isaiah 63:7–9; Hebrews 2:10–18; Matthew 2:13–23

Second Sunday after Christmas—"The Big Deal about Jesus" | 44
Jeremiah 31:7–14; Ephesians 1:3–18; John 1:1–18

Epiphany of the Lord—"We, Too, Are God's Mighty Act" | 50
Isaiah 60:1–6; Ephesians 3:1–12; Matthew 2:1–12

Baptism of the Lord—"Power to Be Meek" | 56
Isaiah 42:1–9; Acts 10:34–43; Matthew 3:13–17

Second Sunday in Ordinary Time—"God's Promotion Policy" | 62
Isaiah 49:1–7; 1 Corinthians 1:1–9; John 1:29–42

Third Sunday in Ordinary Time—"Won to Be One" | 67
Isaiah 9:1–4; 1 Corinthians 1:10–18; Matthew 4:12–23

Fourth Sunday in Ordinary Time—"Blessed Are You" | 73
Micah 6:1–8; 1 Corinthians 1:18–31; Matthew 5:1–12

Fifth Sunday in Ordinary Time—"Uncovering the Light" | 78
Isaiah 58:3–9a; 1 Corinthians 2:1–11; Matthew 5:13–16

Sixth Sunday in Ordinary Time—"First Be Reconciled" | 85
Deuteronomy 30:15–20; 1 Corinthians 3:1–9; Matthew 5:17–26

Seventh Sunday in Ordinary Time—"To Pluck Out an Eye, to Cut Off a Hand" | 91
Isaiah 49:8–13; 1 Corinthians 3:10–11, 16–23; Matthew 5:27–37

Transfiguration of the Lord—"The Meaning of Messiah" | 97
Exodus 24:12–18; 2 Peter 1:16–21; Matthew 17:1–9

Ash Wednesday—"A Proper Lent" | 102
Isaiah 58:1–12; 2 Corinthians 5:20b—6:10; Matthew 6:1–6, 16–21

First Sunday in Lent—"Who Do You Trust?" | 108
Genesis 2:4b–9, 15–17, 25—3:7; Romans 5:12–19; Matthew 4:1–11

Second Sunday in Lent—"Called to Be a Blessing" | 114
Genesis 12:1–4a; Romans 4:1–5, 13–17; John 3:1–17

Third Sunday in Lent—"Life in the Wilderness" | 119
Exodus 17:1–7; Romans 5:1–11; John 4:5–42

Fourth Sunday in Lent—"Sight Restored" | 124
1 Samuel 16:1–13; Ephesians 5:8–14; John 9:1–41

Fifth Sunday in Lent—"To Live Again" | 129
Ezekiel 37:1–14; Romans 8:6–11; John 11:1–45

Palm/Passion Sunday—"What Shall We Do with Jesus?" | 135
Isaiah 50:4–9a; Philippians 2:5–11; Matthew 21:1–11

Maundy Thursday—"Testimonial Dinner" | 141
Exodus 12:1–4, 11–14; 1 Corinthians 11:23–26; John 13:1–17, 31b–35

Good Friday—"A Reading for Three Voices" | 146
Isaiah 52:13—53:12; Hebrews 4:14–16; 5:7–10; John 18:1—19:42

The Resurrection of the Lord—"Already Raised" | 153
Acts 10:34–43; Colossians 3:1–4; Matthew 28:1–10

Second Sunday of Easter—"The Rest of the Story" | 158
Acts 2:14a, 22-32; 1 Peter 1:3-9; John 20:19-31

Third Sunday of Easter—"Love Walks on Wounded Feet" | 163
Acts 2:14a, 36-41; 1 Peter 1:17-23; Luke 24:13-35

Fourth Sunday of Easter—"The Open Door" | 168
Acts 2:42-47; 1 Peter 2:19-25; John 10:1-10

Fifth Sunday of Easter—"The Way of Forgiveness" | 174
Acts 7:55-60; 1 Peter 2:2-10; John 14:1-14

Sixth Sunday of Easter—". . . Who Made the World and Everything in It" | 179
Acts 17:22-31; 1 Peter 3:13-22; John 14:15-21

Ascension of the Lord—"Powerful Witnesses" | 184
Acts 1:1-11; Ephesians 1:15-23; Luke 24:44-53

Seventh Sunday of Easter—"Nobody Said It Was Going to Be Easy" | 189
Acts 1:6-14; 1 Peter 4:12-14; 5:6-11; John 17:1-11

Appendix—"Bearing the Fruit of the Spirit" | 195
Psalm 133; Galatians 5:13-26; Matthew 18:1-7

List of Sources Cited | 201

Introduction

THE FIRST PRESBYTERIAN CHURCH of Dodge City, Kansas, is located on the corner of Vine Street and Central Avenue, along the main route from downtown toward the northern part of the city. Perched on the lawn above a limestone retaining wall at the street corner is an outdoor sign with moveable letters, as many churches have, providing the name of the church and Sunday worship times, and on which it was customary in the 1990s to announce the title of the Sunday sermon. I had never before been pastor of a church that publicly advertised the sermon title, and never really considered that doing so might attract someone to cross the threshold on Sunday morning, but I changed my mind when the young curate of the Roman Catholic church a block north of us mentioned to me on some occasion that he found my sermon titles intriguing. I suspect that, had Jonathan Edwards announced his sermon titles in advance, no one would ever have actually heard "Sinners in the Hands of an Angry God."

Preachers in many denominational traditions, including Roman Catholic, do not typically title their sermons or homilies, of course. I early adopted the practice of jotting down possible sermon titles while reading over the lectionary scripture passages and exegeting them and studying commentaries, and always tried to choose one early in my sermon preparation, mainly as a means of providing a focus for my hermeneutical approach and homiletical intent. Early in my ministry, finding it to be (for me) an artificial technique of adhering to a sermonic theme, I abandoned the ideal of outlining my sermons in favor of using the title—the less prosaic, the better—as my homiletical guiding star while allowing the scripture itself to provide the principal frame of reference and remembering always to honor the context of the passages in question. Admirable and Spirit-led as the work of the Consultation on Common Texts has been, any attempt to delineate the beginning and conclusion of scriptural excerpts either for public worship or private meditation is an exercise that the original writers of the Bible could not have contemplated and for which they did not knowingly prepare. While the homiletical task, at least in the expository style, will involve preaching on specific texts, I have found it appropriate always to regard the anticipated sermon as being an intentional link between what is precedent and what is subsequent in the uninterrupted scriptural record.

This volume resumes my offering of sermons based on the Common Lectionary (Revised) as an encouragement to homilists to consider adopting the discipline and thus enable their congregations to join the many millions of Christians around the world listening to the same readings on any given Sunday and to pray through the week with those scripture passages in mind, and to observe the great feast days of the church calendar with corporate worship, including a sermon based on the readings appointed for the occasion. I suspect that preachers who regularly use the lectionary will find, as I have discovered, that the Holy Spirit faithfully provides insight that discloses one or more of the lections to be fully relevant to issues of global, national, local, and congregational concern, as well as promoting the sacramental richness of both individual faith expression and life together in Christ's church. Beginning with the first Sunday in Advent for Year A, featuring Gospel readings from Matthew, *Love Walks on Wounded Feet* is intended to invite the lay reader as well as clergy to embark upon a three-year adventure in discovering biblical treasures and suggestive dimensions of faithful obedience to the Word made flesh, Jesus the Christ.

My Roman Catholic friend's comment about the sign at Central Avenue and Vine Street came shortly after I preached the sermon from which this volume takes its title. When I entered seminary, in the late 1970s, many clergy and laity alike were being influenced by Henri Nouwen's ironically-titled book *The Wounded Healer*. Pastoral experience and theological reflection have verified, for me, the book's premise that, as our salvation to wholeness is made possible through Christ's suffering on the cross—and, even more generally, his life of Isaiah-like rejection and slanderous abuse—so the wounds that we suffer as servants of God and more generally as a result of the human condition make us better prepared to minister to others. Indeed, it may be impossible to serve others in genuine love except from out of our shared need. God has witnessed human pain and now knows it first-hand through the sufferings of Christ

Jesus his Son; this is one of the meanings of the incarnation, a voluntary taking on of human vulnerability by the compassionate divinity. The love of Christ is characterized by deep empathy through which Jesus was willing to be broken that we might be made whole. To be a follower of Christ is to love with a profound empathy that leads to self-giving and even sacrificial action on behalf of others, as we learn, through Christ's own example, to value others more than we value ourselves. As hymnwriter Mary Chiusano has expressed in a recently-published text addressed to Christ:

> Your bleeding wounds remind us
> that we are wounded, too.
> Your boundless love has taught us
> that we must love as you.[1]

Truly, *agape* walks on wounded feet. It is genuine only if it is compassionate, and the compassion is born of one's own experiences of pain and injury that prompt action that participates in the redemptive work of God's crucified and risen and living Christ. We, the church, are, after all, Christ's hands and feet in the world, and the hands and feet that Christ exhibited to his disciples bore the scars of the cross.

We all, unavoidably and inevitably, have experiences that, as a by-product, prepare us to love with the same love as Christ loves. God does not will the suffering of anyone. It is simply a part of life in which we are loved deeply and specially by God but are not the axis. By God's grace and by the work of the Holy Spirit, our wounds can equip us to minister with wisdom and compassion, as the principal character in the story sermon "To Live Again" herein discovered and as the apostle Paul long ago attested. Perhaps some passerby at the corner of Central Avenue and Vine Street was prompted by the inspiration of the Holy Spirit to ponder a sermon title posted one day outside the "Plains Gothic" church building standing there to consider that we do not live for ourselves, and that even our hurts and disappointments may become a balm for others through the miracle of God's grace.

---

1. "The Way of Sorrow," © 2020, Mary Chiusano, published by OCP, all rights reserved. Used with permission.

First Sunday of Advent
Spanish Springs Presbyterian Church, Sparks, Nevada
December 2, 2001
ISAIAH 2:1–5
ROMANS 13:11–14
MATTHEW 24:36–44

"Empire of Peace"

CLOSE YOUR EYES FOR a moment. Picture in your imagination the scene in today's Old Testament reading. Holy Zion, the mountain of God's own temple, is being lifted up and held in regard above all other mountains, all other high points, all the places where people worship false gods of every name and every description. And long lines of people from all over the earth are flowing to it like rivers meeting in a sea. And they're saying to each other as they walk along, "Let's go to God's sanctuary, where we can learn about how God wants people to live and relate to each other and what God wants people to think about and value and why God's ways are better than the ways of pride and selfishness and greed and fear." And people are bringing their disputes and arguments, even great disagreements between nations, and submitting them to judgment according to the will and purpose of God. And having learned about God's purpose, having laid all the feuds ancient and modern at God's feet so that God's purpose of justice and equity, wholeness and salvation shall prevail, all these people now take whatever weapons they have and refashion them into tools that will help feed people. And, as there are no longer any weapons, so there are no battle plans, and so there are no casualties, and so there are no sorrows, and so there are no tears. Imagine.

You can open your eyes now. How difficult an exercise was that for you? Was it hard, because you have never known a world in which those things happened? Was it objectionable, because it sounded like the idealistic drone of what some people have labeled "peaceniks"? Was it simply unthinkable, because we live in a world where nations have to step on each other to survive, where conflict and contest are as inevitable as death, where everybody knows that you can't trust the other guy, and so you have to be armed to the teeth? Why is it, in a time when some people insist that every word in the Bible be taken literally, to defend the supreme truth of *God*, that we hear so little about the strong biblical testimony that people who have learned the Lord's desires and practice the Lord's ways are people who refuse to lift up swords, one nation against another, and who instead dedicate the resources *once* used for warfare to meeting human needs, such as hunger? Is it just wishful thinking, simply a dream, not very realistic and perhaps not even very responsible? Or is it the will of God by whose instruction the *people* of God, including you and I, have pledged to live?

Sometimes we hear people say that wars will end when God wants them to end—that peace will come in God's time. By that, perhaps, they mean that wars will end when our enemies decide not to be enemies anymore, when those whom we *fear* lay down *their* weapons, when everybody *else* finally agrees with *us* and adopts *our* type of economy, *our* way of government, *our* cultural model, or when everybody else agrees with *our* personal opinions, and stops doing things that hurt or annoy us. Peace will come, in other words, only when God waves a sort of magic wand and makes differences disappear, or, rather, causes everyone else to conform to our ideas. No one has ever yet seen that magic wand being waved, and, so, conflict continues, *must* continue, because God hasn't yet done anything to stop it—conflict between nations, conflict between religions, conflict between classes, conflict between individuals. And some perhaps think that it is even unseemly, unpatriotic, to talk about the subject while we have armed forces engaged in a military campaign overseas and we are still salving the deep wounds of vicious attacks upon our nation and grieving the loss of our countrymen and women to despicable atrocities. But the purpose of God surely remains the same in every season. The teachings of God are equally relevant in every circumstance. The will of God for peace would scarcely need *mentioning* if *all* peoples and nations were in *agreement.*

In the time of Jesus, there was peace, in the sense of orderliness and a lack of armed conflict within the Roman Empire. It was the era of the *Pax Romana,* the "Roman Peace." As some of you know, I was a Latin major in college. All through junior and senior high school, I took

Latin. I was the president of my high school Latin club, and president of the Colorado state Greek and Latin students' organization, and then president of the national Greek and Latin students' organization—one hundred thousand high school kids from nearly every state in the country and beyond, thirteen hundred of them at the national convention the year that I presided at Tulane University. We had Roman banquets. We celebrated the Roman civilization. We lionized Roman values. And we glorified the great Pax Romana, the visionary goal and outstanding achievement of Caesar Augustus. As Roman armies had conquered territory, wars had subsided. As the emperor's decrees were obeyed, civil disturbances ceased. The Romans thought they were bestowing a great gift upon the world—the benefits of their legal system, the benefits of their arts, the benefits of their way of governing. Who wouldn't want to be a Roman? Even the apostle Paul was proud of his Roman citizenship. And as the empire spread, people in faraway corners of the known world came to be included, whether they wanted to be or not.

Not a day goes by that I do not draw on my Latin background—both the language itself and its literature and ideas, and the experience of leading and planning and public speaking and everything else that was invoked in my participation in the Junior Classical League. I think that school districts that have dropped Latin from the curriculum have done students and society a tremendous disservice. But, upon more mature reflection, I think that my youthful zeal for ancient Roman *culture* should have been tempered with some critical analysis of its assumptions and its methods—the very assumptions and methods that, after all, put Jesus on the cross. Maybe I was misled by all of those nuns in togas.

"The Roman Peace," you see, was not really peace. It might have been an absence of war, it might have been an orderliness of government administration and an efficient method of distributing goods and carrying on commerce. It might have been a time of unprecedented wealth and luxury for some, and at least sufficiency for many. But it was not peace. Whatever lack of *conflict* there was, it was because of fear of the Roman *army*. Whatever *orderliness* there was, was *imposed*, without consultation or compromise. Whatever *prosperity* there was, it was created on the backs of slaves and the working poor. So, people in places like Palestine, oppressed by unfair taxes, despised by their governors, their customs and language and religion ridiculed by their Roman overlords who chauvinistically asserted *their* superiority in everything, yearned for peace, longed for a great national hero to create peace by vanquishing the Romans, by destroying them with the sword, or if not destroying them, at least forcing them out of their land. A great messiah to do it all *for* them—that was their dream. A leader designated and empowered by God to snap his fingers and make everything right—that was their expectation. And whenever some self-appointed hero appeared on their horizon, roused them with nationalistic speeches and asserted his bravado, they hailed him as their savior, their peacemaker. And they looked for signs that the end of their suffering was near, and they listened to false promises and nursed vain assurances until, at last, they rebelled, these beneficiaries of the Roman Peace, and the Roman army destroyed Jerusalem and demolished the house of God as easily as a person can crush an ant under his or her heel. And there was peace—only in the sense that there was no warfare.

Of course, peace will come in *God's* time. But the Bible is not a book about magic. It is a book about the purpose of God, and God's stubborn progress toward that purpose within, and in spite of, human history. The Bible does not approve our being passive in the face of God's purpose. Our hope in God is not wishful thinking. It is faith that God's goodness will inevitably prevail over everything that *opposes* God's goodness, and faith calls us to action and prompts behavior. But God gives us no authority to impose Christian imperialism, no matter how good we think it would be for nonbelievers. The *Crusaders* decimated *Muslim* Jerusalem quite as thoroughly as the *Romans* decimated *Jewish* Jerusalem. Their methods were no different, but created the same sort of suffering. And what *Christian* purpose could *possibly* have been served by the Spanish conquistadors who first forcibly baptized and then immediately beheaded the Pueblo Indians when they encountered them as they marched through New Mexico searching for gold?

Isaiah tells not about a wish or a dream. Isaiah tells about an event that is going to happen in the days ahead within history at a specific place. Isaiah speaks of God's will coming about not through the establishment of an empire of soldiers and prisons and treaties and alliances, but an empire of peace. Isaiah tells of a day when humankind shall live together and walk together in love and righteousness and mutuality. *Within* history, not at its *end*, but as its *climax*, the earth will be transformed, and all people will acknowledge the *source* of genuine wisdom and authentic teaching. Every dispute and every disagreement will be settled according to the teachings of God as people seek together God's will for humankind. Fear will be at an end, because the falsehood of the powers that threaten us and make us afraid in the world will be uncovered by the light of God, and so they will be powerless. Nations will be united not by treaties forged in common fear or common lust, but will be united by the bonds of a common faith and a common commitment. People will be reconciled not by judgments and fines and penalties, but by mutual respect and self-giving and forgiveness. It will be a day of peace—not just absence of war, but a correction of the conditions that make for poverty, an exposing of the attitudes that lead to injustice, a rejection of the ways that inflict oppression. And the One who *alone* is deserving of worship shall be worshiped by *all*, and rightly—not false gods of wood or stone and not false gods of money or technology; and the One who alone is wise to teach us shall be heeded by all, and rightly—not the false truisms of this ideology and that and not the false truisms of marketplace and pundits; and the One who alone offers salvation shall be the sole source and object of our faith, and rightly, so that, in reliance upon *that One, we* practice the forgiveness and self-giving and compassion and generosity and acceptance that alone will result in the empire of peace for which the world has yearned for thousands of years—the peace of God. The motive of human behavior will no longer be mutual suspicion and distrust, desire for advantage or revenge, but God's loving purpose. And every problem between people will be addressed in light of God's purpose for all humankind. There will be peace on earth *because* there is good will among men and women—the good will that can *only* come by subjecting all of our *individual* wants and desires to the will of *God* for *all* creation.

The old order, the night, is going to pass away. Don't be anxious. You and I, as people of God, redeemed by Christ, don't belong to the old order, to the night. We belong to the *new* order, to the day that Isaiah foresaw and Jesus promised and which is breaking upon the world even now. That means that we need not, must not, wait for all people everywhere to live in accordance with God's will before *we* start to live in accordance with God's will. An empire of peace is surely coming—the kingdom of God on earth, which Christ announced and of which Christ will be the ruler and judge. It is coming not by magic, not by wishing, not by dreaming, but by God's will being worked out within history, and that means through the *people* of God living as citizens of God's kingdom *today*. We cannot *force* its coming. It is not up to *us* to *create* the empire of peace—peace, after all, that is *God's gift*, not *our achievement*. But it *is* up to us to live and work and pray *now* as people who *already* acknowledge God's will, who *already* submit to God's wisdom, who *already* witness to God's purpose, and who *already* trust God's promises and expect them to be fulfilled at any moment. We must be ready for the coming of the Son of Man and the arrival of the kingdom of God and this empire of peace. That means *not* waiting for the *other* guy to ask our forgiveness. That means *not* waiting for those *other* nations to change *their* ways. That means *you* and *I* taking *now* the first steps on the path that *all* peoples and *all* nations will one day tread.

The word of the Lord came to Isaiah:

> In days to come
> > the mountain of the Lord's house
> shall be established as the highest of the mountains,
> > and shall be raised above the hills;
> all the nations shall stream to it. . . .
> For out of Zion shall go forth instruction,
> > and the word of the Lord from Jerusalem.
> He shall judge between the nations,
> > and shall arbitrate for many peoples;
> they shall beat their swords into plowshares,
> > and their spears into pruning hooks;
> nation shall not lift up sword against nation,
> > neither shall they learn war any more.
> O house of Jacob,
> > come, let us walk
> > in the light of the Lord! (Isa 2:1–5)

That means *us*. And that means *today*.

Second Sunday of Advent
Spanish Springs Presbyterian Church, Sparks, Nevada
December 6, 1998
ISAIAH 11:1–10
ROMANS 15:4–13
MATTHEW 3:1–12

"Broaden Your Hope"

I WAS BORN RIGHT in the middle of the twentieth century. Like others in the baby boom generation, I experienced the tremendous post-World War II period of affluence in America, lived the transition from one-car garages to two-car garages, witnessed the birth and the growth of the "pop culture," watched the horrors of a controversial war on television just before or after dinner every night until I became almost numb to the obscenity of weekly body counts, read of people being taunted with words and beaten with sticks because they happened to be born with a certain skin color, discovered from the headlines that there are as many *s*'s in the word "assassination" as there are in the word "Mississippi," wondered *when*, not *if, my* city would go up in flames.

The sixties was the decade when I learned, like millions of others, that the world is not yet the happily-ever-after of fairy tales and certainly is not yet the peaceable kingdom prophesied in the Bible. From astronauts walking on the moon to four college students shot dead by national guardsmen on their university campus, it seemed like life was all mountains or valleys without much level ground in between. I became aware of poverty, and my own privileges; became alert to injustice, and my own prejudices; became sensitive to unfairness, and my own sin. I was far from radical as a teenager—one of the most conservative kids you can imagine in matters of dress and recreation, and yet singing along with Peter, Paul and Mary records pricked my conscience about war, serving on the executive board of a statewide student organization alongside an African American pricked my conscience about race, and the accusing response of a girl from a low-income family in my high school class whom I asked out for a date pricked my conscience about poverty. And as I began to read the Bible more carefully in confirmation class and youth group, and to pay closer attention to the themes of scripture that I was singing in choir, and to listen more keenly to the words of Jesus as our minister quoted them in worship, I came to have an enlarged understanding of God's will of salvation for the whole world that God created.

I was fortunate, growing up, to have ministers who did not neglect the Old Testament prophets in their preaching, and who recognized that prophecy is not so much a matter of predicting some event way off in the future as it is a matter of proclaiming the timeless truth of God in *today's* situation. The difference can perhaps be shown best in the force of the verbs the prophet used—it isn't simply that the wolf *will* live with the lamb sometime in the *future*, and the leopard will lie down with the kid and the calf and the lion and the fatling together in the days to *come*. "The wolf *shall* live with the lamb, the leopard *shall* lie down with the kid, the calf and the lion and the fatling together" (Isa 11:6a–c). It is the will of God *now*. It *must* be accomplished. It is what is *right*. It is what is *good*.

Prophecy is a matter of focusing the light of the kingdom of heaven upon the nations of the world. Prophecy is a matter of exposing the falsehood of human fantasies to the judgment of God's reality. Prophecy is a matter of stripping away our personal and social illusions and sizing us up, ourselves and our concoctions, against the standard of divine truth. *That* is what *prophecy* is. Prophecy searches every corner of the human heart and bares the condition of the human soul and exposes the rationalizations of the human mind, and so it is deeply personal. Prophecy measures the distance between the world as it *is* and the world as God *intended* it to be and condemns the gap between the haves and the have-nots and calls "injustice" whatever protects the interests of the powerful and the privileged, and so it is profoundly social. And a large proportion of the Bible is prophecy.

But in today's political and economic and social atmosphere, we are not hearing much about the biblical prophets, even in Christian circles. It isn't popular to quote the verses that speak God's judgment upon Israel, its government and its religious leaders, for neglecting the poor or turning away the stranger or trusting in riches and armaments rather than in truth and righteousness. And it's a paradox; after all, it's the peace-and-love-and-justice generation that's at the controls of politics and business today. And ministers are being advised that, if they want their churches to grow, they need to stay away from controversial subjects, not be too concerned with social ministries, fit the church's message to the postmodern outlook, just talk about what Jesus Christ can do for *you*. The generation that marched for equality and denounced poverty was also the "me generation," and many of the same people who left the church in the sixties and seventies because they thought it was *socially irrelevant* are being attracted now by religious messages, Christian, non-Christian, and anti-Christian, that are all highly individualistic, not taking much interest *in* or responsibility *for* anyone else.

Back in *ancient times*, prophets were not popular people—not because they were predicting blessings and woes way off in the *future*, but because they were declaring that God wanted changes that very *moment*. They were ridiculed and condemned. Back in the *sixties*, prophets were not popular people—not because we didn't have a sneaking suspicion that they might be right, but because they challenged the existing power structures, seemed to threaten the stability of society and the people who benefited from it, which was most of us, one way or another. *Today*, prophets . . . do we even have any left? Everybody's horizon of interest seems narrower these days. The more interdependent the world becomes—global economy, world wide web, international banking and the rest—the more we are tempted to retreat into our own closet of self-concern. It is certainly reflected in politics, not only in America but in all of the Western world. And I have to say that I see it reflected more and more in the church.

It was not long after the crucifixion and resurrection of Jesus that Christianity found its way to the heart of the Empire—Rome, the capital of the Caesars, whose soldiers mocked Christ's kingship by pressing a crown of thorns on his forehead, hoisted Jesus up on a cross, pierced the side of God's own Son with a sword. Every human instinct must have tempted the apostles to retrench, to shut themselves off from the world, to preserve their precious faith in a close cocoon of private interest and personal salvation. Some of them argued for taking just such a course. Surely, they thought, they owed nothing to people who might ridicule them, might arrest them, might even execute them. Why not just live quietly within the security of the family circle, trusting that God would put bread on their own table and that Jesus would take them into his arms at death? Others wanted to confine the message to the Jewish people, whose own scriptures Jesus had fulfilled. Why share their faith with people who didn't know or care about the law of Moses, who built temples to pagan gods that acted out the same passions and pursued the same vices as the most notorious sinner?

But others realized that to keep the good news a private affair, an individualistic gospel of salvation for a select few, would be denying their responsibility to care for God's creation, would be disobeying Christ's command. One apostle in particular—Paul—felt keenly the responsibility to carry the message of hope not only beyond home and family but even beyond the Jews to the Gentiles. "May the God of steadfastness and encouragement grant you to live in harmony with one another," he wrote to a congregation of new Christians in Rome, a congregation that had in it people of both Jewish and Gentile background, "in accordance with Christ Jesus, so that *together* you may *with one voice* glorify the God and Father of our Lord Jesus Christ. *Welcome* one another, therefore, just as *Christ* has welcomed *you*, for the glory of God. For I tell you that Christ has become a servant of the circumcised"—that is, the Jews—"on behalf of the truth of God in order that he might confirm the promises given to the patriarchs"—that is, to Abraham and Isaac and Jacob—"*and in order that the Gentiles might glorify God for his mercy*" (Rom 15:4–9a). No one should be excluded from the good news. No promise of God should be withheld from anyone. "The root of Jesse shall come, the one who rises to rule the Gentiles; in him the Gentiles shall hope," Paul reminded his readers, both the children of Abraham and the children of idol-worshipers. "May the God of hope fill you with all joy and peace in believing, so that you may abound in hope by the power of the Holy Spirit" (15:12–13).

In Jesus Christ, God did not work a miracle of salvation just for a select few. In Jesus Christ, God did not offer himself on a cross so that the intelligent might pass tomorrow's exam or so that the privileged might have yet another vehicle in the driveway or so that the wealthy might quadruple the profit from their stock holdings or so that the powerful might eliminate their competition by bankruptcy or by merger. In Jesus Christ, God did not seat the risen Lord of creation at his right hand to judge between retirement investments or teams on a football field or soft drinks in a national taste-test.

But see how narrow our hopes become when the *testimony* of the *prophets* is forgotten or ignored—how individualistic our understanding of good news, how self-absorbed our prayers, how private our faith. And if we hope for too *little*, we are likely to miss the urgent summons to repent, and to give witness with our lives that the kingdom of heaven has come near. Without the testimony of the prophets, we haven't a clue what it means to prepare the way of the Lord, to make straight the paths of the one who is coming again to judge not by appearances, not by popular wisdom or rumored truths, but with *righteousness* he shall judge the poor, and decide with equity for the *meek* of the earth, who decrees that the cow and the bear shall graze, their young shall lie down together, and the lion shall eat straw like the ox.

Jesus Christ is coming to fulfill God's promise of peace and justice and plenty and joy. And it is the responsibility of everyone who believes that Jesus Christ is the fulfillment of the prophecies to give *witness* to that promise: to prepare the *way* of our Lord by repenting of *anything* that obstructs the kingdom of heaven, and by living out and giving testimony *now* in our words and our deeds to the truth of God's promise of peace and justice and plenty and joy, in our home, in the marketplace, at school, in the voting booth, in the soup kitchen, in the halls of government, in the office and in the shop and in the fields. Do not hope for less than *everything* that God has promised. Do not hope for less than the fullness of Christ's peace and justice and forgiveness in your home and in every land. Do not hope for less than a full share of God's bounty for yourself and for every person on this earth which *God* waters and upon which *God* makes the sun to shine and in whose soil *God* causes the seed to germinate and grow and yield fruit. Do not hope for less than salvation for *all* people. Let your hope be all that the prophets have declared, and *live* in that hope, so that *you* will be *prepared*. Broaden *your* hope. The Lord is coming.

Third Sunday of Advent
Spanish Springs Presbyterian Church, Sparks, Nevada
December 12, 2010
ISAIAH 35:1–10
JAMES 5:7–10
MATTHEW 11:2–11

"What We Hear and See"

FOR MANY CENTURIES, THE four Sundays leading up to Christmas have been identified by the Christian church as a season of *hope*. Advent is a season of *repentance*, as last Sunday's introduction to John the baptizer made clear, but Advent is *also* a season when we hear anew God's promises of *fulfillment* and *consummation*. So, in addition to *contrition*, Advent is a season of *expectancy*. We aren't so much waiting for Christ's *birth*, promised by God through the Old Testament prophets—that already happened two thousand years ago. We don't wait for what has already occurred. While the stories of the manger are still glad tidings, for those of us who are already believers, they are old news, though eternally joyful and worthy of praise. The coming of which *Advent* speaks foremost is Christ's *return*, promised by Jesus himself and by the apostles. And the reason for *repentance* isn't so much to be ready for something that happened twenty centuries in the *past*, but to be ready for something that is yet to *come* to pass. And when it *does*, the Bible testifies, all of the *other* promises of God will come to fruition as well—all those assurances of peace and wholeness and satisfaction and contentment given us in Isaiah and many other places in scripture.

I have to confess, though, that, even though I am a minister of the gospel, which means, among other things, being a preacher of good news, I often get pretty depressed by what's going on in the world, and the habits into which our nation, our entire culture, seems to be falling.

North Korea, Afghanistan, Iran, Pakistan—the list of trouble spots this Advent season seems to form a litany of impending *war*, not *peace*. Sao Paolo, Juarez, Oakland, Stockton—war is already raging even in the streets nearby, not because of competing political ideologies, but because of unprincipled greed that recognizes no limits. And then there is unemployment and poverty, and a political system that, fueled by talk-show demagoguery and the desire to destroy the opposition and sheer lust for power, is more adept at drawing partisan lines in the sand than exercising compassion toward the needy. It becomes pretty hard not to be habitually depressed and deeply cynical, especially if all that one reads is headlines and if all that one looks at is the evening news. There is dangerous wilderness everywhere we turn, and it is full of lions and all manner of ravenous beasts.

Sometime after he had baptized Jesus in the Jordan, John was arrested and imprisoned. For trying to be obedient to God and faithfully to prepare the way for the Messiah, John had offended Herod and other powerful people in Israel, and now he was having to pay the price for his devotion. Ultimately, we know, John was beheaded. During his ministry, he had come to have a number of followers, disciples, many of whom continued to be loyal to him even after Jesus' baptism and the start of Jesus' ministry. Somehow, they were able to remain in communication with John even while he was Herod's prisoner—John was able to get messages to them, and they were able to inform John of what was happening, including, apparently, what *Jesus* was doing and what Jesus *wasn't* doing. The baptizer, according to the writers of the Gospels, thought at the time he baptized Jesus that this person was very special, favored by God. Perhaps John even believed him to be the Messiah. But either because Jesus seemed to be slow at bringing about the kingdom of God, or because the sorts of things Jesus was doing didn't seem to fit his expectations of what the Messiah would be like, or simply because he was receiving only secondhand reports and was uncertain about the accuracy of what he was hearing, John instructed some of his disciples to go to Jesus and ask him bluntly, "Are you the one who is to come, or are we to wait for another?" (Matt 11:3).

John's question is usually interpreted as evidence of a wavering of faith on his part, although Jesus seems not to hold it *against* John, but *praises* him just a few verses later, calling the baptizer *more* than a *prophet*, since John had not only *prophesied*, but took part in the *fulfillment* of his prophecy. Whether impatient or confused or simply wanting confirmation from Jesus' own lips, John's question was really no different from the doubt or uncertainty that many *Christians* show about Jesus, perhaps not with their *words*, but with their *deeds*. "Are *you* the one who is to come, or are we to wait for another?" "Are *you* the one whose authority is true enough for us to stake our future upon, and the future of our families and our communities?—to trust that, in your words of peace and forgiveness, we are hearing about how we should behave toward our enemies, and to honor, with the way that we spend our money and our time, as Lord of all? Or, since there are still wars and sickness and poverty and disappointment in the world and perhaps in our own homes, should we be placing our hope in and giving our allegiance to *another*?—some politician, perhaps, or some self-help expert, or some financial wizard?" Let us be honest. Just about *all* of us, in *some* area of our life, seem still to be waiting for some *other* Messiah than the one whom Christianity contends God has already sent, because we find his teaching and his example and his promise somehow deficient, or simply too difficult, based upon our reading of the headlines, our hearing of the news, our self-centered desires, and our self-consuming interests.

Advent is not only a season of repentance and hope and expectancy. For all of those reasons, it is also a season of *discernment*—not only of *waiting*, but of *watching*, of observing, of interpreting in the light of the totality of what is going on. "Jesus answered [the disciples whom John had sent to inquire of Jesus], 'Go and tell John what you hear and see: the blind receive their sight, the lame walk, the lepers are cleansed, the deaf hear, the dead are raised, and the poor have good news brought to them. And blessed is anyone who takes no offense at me'" (Matt 11:4-6). I wonder if we are as practiced at reading the signs and hearing the stories that confirm Christ's *messiahship* as we tend to be at reading the daily headlines and listening to the newscasts that confirm the world's *need* of a messiah. Skeptics and advertisers both may have conditioned us to notice only whatever is spectacular and overwhelming, the events that take little concentration or patience for us to notice, the occurrences that produce monetary profit or corroborate our prejudices and our preconceptions. We have become so used to overlooking daily miracles of sunrise and rainfall and harvest that we may have neglected to credit Christ with those things to which Jesus drew the attention of John's disciples, which are the very sorts of things that the prophets said would signal the arrival of God's promised day of salvation.

We shake our heads at news that yet another country may have a nuclear weapon, or that drug lords have committed yet more outrageous atrocities, or that a place where poverty is already common has been struck with yet another natural disaster. Why do we not jump in ecstasy when we hear of eyesight restored and lameness overcome and the spiritually insensitive awakening to faith? The *former* set of events may suggest that God's final *triumph* has not yet *arrived*. But the *latter* set of events testifies that God's *purpose* for *creation* is *inevitable*, and has drawn even closer than it was before, is more encompassing than any of us might have supposed. "Be patient, therefore, beloved" (Jas 5:7a), counsels the letter of James, written for Christians during a time of persecution and hardship when it would have been easy indeed to wonder whether the captain of their faith was truly the same one to whom the prophets had testified. All the words of peace must have seemed a cruel mockery to those who were facing arrest and imprisonment and torture and perhaps death. "As an example of suffering and patience, beloved, take the prophets who spoke in the name of the Lord" (5:10)—who tasted persecution just as severe, some of them, as the early Christians, but whose testimony to the certainty of the Messiah's coming was undiminished. So, the early Christians who had been promised that the Messiah would come again must also be patient, like the farmer who knows that the early and late rains will bring a crop from the earth. "See, the Judge is standing at the doors!" (5:9b)—the Judge over all wrong and over all unfairness and over all infirmity and over all that robs people of the life that we were created to enjoy, to whom we should be giving praise and thanksgiving in confident hope whenever "the blind receive their sight, the lame walk, the lepers are cleansed, the deaf hear, the dead are raised, and the poor have good news brought to them" (Matt 11:5).

The promise is that those people who so treasure the presence of God's kingdom in Jesus Christ as to detect the authority of the Messiah in *any* healing, in *any* forgiveness, in *any* coming to life in its fullness, rather than to curse the failure of everything to be made right on *our* timetable, in the manner *we* would prefer, according to *our* specifications—those persons whose eyes of faith perceive confirmation that Jesus Christ is the Messiah—are blessed. *They* are not waiting for *another*, but are eager to be the instruments through which Christ works miracles daily, even the miracles that the world takes for granted or overlooks or shrugs off or denies altogether. And in the two chapters of Matthew's Gospel that follow the encounter between Jesus and the disciples of John, Jesus was criticized for allowing his own disciples to feed their hunger on the sabbath, and for his healing of a man with a withered hand, and for curing a man whom demons had rendered blind and mute. After all that, "some of the scribes and Pharisees said to him, 'Teacher, we wish to see a *sign* from you'" (12:38b). What *more* could he do to answer the question, "Are you the one who is to come, or are we to wait for another?" (11:3). They had seen with their own eyes, and criticized him for it, the *very* things that, according to their own scriptures, identified him as the bringer of the messianic age. Why would anyone *then*, why do so many of us *now*, even those of us in the *church*, speak and act as if Jesus' teachings were insufficient, that his wisdom were flawed, that his example were unclear, that he were *not* in fact the Messiah, but rather take offense that he just didn't seem to know about financial realities, about human psychology, about national security? Are we waiting for some *other* Messiah? Have we not heard and seen?

Among the things for which we ought to repent during Advent should be our repeated failure to observe, to notice, to perceive, and, therefore, to believe. Among the paths that we should abandon and turn our steps away from are the habits of cynicism and skepticism and doubt. Among the practices that should mark us as believers that Jesus is the Messiah who has come is acting in faith that the Bible's testimony to miracles is true, and among the practices that should mark us as believers that Jesus is the Messiah who will come *again* is acting in faith that the Bible's testimony is true that the miracles are not *over*, but are only awaiting our offer to be Christ's instruments in bringing them into being, so that all flesh shall hear and see and rejoice that Christ has not only *come*, but live in conviction of the truth that Christ is coming *again*.

Fourth Sunday of Advent
First Presbyterian Church, Dodge City, Kansas
December 20, 1992
ISAIAH 7:10–16
ROMANS 1:1–7
MATTHEW 1:18–25

"A Promise Kept"

DEEPLY EMBEDDED IN THE Jewish mind of the first century was the prophecy that, one day, a descendant of David would again rule in Jerusalem. A king from the lineage of Jesse would establish anew a kingdom such as Israel had known under its *greatest* king, yet a kingdom which would be *even greater still*. This kingdom would be known far and wide for its justice and prosperity and faithfulness and peace. No more would the wealthy afflict the poor, no more would the privileged abuse the powerless. Warfare would be a thing of the past, for all nations would praise the God of Israel with one voice and obey him with single mind. Weapons would be refashioned into farming tools. All people would worship God rightly, and the wilderness would blossom and refreshing springs would well up in the desert.

The hope for a messiah was more than just a wish. For the people of Israel remembered how their nation had known God's favor during the reign of David, and they recalled how God had made a promise to David through the words of the prophet Nathan:

> Thus says the LORD of hosts: I took you from the pasture, from following the sheep to be prince over my people Israel; and I have been with you wherever you went, and have cut off all your enemies from before you; and I will make for you a great name. . . . And I will appoint a place for my people Israel and will plant them, so that they may live in their own place, and

> be disturbed no more; . . . and I will give you rest from all your enemies. . . . When your days are fulfilled and you lie down with your ancestors, I will raise up your offspring after you, who shall come forth from your body, and I will establish his kingdom. . . . Your throne shall be established forever. (2 Sam 7:8b–12, 16b)

The prophecy was more than the prediction of a mighty dynasty. Israel understood God's promise to mean that she would be blessed forever; the rule of a descendant of David would be a *sign* of that blessing. As the generations rolled on, God gave specific pledges to each of David's successors concerning their own duty and destiny, but each pledge rang with the promise that had been made first to David, and through him, to all of Israel.

In *fact*, the history of the nation of Israel was one of alternating hope and despair. There were times when the people felt not so much *blessed* as *cursed*. Among David's successors, there was wickedness at court, and even during the reign of David himself there was corruption in the palace. Eventually, there was division within the country, antagonism between the northern and southern kingdoms that David had united. There was foreign invasion. There was exile into Babylon. There was subjection by the Assyrians and the Egyptians and the Greeks and finally the Romans. Still, the promise of God was not forgotten by the faithful. They might wonder why disasters befell them, they might cry out, "How long, O Lord?" (Ps 13:1). But they did not forget. And they did not give up hope.

The prophets read the human heart well. They realized that kings and princes could *break* promises as easily as they *made* them. But in the God of Israel, they recognized one who guides the whole of human history in accordance with a promise which *God* made and *will not break*. In the God of Israel, they recognized one whose very nature *compels* him to remain *true* to his purpose just because he *is* a *faithful* God—faithful to his *creation* and faithful to *himself*. In the God of Israel, they recognized one who was dependable even when everything around them seemed awash in crisis and teetering on the edge of disaster.

Human treachery and deceit and insincerity are so common in human affairs that we have become skeptical about promises made to us. A single half-hour of television demonstrates just how cheap promises have become in our world. Think of the pledges made in all of those commercials—claims that a certain perfume or cologne is going to render us irresistible to members of the opposite sex, that a certain airline is going to get us to our destination on schedule, that a certain moving company is going to treat our furnishings as if they were their very own. We have learned to anticipate that many such promises will be broken. Now, when we buy products, we assume that indeed they are *not* likely to be durable, so we buy service agreements, wagering that our appliances and automobiles will *not* continue to operate satisfactorily. We rather expect that our flight will neither depart nor arrive on time, and so we make contingency plans when we travel. We purchase insurance in the expectation that the movers will lose or break our precious heirlooms.

And then there are casual promises that are made to us daily, and that we ourselves make—the promises of acquaintances to keep in touch, the promises of children to clean their room and the promises of parents to read a bedtime story, and all of the promises made out of convention or custom and easily neglected without penalty. And there are the more solemn vows, the promises children make always to be best friends, the promises teenage girls and boys make to remain forever sweethearts, the promises spouses make to be faithful to each other until death, the promises nations make not to wage war upon each other.

The life-task of the heart is to seek and find someone who will be faithful to the promises that he or she makes to us. Our first friendships in childhood are formed through the process of testing to see who does and who does not show faithfulness—faithfulness in the matter of abiding by the rules of the game, and keeping confidences with us, and sticking up for us when it's not easy to do so. Occasionally, children will be so hungry for acceptance that they claim as friends those who in fact are *not* trustworthy. Did you, as a child, ever count as a friend someone who failed to honor the friendship by being unfaithful to it, someone who seemed only to want to take advantage of you, someone who only remembered you at his or her own convenience, someone who acted the part of a friend only when he or she wanted something from you?

The testing becomes more serious in the teenage years, as we become anxious about personal image and we begin to deal with the feelings of sexual attraction and attractiveness. How pitiful the youth who lives at the beck and call of someone who is unfaithful as a friend or as a lover! And then in young adulthood, the search for a mate is acutely the quest for a spouse who will honor the promises he or she makes to us. The likelihood is that, at some time, we will be disappointed, either mildly or bitterly. Even the most solemn promises are sometimes not kept. Inevitably, *someone's* unfaithfulness will astonish us, perhaps devastate us. We may be surprised to realize that it is *we* who have been unfaithful to someone else. For human beings, including ourselves, are not very good at keeping promises. Circumstances change, feelings change, interests change. Or perhaps we never adequately counted the cost of the promise, the cost of being faithful.

The writers of our epistle and Gospel readings this morning were deeply concerned to show that *God has been faithful* in honoring God's promises to God's people. The Gospel of Matthew was written especially for Jews as testimony that Jesus was the promised and long-expected Messiah. It begins with a genealogy tracing the lineage of Jesus, through Joseph, the husband of Mary, back to David, and then through David's father Jesse back all the way to Abraham. The people of Israel *still* hoped for a king who would rule in Jerusalem, a king who was of the line of David and who would fulfill the promise that God had made. After Mary's betrothal to Joseph, Matthew testifies, she was found to be with child—what might well have seemed to Joseph a breach of her promises and of his trust. An angel appeared to Joseph in a dream to dissuade him from divorcing Mary and to encourage him to conclude the marriage. "Joseph, son of David, do not be afraid to take Mary as your wife, for the child conceived in her is from the Holy Spirit" (Matt 1:20b). Matthew understood it all as fulfilling Isaiah's prophecy concerning the birth of a son to be named "'Emmanuel,' which means 'God is with us'" (1:23b). And so Jesus, by human reckoning, was a descendant of David to whom God had made a promise so many centuries before.

Paul testified, too, that the gospel that he preached was a witness to the Son of God, "who was descended from David according to the flesh" (Rom 1:3), the fulfillment of God's promise made through the prophets. But in the birth of Christ, God had done more than merely keep his promise to his chosen people Israel. In Christ, God had reached out beyond the covenant people to extend the promise among all nations and all races, crossing the boundaries of time and of oceans to proclaim God's redeeming love for you and for me and for all of God's creation. The covenant with Israel had been founded upon God's grace. In Christ, God offered that unspeakable grace even to the Gentiles who never before heard the promise, and to millions yet unborn. In Jesus, God made a new and startling beginning with his creation, and now *all* people are invited to be "God's chosen" (Col 3:12). A new age has begun, a new chapter in the story of God's dealing with humankind, and the title of that chapter is "God is with us" (Matt 1:23). The kings of the history books failed to bring to God's creation *lasting* righteousness, justice, and peace. *Their* promises were like yours and mine—well-intentioned and solemnly vowed, perhaps, made in the confident zeal of the moment, but changeable and transitory. If God's creation is ever to know *true* righteousness and justice and peace, it will not be on the basis of *human* faithfulness and *human* promises, but because *God* has been faithful to keep *God's* promise, sending one to rule in the Spirit of holiness, one who is fully obedient to God even unto death on a cross, and who will return again to establish his kingdom in every land and in every heart.

Can it be that the babe lying in the manger is the long-awaited Messiah? Can it be that this son of David is also the Son of God, who will bring righteousness and justice and peace wherever he is honored as Lord? Can it be that this tiny gift from God will blot out our sin and lift our sorrows and awaken our spirits? Can it be that this little child born long ago in Bethlehem is the King, whose kingdom shall have no end? The lines of the Advent hymn run:

> Comfort, comfort you my people, Tell of peace, thus says our God;
> Comfort those who sit in darkness Bowed beneath oppression's load.
> Speak you to Jerusalem Of the peace that waits for them;
> Tell them that their sins I cover, And their warfare now is over.
>
> For the herald's voice is calling In the desert far and near,
> Bidding us to make repentance Since the kingdom now is here.
> O that warning cry obey! Now prepare for God a way;
> Let the valleys rise in meeting And the hills bow down in greeting.
>
> Make you straight what long was crooked, Make the rougher places plain;
> Let your hearts be true and humble, As befits God's holy reign.
> For the glory of the Lord Now o'er earth is shed abroad;
> And *all flesh* shall *see* the token That *God's word is never broken*.[1]

The good news of the Christian gospel is that *Jesus* is God's promise *kept*.

---

1. Olearius, "Comfort, Comfort You My People" (emphasis added).

Christmas Eve (Early Evening)
Spanish Springs Presbyterian Church, Sparks, Nevada
December 24, 2004
ISAIAH 9:2–7
TITUS 2:11–14
LUKE 2:1–20

"A Lamb's Tale"

"OH, MARES EAT OATS and does eat oats and little lambs eat ivy, kid'll eat ivy too, wouldn't you? Oh, mares eat oats and—" Oh, hello. Pardon me, but I just heard the best news that makes me feel like singing. Did you hear it, too? No? Well, Clarence, that big ram over in the next pasture from ours, told me that *he'd* heard that there weren't ever going to have to be any sacrifices anymore. No sheep or goat is *ever again* going to have to be taken into that big building in Jerusalem where the smoke goes *up* and no animal ever comes *out*. I haven't ever known exactly what happens in there, but it's always been something that I've dreaded. And not just *me*, but all my *friends, too*. It had something to do with making an offering of our blood for the wrongdoings of human beings. Isn't that just about the most gruesome thing you've ever heard? But now, from what Clarence told me, we no longer have to live in fear that we'll be sold for sacrifice. Something's happened that makes sacrifices unnecessary from now on! And, although Clarence didn't quite understand the connection, it seems that it all has to do with something quite wonderful that happened to *me* a long time ago, yes, way back many winters now, on a cold, cold night.

Hymn "In the Bleak Midwinter"

Oh, excuse me. Where are my manners? My name is Hermione. As you can see, I am a sheep, a ewe. No, not "*you*," as in you-out-there, but a "*ewe*," a girl sheep. My mother's name was Gretchen, and my father was Elmer. He was a prize-winner, you know—best of show in the Jericho County Fair, 6 BC. I've heard others say that's why he was never offered for a sacrifice—he was so valuable that our owner wouldn't allow him to be sold to be taken up to Jerusalem. He got his blue ribbon just a few years before I was born. So I wasn't very old the night it all happened.

At first, there didn't seem to be anything special about that night. It seemed pretty normal. We were out in the field on the hillside as usual, with our shepherds and the sheepdogs and a goat or two. Do you know the place, just a little ways from Bethlehem? Pretty soon, we would be kept in the sheepfolds at night, because it was getting into deep winter when it would be too cold for little ones like me to be out on the chilly hillsides. I was ready for that. I mean, I've always had a nice thick coat of wool—I've contributed my best to many a warm blanket—but I'm not a fanatic!

Well, we had been out on the hillside since dark. I was lying down after a long hard day of frolicking about, wiggling my ears and my tail, and eating grass, but I wasn't asleep. There was still too much bleating going on for me to sleep—some of those sheep just loved to keep it up even though they really didn't have anything to say. That included this teenager named Gwendolyn. "Hey, mutton-breath, knock it off!" someone would say, or, "Yo, cardigan-brain!" but they'd just get "Baaaaa" for an answer. One of the shepherds got me a pair of earmuffs to help me sleep better, but they kept sliding off my very silky ears! Baaa-baaa, I'm only kidding—that didn't really happen. It's just a little lanolin humor.

So, anyway, I remember it was quite dark, except for the starlight, and, other than the incessant bleating of some of my neighbors, the night was very quiet. No wolves. No rustlers. The shepherds had been talking among themselves after their supper, but even *they* had gotten quiet by midnight, pulling their cloaks tighter around themselves against the cold. Dark, quiet, cold. Then suddenly, there was this great commotion up in the sky.

Hymn "It Came upon the Midnight Clear"

Now, this is going to sound to you like a yarn—ha, ha!—a yarn, get it?—but I'm not trying to pull any wool over your eyes. It really happened! It was like the flutter of a bird's wings, but louder, and bigger. The shepherds were frightened. The sheep were frightened. Gwendolyn was shaking so much that the bell around her neck was ringing. It wasn't a bird that we had heard. This *man* had appeared from out of nowhere, all dressed in white robes, and there was a great white light shining on everything, and the whole hillside was lit up.

The dogs were barking furiously. I scrambled to my feet—I was still a little wobbly getting up in those days—and looked around for my mama! But almost as soon as the man appeared, he began telling the shepherds not to be afraid. I could tell that they were, of course, and that made me *more* afraid. But the dogs immediately stopped barking, and as the man spoke, the expression on the faces of our shepherds turned from fear and alarm to happiness and excitement. I can still remember the words he said to them: "Do not be afraid; for see—I am bringing you good news of great joy for all the people: to you is born this day in the city of David a Savior, who is the Messiah, the Lord" (Luke 2:10–11).

I still don't know what all of that means, but I *do* know that Bethlehem is sometimes called the "City of David," and I've heard people—human beings, I mean—speak from time to time about looking forward to the Messiah, because he will bring an end to hurt and sadness. That would be pretty good news, I think.

Hymn "While Shepherds Watched Their Flocks by Night"

And then the man said something else: "This will be a sign for you: you will find a child wrapped in bands of cloth and lying in a manger" (2:12). Now, that was a funny thing to say. You *know* what a *manger* is, don't you? It's a box or a trough where cattle eat from when they're in the barn. What in the world would a *baby* be doing in a *manger*? I looked at Gwendolyn and at some of the other big kids, and I could tell *they* were confused, too. It wasn't just me!

But before I could ponder that one very long, the light got even brighter, and the whole sky was filled with people, all dressed in white and singing, "Glory to God in the highest heaven, and on earth peace among those whom he favors!" (2:14). And that went on for quite a while, and then suddenly they all went up into the sky, and once again the night was dark and cold and quiet, quiet, not a sound—not even Gwendolyn. But then the shepherds began talking real loud all at the same time among themselves, waving their arms all excited, and off they went, running up the hill toward Bethlehem, leaving us behind in the dark. But one of them stopped and turned around and raced back and grabbed me under my belly. I was the youngest in the flock, and I guess he thought he shouldn't leave me out on the hillside—I would have been a little scared, after everything that had happened. Anyway, we trailed the others, still running, all the way into Bethlehem, looking in every barn door on the outskirts of the town until we came to one barn that was lit up—a sure sign that there were people inside.

Hymn "O Little Town of Bethlehem"

Most of the town was dark—people were asleep in nightclothes and under blankets made from the wool of my friends and relatives. It looked just like any other night, nothing unusual except for these shepherds running wildly through the streets, and most people probably thought it *was* like any other night. But there must have been something very special happening in that one barn. And I was going to be the only one from our whole flock to see it! Imagine! What could it be? What was so special about a baby being born?

Hymn "Lo, How a Rose E'er Blooming"

We'd caught up with the other shepherds by now as they had been going from barn to barn, peeking in the doors. But now, we knew this must be the place. And the shepherd who held me gently pulled open the door. He was careful not to make a loud noise. All the familiar smells of a barn came out to us, and we went in. At first, the light sort of hurt my eyes, and I blinked a few times without really seeing anything. But, as my eyes became accustomed to the light, I could see that it was coming from some lamps that had been hung above a cattle stall. The shepherds walked toward the lighted stall kind of slowly, and when we got up to it and could look in—it was just like the man had said out on the hillside! A baby, wrapped up in cloth and lying in a manger!

Hymn "Away in a Manger"

There were a man and a woman there, too—the woman was kind of lying down and didn't look exactly well, but she seemed happy. The man, who was kneeling beside her, seemed excited, and he was looking from the woman to the baby and back again when he noticed us and stood up, sort of anxiously, I thought. Then the shepherds, who looked a little sheepish—ha, ha, "sheepish," get it?—told the man what had happened to us out on the hillside, and he spoke to the woman, and the two of them looked surprised and then confused and then happy. Then the man smiled and motioned us toward the manger. The one shepherd was still holding me, more tightly now with his one arm as he patted my head with his other hand. My ears were all a-twitch with excitement as we got nearer, and then I could see over the edge of the manger the beautiful little baby asleep in the hay. "Look here, Hermione," he said to me as he held me higher and we peered together into the manger. "What a precious child!" he said.

Then the woman spoke up for the first time. "His name," she said, "is Jesus—Savior."

Hymn "Infant Holy, Infant Lowly"

We all stayed there for several minutes just looking at the baby. Finally, one of the other shepherds said, "We'll be going now." I think he could see that the woman was tired. I would have been happy to stay there all night in the soft light and warmth of the barn, but I supposed the rest of the flock would have gotten worried about us. And, as it was, I could hardly wait to tell them what we had seen. It's not every night that you see a baby in a manger! Come to think of it, it's not every night that I get to see a baby! I wished that I could have given him some of my wool right then and there to help him stay warm through the night. I bleated a greeting to the little baby as we withdrew from the manger. But then, within a few seconds, or just a few shakes of a lamb's tail, we were back out in the dark, cold night—but no longer a *quiet* night, because the shepherds were singing and talking and praying all the way back down the hillside.

Hymn "Good Christian Friends, Rejoice"

And when we got back to our pasture, all the other sheep gathered around me, wanting to know everything that had happened in Bethlehem. Gwendolyn looked jealous. But, more than jealous, she looked genuinely excited. Everyone huddled together around me, and the night seemed a lot less cold. And I felt pretty special as I told them the whole story.

Hymn "Go Tell It on the Mountain"

Now, about what Clarence said—something about a Lamb being sacrificed, over in Jerusalem, but this Lamb's not a sheep, but a Shepherd, and so no sheep or goat need ever be sacrificed again. I still don't understand it all, and Clarence looked a little puzzled, too, but relieved. But he said that the Lamb's name is Jesus, which is what the woman said the *baby's* name was that night so many years ago. I wonder if he ever had a blanket made of my wool? Or a robe?

"Oh, mares eat oats and does eat oats and little lambs eat ivy, kid'll eat ivy too"—

> *"Joy to the world! The Lord is come: Let earth receive her King; Let every heart prepare Him room, And heaven and nature sing, And heaven and nature sing, And heaven, and heaven and nature sing."*

Christmas Eve
Spanish Springs Presbyterian Church, Sparks, Nevada
December 24, 2007
ISAIAH 9:2–7
TITUS 2:11–14
LUKE 2:1–20

"Insiders Now"

I REGRET THAT MY children don't have the opportunity of seeing on television some of the shows that I was able to watch as a youth. I am especially aware of the loss this time of year, when those of us who are middle aged and older used to be entertained and uplifted by the Christmas specials—Perry Como, Bob Hope, Bing Crosby, Andy Williams—and the Christmas episodes of the variety shows. The recent death of the great French pantomime artist Marcel Marceau brought to my mind that *other* great pantomime artist, Red Skelton. They were different—Marceau more subtle, Skelton often slapstick. *Each* of them thought that the *other* was the world's greatest mime. I am grateful that I got to see Marcel Marceau when he was in town at the El Dorado a few years ago. I never got to see Red Skelton in person, but I would think that that would have been a real treat.

Red Skelton's most famous character was Freddie the Freeloader, the hobo whose sense of justice was so frequently offended by the habits of the world, but who always, by the end of the skit, was smiling and accepting of life as it came to him. One of the programs that endures in my memory was a Christmas special in which Freddie is walking along the sidewalk on Christmas night outside a swank restaurant which, of course, he could never have afforded and to which, dressed as he was, he would never have been admitted under ordinary circumstances. He pauses in the cold to look in through a window into the warm dining room where the food is plentiful and the people are genteel and the trappings of the holiday are oozing out of the walls and upholstery. And he licks his lips.

The whole premise of this Freddie the Freeloader character was based on the distinction between the "have's" and the "have-not's," but I think that no portrayal by Red Skelton captured so perfectly the difference between being an "insider"—someone in the warmth and plenty of the restaurant on Christmas night—and an "outsider"—a hobo looking in through the window from the cold sidewalk outdoors. Finally, through a series of incidents and accidents, Freddie gets inside the restaurant and gets to have a Christmas meal. It's a simple idea, this Christmas story. But in his perfect mastery of the art of pantomime, Red Skelton, intentionally, I would think, portrayed precisely what the second chapter of Luke is ultimately about.

"In those days a decree went out from Emperor Augustus" (Luke 2:1a). Augustus was the ultimate insider. Theoretically, he was the most important person on earth—at least, that's what everyone would have told you at the time. That's what everyone supposed. He was the *emperor*. He could issue *decrees*. He could command that people pay *taxes*. He could invade *countries*. He could order *executions*. He had gotten to the royal palace by ruthlessly eliminating his competition, and the whole world was now expected to dance to his tune, and pretty much *did*. Everybody tried to cozy up to him, to get into his good graces, to be in the inner circle of his favored ones.

In one degree or another, everyone *else* in this *first* Christmas story is an *out*sider, as far as the world is concerned and the way that the world works. Joseph and Mary were just two of thousands of people whose lives were disrupted by the decree that everyone should travel to the city of their birth to be registered, which seems to have been a census for the purpose of providing notice of their whereabouts to the tax collector. Only, Joseph and Mary were inconvenienced even more than *most* people by the decree, for Mary was nearing the full term of her pregnancy. What could Joseph *do*? He couldn't leave her at home in *Nazareth* at a time like that. Things had been hard *enough*—a rapid wedding after what most delicately could be called an unplanned pregnancy, probably surrounded by vicious rumors and Joseph's own share of doubt. But such people as Joseph and Mary couldn't *expect* the emperor's ruling to be amended on *their* account. In the *government's* eyes, they were nobodies, nothing more than a source of revenue. And when they got to their destination, Bethlehem, they were even *more* outsiders—strangers, whose condition of advanced pregnancy made them less than welcome at any public accommodation. While other visitors were warm inside their lodgings, Joseph and Mary were put up in a stable, "because there was no place for them in the inn" (2:7b)—either because the inn was full, or because the innkeeper didn't want to be bothered with the noise and mess of childbirth. We can imagine the couple going from inn to inn, peering in from the cold sidewalk through the windows at the favored people eating in the warmth and pleasant aroma of a dining room. As far as the story goes, they were alone—no female relatives to attend the young mother—and forgotten—Luke tells of no innkeeper's wife or anyone else giving a second thought to the humble couple who ended up billeted with the livestock.

Then the scene shifts to some people who were even *more* outside the circles of power and influence and gentility. "In that region there were shepherds living in the fields, keeping watch over their flock by night" (2:8). The imagery peddled by Hallmark and Precious Moments notwithstanding, shepherds in those days were universally considered to be undesirables, dirty and shiftless, not even welcome on the *sidewalk*, much less inside the *restaurant*. And so it was *especially* amazing—*scandalous*, in fact—that it was to *shepherds* that God chose to send an angel, bringing news that would be good for *all* people but was entrusted *first* and *especially* to *them*: "to *you* is born this day in the city of David a Savior, who is the Messiah, the Lord" (2:11). Not to the priests was the news entrusted. Not to the rabbis. Not to the governor. Not even to the great Emperor Augustus. Not to any *insider*, but to those whom society always left out on the street, shaking its head and holding its nose.

The birth of Christ inaugurates a new world order—a world not under the control of Augustus or any *earthly* power or authority, but under the power and authority of *God*. And God exercises power and authority for the redemption of *all* peoples, just as God has created all people in his own image, and therefore they are all to be treated with dignity and respect and compassion. There *is* a place for the humble in this world, God declared in the birth of Jesus. There is a place even for shepherds and for unwed mothers. There is a place for village-folk-made-refugees. The widow and the orphan and the leprous are not forgotten. There is hope for the imprisoned and the oppressed. And for anyone who knows him- or herself to be needy, to be unimportant in the eyes of the world, to be always on the outside looking in, there is *special* joy in the angel's message that God thinks so highly of such folk that the news of a Savior was delivered *first* to people like *them*. While emperors and the like extend their empires with armies and swords, *God* extends his kingdom by inviting the poor and the maimed and the blind and the lame, the forgotten and the friendless and the bullied and even the scandalous, to have a seat at the dinner table. So it was shepherds who had the distinct privilege of being the first to see God's newborn Son laid in a feeding trough, tiny and helpless, totally insignificant in the reckoning of Augustus and his pals. For everyone who has ever felt an outsider, one cold night long ago in a stable in an unimpressive little hamlet, God was setting places for *them* at the great heavenly banquet in the new age he was preparing.

None of us here is a shepherd. Probably, not one of us knows much about sheep or has ever spent a night on a hillside watching after them. But at one time or another, very likely each one of us has felt an outsider, has been excluded, has been left off someone's guest list, has felt rejected by other people, forgotten by the world. We must not miss or discount the special care that God shows toward the poor and the oppressed throughout the Bible—the *really* poor, the *really* oppressed—but to the degree that *any* of us has ever felt on the outside looking in, whether it be on the schoolyard or in the workplace or in the family or even perhaps in the church, with the selection of Mary to be the mother of the Savior of the world, with the selection of Joseph to be his provider, with the selection of the shepherds to receive the angel's glad tidings, we can see *ourselves* in *their* place, and *we* can recognize the Christmas story as good news.

No less a dignitary than *God himself* that night turned the ultimate *outsiders* into the ultimate *insiders*. Now *they* had the inside track on salvation, now *they* were given a front-row seat at the most important event in all of history. While great Augustus plotted and partied, a maiden and a carpenter and some shepherd lads were the ones God included as his personal guests at the great drama of salvation. Emperors, tycoons, celebrities—*their* attempts to win fame and seize riches seem suddenly pitiful in comparison, don't they? The world would probably have been little impressed with a humble birth in a stable even if it had known about it. But all the people who thought themselves to be important, or who spent their lives trying to be, were suddenly the outsiders. The great reversal of roles had begun. God had drawn up the guest list for the heavenly banquet, and a lot of people would be surprised. The kingdom of God was coming near. Freddie the Freeloader, and everybody like him, was being welcomed to the feast.

It's not too late to find ourselves invited in off the street—to find ourselves welcomed into the warmth and cheer of the banquet God first began laying out in the stable at Bethlehem. It requires, of course, not being offended by the presence of people like Mary and Joseph and even the shepherds. Perhaps that starts with realizing that they really aren't that fundamentally different from *us*, and certainly not in *God's* eyes. In fact, if we strive to be more like them, humble, grateful, willing to be amazed at the everyday miracles of God and open to the bigger ones, eager to proclaim in our own words and in our own deeds the undeserved generosity and mercy that God has shown to us, we may find ourselves to be sisters and brothers of the one whose birth we celebrate at Christmas—to be insiders, now, in God's program of redeeming creation, embraced in God's love, embracing with *our* love anyone and everyone who is still out on the sidewalk in the cold and dark, so that they can be insiders, too. "In that region there were shepherds living in the fields, keeping watch over their flock by night. Then an angel of the Lord stood before them, and the glory of the Lord shone around them, and they were terrified. But the angel said to them, 'Do not be afraid; for see—I am bringing you good news of great joy for all the people: to *you* is born this day in the city of David a Savior, who is the Messiah, the Lord'" (2:8–11).

Nativity of Jesus Christ / Christmas Day
ISAIAH 57:7–10
HEBREWS 1:1–4
JOHN 1:1–14

"A Christmas Carol—Epilogue"

IT WAS NOT MANY years, by earthly reckoning, after the remarkable visit to Ebenezer Scrooge by the ghost of his deceased partner, Jacob Marley, and the successive appearances of the three spirits on a single night, Christmas Eve, that the surviving member of the firm Scrooge and Marley passed from this worldly life to the next. By coincidence, or by irony, or by divine intention perfectly wrought, death came to Ebenezer Scrooge on a Christmas night.

It was now the third day since. Snow was falling lightly on the street outside the undertaker's establishment, and, within, the proprietor was making final preparations for the conveyance of the coffin bearing the mortal remains of the legendary, some might not long ago have said "infamous," businessman from the funeral parlor to the nearby church where Mr. Scrooge had become a regular presence on Sunday mornings and a liberal supporter of the parish's benevolences. The intervening holiday of Boxing Day had delayed newspaper announcement of Scrooge's death and arrangements, but there had been no interruption in the arrangements themselves, and today was the time appointed for the funeral. The undertaker had only the dimmest memory of the funeral of Scrooge's partner, Jacob Marley, some years past, perhaps because it had been such a modest affair of even more modest expense and with a yet more modest attendance of but one mourner, being Ebenezer Scrooge himself.

The undertaker assumed his habitual and practiced expression of somber dignity at the tinkling of the bell above the door. He emerged from the inner dominions of the funeral parlor to see a man, just stepped in from the now snow-covered street, dressed in topcoat and hat and scarf. "Is this where Mr. Ebenezer Scrooge is laid out?" the man inquired without either ceremony or sentiment.

"Mr. Scrooge is resting within," the undertaker responded, bowing slightly and indicating with his hand a passageway beyond velvet curtains tied back to a doorframe. "We will be transiting to the church shortly."

"I felt obliged to pay respects," the other man said. "I've just returned from several years abroad, and saw the announcement in the newspaper this morning."

"Would you come with me?" invited the undertaker, drawing aside further one of the curtains for the man's passage.

Upon entering a small candle-lit room, the new arrival walked without hesitation directly to the coffin and peered at its inhabitant.

"No, no. I wanted to see Mr. Ebenezer Scrooge."

"This is the late Mr. Scrooge," the undertaker answered patiently.

"I think not," retorted the man. "Though I've been abroad in Canada these past several years, I know his face all too well, with a scowl so perpetual as to be chiseled in cold stone."

"This is indeed Mr. Scrooge, sir. I transported him here myself from the house of his nephew."

"See here. You're quite mistaken, I tell you. That smile and contented countenance are not those of the man I know, or, rather, knew. No mortician's artifice could so transform a disagreeable character long written so plainly on a face."

"I'm sorry, sir, but I really must now close the coffin. The hearse will be here any minute. Perhaps you would care to sign your name in the condolence register?"

"Surely no one will ever be interested to consult a record so thinly used," the man said with a sarcastic sneer. He glanced around the room and noticed a wooden stand with an open book. Walking over to the register and taking pen in hand and, dipping it into the inkwell, he glanced at the page in front of him, and a look of amazement came over his face.

Ebenezer Scrooge's nephew Fred, the son of his sister Fanny, of whom Scrooge had been so fond in their youth, now herself deceased many years, led the procession into the church behind the coffin and accompanied by his wife and small children. His wife's sisters and their husbands were already in their places, as were the many score of other mourners who had defied the snow, still falling softly. Seated directly behind the family, in a location, as it were, of some special significance, was another family of husband, wife, and several children, one of whom was seated on the lap of his father. Just behind them were three women whose likeness of features hinted at their being sisters, perhaps slightly younger than Scrooge would have been, with their husbands, and then another older woman, seated by herself in mourning clothes, her face a study in deep introspection. At the front of the nave was an abundance of flowers in just a few rather elaborate displays but mostly in a large number of more modest arrangements. Quite a few of the mourners were weeping quietly, but despite their obvious sadness, they also bore, so far as an observer could interpret, gentle smiles suggesting warm memories.

It was more out of curiosity than any other motive, certainly not affection, that the man who had lately come to the funeral parlor was squeezed into one of the pews far to the rear of the sanctuary, somewhat uncomfortably crowded on this occasion. He could hardly credit the outpouring, which made him again question whether the man in the coffin was Ebenezer Scrooge and whether, indeed, he had come to the right church. "His poor heart just finally gave out, I understand," he had overheard a woman explain to her neighbor, a comment which further cast doubt on the identity of the deceased in his mind, for, like so many who had had business dealings with Scrooge and Marley, he had long since concluded as a certainty that the individual in question did not possess that bodily organ.

"The Word was made flesh, and dwelt among us," the priest's voice awakened the man from his long muse on the crowd that had responded to the announcement in print and by word of mouth of Scrooge's death. "That testimony refers, of course, to our Lord, whose birth we celebrate this holy season. But it is no blasphemy to testify that our Lord's words themselves became flesh and dwelt among us in the person of Ebenezer Scrooge."

"Bless him," the man heard someone seated nearby murmur as others, in unison, as it were, nodded their heads in assent and confirmation at the words of the priest.

"No one among us was more generous toward those whom our Lord specially loves," the priest continued—"the poor, the sick, the hungry, the imprisoned, the lonely. Ebenezer Scrooge visited them, carried food and medicine to them, gave without calculation his fortune for their care and support with the oft-stated goal that there need be not a single almshouse or prison in all of London."

The man's mouth fell agape. Had he not himself entered into arrangements with Scrooge to transfer notes whose payment was in severe arrears, and then watched from afar as Scrooge foreclosed without regard for circumstance, turning out widows and infants without delay? Had he not himself received only a blank look and sneer when he questioned Scrooge where the destitute were to turn for shelter and sustenance? He did not regard himself in the least bit sentimental, but he still harbored some feeling of humanity despite his belief in the sanctity of contract and the justness of return on investment.

"And, as if his daily liberality could be surpassed, this season of the year brought out from Ebenezer an especial sense of urgency to do good and to elevate the unfortunate to dignity and hope," said the priest. "Though it was certainly not his intention, his embrace of the Christmas spirit, shown brilliantly year 'round, many a time put my own humble efforts to shame." Here, the priest removed his monocle and dabbed his eyes with a handkerchief. "But, oh, what an example of Christ-likeness with which he has blessed us!" he resumed after replacing his eyepiece. "It is said that he retained only such portion of his income, much more modest than many of us would claim by right, as was required to provide for his simple needs, and that he regarded any surplus as stealing from the poor."

The man sat as if in a daze. He noticed as for the first time the fact that many of his companions in the church were dressed rather more simply than he himself was, and, despite their efforts to primp and coif for the occasion, they could not conceal broken and missing teeth, many of them, and other evidence of hard lives.

"Abandoning the pleasures and privileges which others in his position of business and fortune might demand as their due," the priest went on, "Ebenezer Scrooge, as it were, eschewed the mansions of human ambition to make common cause with the wretched and the dispossessed. But never did he abandon his good cheer, on such full display this very season and up until just a few nights ago as he partook so joyfully and gratefully in the warmth of hearth and table at his nephew's house in celebration of our dear Lord's birth. Indeed, it could well be said, and truly, that he knew how to keep Christmas well, if any man alive possessed the knowledge. And indeed," the priest concluded, "may that be truly said of *us*, and all of us."

"God bless Us, Every One!" a child exclaimed from near the front of the nave, and the congregation turned toward the angelic voice, that of the boy seated on his father's lap, with nods and smiles and tears.

At the conclusion of the service, the mourners followed the coffin, borne by six pallbearers, into the churchyard and toward an open grave near the outer wall that enclosed the sacred precinct. The snow was no longer falling, but the sun was even beginning a rare peek through the wintry London overcast, scattering the customary greyness and awakening a flock of sparrows to song. The man followed in turn, and was beginning to wish that he had known the deceased man being carried to his final resting place in these his final few years. For the man in the coffin was one, from what he had heard that day, far different from the miserly curmudgeon whose memory he had come, out of a sense of hoary duty rather than tender affection, to honor in sterile custom, and mutter unfelt thanks to God for his brief sojourn on earth. He did not personally know these other mourners, so clearly and deeply affected by Scrooge's death, but recognized among them a few of the city's renowned philanthropists. Close by the grave, shoveling spades-full of earth upon the coffin following the priest's commendation, were those whom the man supposed were Scrooge's nephew and family, but also the man whose wife and children had sat close behind the nephew inside the church, seemingly most deeply moved of anyone by the ritual farewell. Curious, the man lingered behind the other mourners, none of them quick to leave the graveside after the gravediggers had completed their labors, to speak to the humble-looking fellow to learn more of the dead man's final years.

"Pardon me, sir, in your grief, but I was moved by your manifest esteem for Mr. Scrooge and wished to offer my condolences." He introduced himself as he reached out a hand from which he had removed his glove.

"Thank you kindly, sir," said the little man. "I was Mr. Scrooge's clerk these many years. My name is Bob Cratchit. And never was there a kinder, more considerate employer, and that's a fact."

"I knew Mr. Scrooge in former years, and, if I may say so without offense, few people I knew then would have described him in such words."

The little man turned and looked at his family, who were standing near the grave in consoling embrace. Turning back toward the businessman, Bob Cratchit explained simply, "He was a good and godly man, and no one can rightly say different. We're none of us perfect. We live by God's grace, bless the Lord. And Ebenezer Scrooge showed many a person the face of Christ and the love of him who created us and sustains us from cradle to grave. None knows that better than me, I should think."

"May I offer any assistance you might require in finding a new position?" the man asked, moved by Bob Cratchit's testimony and suddenly feeling no need of further attestation of the goodness of Ebenezer Scrooge.

"Thank you, most sincerely. Mr. Scrooge already saw to that, I am grateful to say."

"Well, then, goodbye. And I am most heartily sorry for your loss. I am grateful myself that Ebenezer Scrooge had such a loyal and faithful employee as yourself, and hope that I may someday come to inspire such esteem from those who work for me and with me. Indeed, you prompt me to start earning such respect this very day."

They shook hands, and the man departed from the churchyard.

By some mysterious gravitation, the man was moved to revisit the churchyard the next day and gaze upon the newly mounded grave. And when he did, he saw a curious thing: lying on top of the mound, nestled among a plethora of inexplicably fresh and unwithered wreaths and flowers, were a small child's leg brace and crutch.

First Sunday after Christmas
First Presbyterian Church, Dodge City, Kansas
December 31, 1995
ISAIAH 63:7-9
HEBREWS 2:10-18
MATTHEW 2:13-23

"Not Ashamed of Us"

OF ALL THE VERY remarkable statements in the Bible (and there are many), few make as astounding an assertion as one of the verses in our reading from the Letter to the Hebrews. Speaking of us whom Jesus sanctifies by his life, death, and resurrection, the writer of the letter says, "Jesus is not ashamed to call them brothers and sisters" (Heb 2:11b). The very same *sinners* that Jesus entered the world to save, the very same people whose rebellion against God was the reason that God, from all eternity, planned to enter the world in the form of Christ to rescue from our self-destruction, "Jesus is not ashamed to call ... brothers and sisters" (2:11b). Shame seems to be a vanishing phenomenon in our culture, as has been recently pointed out about talk shows which feature such topics as "chain-saw masochists and proud of it." Still, one must wonder that the sinless Christ would not be ashamed to call gossipers, warmongers, and egotists "brothers and sisters," much less adulterers, murderers, and those who love money. But then we remember that, according to the Bible, it was just such people with whom Jesus spent his time, it was just such people from *among* whom Jesus called his disciples, it was just such people that Jesus, the Great Physician of the soul, said he came to heal. Indeed, he did not seem to enjoy very much the company of people who considered themselves to be sinless, to be *deserving* of God, to be God's favorites.

Strange, isn't it?—the sinless one being so "soft on sin" while so often rebuking the righteous keepers of the law as hypocrites and vipers? But Jesus recognized with those who were being saved a common relationship as spiritual children of the heavenly Father, and so, Hebrews says, he was not ashamed to call them brothers and sisters. And because they were brothers and sisters of Christ, Hebrews goes on to explain, Christ had to share with them flesh and blood, suffering and death. "For it is clear that he did not come to help angels, but the descendants of Abraham. Therefore he had to become like his brothers and sisters in every respect" (2:16–17a). And he is not *ashamed* to call *us* brothers and sisters.

If I were Jesus, if I were God in the flesh, if I were holy and sinless, I would think that I would not want to be seen with just *anybody*. I think that I would want to keep my reputation unsullied, so I would probably keep company with the priests and the Pharisees. I would never touch a leper or a demoniac, I would never speak to a prostitute, I would never go to dinner with a tax collector. I would be much like the common picture of angels, living in an antiseptic realm far above the earth, walking on a cloud that never let my feet quite touch the dirtiness of the world. Indeed, there *are* some Christians who live their lives that way, never quite coming into contact with the world. But if their aversion to dealing with sinners means failing to recognize a shared brokenness, as it often seems to, a common need for God's mercy, that the sin of *any* of us is a burden to be shouldered by *all* of us, then it must be that such Christians are often ashamed of Jesus, who did not regard himself as too pure to eat with tax collectors or forgive prostitutes or wrestle the devil out from those who were possessed or look with pity upon those who were deformed with leprosy.

Jesus was not an angel, but the Son of God, and the fact that Jesus did not come to help angels, but the children of Abraham—the sinful, quarrelsome, scruffy descendants of Abraham who were in need of *salvation*—tells us a lot about the *Father* of the one who sanctifies *and* of those who are sanctified. God does not deem it adequate to send us a memo about the need to shape up. God does not dispatch a press secretary to read us God's thought-for-the-day. Our salvation is not by a messenger or an angel only—a *representative* of God—but by the one who is the very *presence* of God, God himself in human form. And this Jesus, this very presence of God, is so far from being ashamed of identifying with humankind, and bearing the burden of human sin, and suffering the judgment of human accusers, that he was born in the lowliest of surroundings because the good people of the time would make no room for him in their own dwellings, his parents had to secrete him out of the country in order that he escape brutal murder in infancy, he grew up in an insignificant hamlet in the hills where he learned to work with his hands, he died in the way of a criminal—a sinner against the law. And this was the Son of God!

It is sometimes easy for us to lose the point of Christmas by romanticizing the picture of shepherds and stars and motherhood and wise men. The main point of Christmas is about God coming to us in Jesus Christ. That is a wondrous miracle. And it becomes more and more wondrous when we think about Christ's coming into *our* world—into our messy, sin-ridden world—*demonstrating* that the Son of God is not ashamed to call us brothers and sisters. No matter what our past, no matter how many times and no matter how many ways we may have tried to shut God out of our own private worlds, Jesus Christ in our lives means that God's very *self* is in our lives, remaking us into the beings that God wants us to be, but also accepting us as his children when we are still far short of the goal. And having the same Father that *he* does, Jesus is not ashamed to call us brothers and sisters, to feel our temptations, to suffer our disappointments, to cheer our spiritual achievements, to love us in every circumstance. Jesus does not simply bend down a little bit from his heavenly perch, high above the swirling waters of greed and pride and selfishness, to remind us that we really shouldn't be so sinful. At Jesus' birth that night in Bethlehem, God plunged into the waters with us, to be buffeted by the waves as we are, to struggle against the undertow as we do, to offer us not just an encouraging shout from the beach, but Christ's own example of how to swim, and to grab us secure in his arms as he pulls us toward the shore when *our* arms and legs give out.

God's presence with us in Jesus Christ may not always strike us in such heroic terms, as he walks through the seamier alleys of human existence. But Christ works the grand and glorious salvation of all creation through little acts of humble service to people who, from a human point of view, are not particularly *deserving* of salvation—drug addicts, thieves, adulterers—and ultimately, but identifying with us at the point of our greatest need, dying on the cross, a crude and horrible execution.

Most of the disciples of Jesus—people who, until the grace of God touched their lives to bring them to repentance, had lived in less than exemplary style—were not even there at the cross. They were afraid, to be sure, they were confused, but they were also ashamed. We can imagine that many of them had been uneasy with much of what Jesus had done—forgiving those whom the law said should be stoned, healing on the day which the law said was for rest, riding into Jerusalem to the treasonous shouts of "Blessed is the king who comes in the name of the Lord!" (Luke 19:38a), making a scene in the temple, which all thought should be a place of reverent decorum. Then he was arrested and tried and executed by those whom everyone supposed were in a position to know what was right and what was wrong. And the disciples' shame caused them to doubt that Jesus had ever been the presence of God in their midst at all. And then came the resurrection, and the shame turned to faith.

The birth and life and death of Jesus demonstrate that he is not ashamed to call *us* brothers and sisters. Let us never be ashamed of *him*! Let us never show shame at his birth in a stable by disregarding the poor in our community. Let us never show shame at the company he kept by deciding that we will not involve ourselves in the needs of those who are sick with messy diseases contracted in messy ways. Let us never show shame at his identifying with sinful humanity by refusing to admit that we *share* guilt in the misdeeds of our brothers and sisters, in the misdeeds of the church, in the misdeeds of our nation. Let us never show shame at the things he taught by explaining away the plain commands of the gospel to give and to forgive. Let us never show shame at the way he died by refusing to speak the truth of God regardless of the risk to our reputation, our popularity, even our life.

We peer into the manger once again this Christmas and see the very presence of God nestled in the straw and wrapped up in strips of cloth, squirming and chirping, eyes opening and closing, not yet focused, mouth yawning, lips seeking mother's milk. How dear, how precious, how innocent, how beautiful. We pass by the Jordan and see the very presence of God kneeling in the water to receive baptism from the one who calls sinners to repentance. How odd, and yet how appropriate to fulfill all righteousness. We hear of the very presence of God being driven out into the wilderness for forty days and being tempted to take an easier road, a more spectacular road, a more popular road, and that he refused to do so. How strange, and yet how reassuring to *us* who face hardship, anonymity, and rejection. We sit in a courtroom and see the very presence of God being condemned on vague charges of upsetting the order of things. How unfair, how presumptuous, how self-serving of those who sit in judgment, and yet how necessary it is for the salvation that God has always planned. We stand looking up at a hilltop and see the very presence of God hanging on a cross and gasping, "Father, forgive them" (23:34a). How extraordinary, and yet how like God to sacrifice what is dearest to him so that we might have eternal life. The very presence of God, with us, all that we need for salvation, sharing so much with us, unashamed to call us brothers and sisters. The very presence of God, healing, encouraging, feeding, comforting, forgiving, confronting, dying, but then rising from the grave. Let us never be ashamed of him!

Second Sunday after Christmas
January 5, 2014
First Presbyterian Church, Ponca City, Oklahoma
JEREMIAH 31:7–14
EPHESIANS 1:3–18
JOHN 1:1–18

"The Big Deal about Jesus"

ONE OF THE HARDEST things about Christmas shopping is resisting the temptation to buy something for yourself when you are supposed to be out selecting appropriate gifts for other people. Nearly every year, I have at least one of those moments—some years, more than one. I'm not a person who goes shopping very often, that is, just looking around. For instance, I could probably count on both hands the number of times I've been inside a store during the past year except to buy some very specific necessity. But I have a hard time passing up a book store, and I can't go into a book store without browsing—very dangerous. And so it happened that, in a book store not long ago, while looking for something to give someone else, I saw and picked up and leafed through a collection of photographs from the Hubble telescope.

I had a year of astronomy in college and have always had an interest in it, from the time that my parents gave me a telescope for Christmas when I was about ten or eleven years old. From time to time over the past several years and in different places, I have seen some of the astounding pictures from Hubble that NASA has released, but I had never come across such a large collection of color prints of wonders that exist many, many light years from earth. What we are seeing, scientists tell us, are, in many cases, images of the way the universe was billions of years ago, before our own solar system even was formed. What these faraway worlds look like today, or whether they even still exist, no one knows. Whole galaxies have come and gone in the time it has taken for the light from some of these wonders to reach us. Compared with such eons of time, our own lives are but a speck on the cosmic record. But, the Bible testifies, our existence is a part of the same grand scheme that created the heavens, wide and deep. The same purposeful and skilled power and wisdom that brought into being constellations and nebulas lovingly brought into being each one of us, so small in comparison with the vastness of space, but cared for, each one of us, intensely, by the one who willed the universe.

The writer of the Fourth Gospel knew nothing of telescopes or what they can show us of the far-away stars or even other planets. But he knew the testimony of the scriptures and the promises of the prophets and, most importantly, he knew what the church had experienced in the person of Jesus, who, though seemingly oblivious to the amazing complexities of the universe, was nevertheless, *another* Gospel writer tells us, born under one particular star whose light guided sages from distant lands to his crib in Bethlehem. Indeed, only in and through him do we encounter the light that sheds the truth on all eternity. More truly even than the billions of stars that the Hubble telescope has revealed and the billions more *beyond* the reach of its vision, his birth brought light into the world—the perfect light that illumines whatever darkness there is, and is so powerful that no darkness can dim it or extinguish it.

John begins his Gospel with a phrase that brings to mind the very first words of the Bible—"In the beginning" (John 1:1). In the book of Genesis, in its epic poetry about the creation of the heavens and the earth, we are told that God spoke, and there was light. And God spoke again, and the sky was separated from the sea. And God spoke again, and there was land, and yet again, and there were trees and plants of every kind. And God spoke again, and the sun and the moon came into being. And God spoke again, and the waters and the sky were filled with creatures. And God spoke again, and animals began to live upon the dry land. And God spoke once more, and humankind was created in God's own image, male and female. And God blessed them. And God saw everything that had been made and judged it to be good.

John tells us that God has always been, before even any of the universe came into being, before time began. And John also tells us that, with God, there has always been that *part* of God, that feature, that dimension, that faculty that, in human beings, we call "thought," "word"—the part of us that expresses who we are, what we desire, what we intend, what we value, without which we would not *be* who we are.

> In the beginning was the Word, and the Word was with God, and the Word was God. He was in the beginning with God. All things came into being through him, and without him not one thing came into being. What has come into being in him was life, and the life was the light of all people. The light shines in the darkness, and the darkness did not overcome it. . . .
>
> He was in the world, and the world came into being through him; yet the world did not know him. He came to what was his own, and his own people did not accept him. But to all who received him, who believed in his name, he gave power to become children of God, who were born, not of blood or of the will of the flesh or of the will of man, but of God.
>
> And the Word became flesh and lived among us, and we have seen his glory, the glory as of a father's only son, full of grace and truth. (1:1–5, 10–14)

God and the Word of God are in such intimate relationship that they cannot even be conceived of, each other, without thinking of them both, as a parent can only be a parent if there is also a child, and the very term "son" or "daughter" means that there must also be a "father" and a "mother." Each is necessary for the other to be a reality. The Word is the aspect of the divine through which God acts, whether that act be creation or salvation. And at a particular point in history, in a particular human being, that eternal Word which has existed with God from all eternity became visible, three-dimensional, sentient, in the person named Jesus.

Non-Christians sometimes ask Christians, "What's the big deal about Jesus? Sure, he was a good person. He spoke some wise sayings. He did some good deeds. But why, in the end, do you worship him?" They may or may not know that, at the time of Jesus, there were other wise teachers who said things both insightful and memorable. They may or may not know that, at the time of Jesus, there were other healers, people who seemed able to cure those whom physicians could not help. They may or may not know that, at the time of Jesus, there were priests who pronounced absolution of sins upon the making of a proper sacrifice or the chanting of the proper formula. And some people today, who would not describe themselves as Christians, nevertheless try to live their lives more or less according to the way Jesus said people should behave—try to do unto others as they would have others do unto them. But they would have admired *whoever* might have taught such things, and *do*, without *worshiping* them, without considering that the eternal destiny of their souls depends upon actually *believing* anything and everything that

Jesus taught, without considering that the eternal destiny of their souls depends upon actually *following* the example of anything and everything that Jesus did. What's the big deal about Jesus? After all, even the disciples of John the baptizer thought that *he* was just as worthy of being followed as *Jesus* was, and *they* were *there*.

The words that Jesus said and the stories of what Jesus did were well known by the time the Fourth Gospel was written. Most people would have been impressed by the parables, by the miracles, by the sacrificial death, and by the resurrection as Mark and Matthew and Luke recounted them. But in a way, there was needed a clear reflective voice to bring people a step backward from all the trees, so to speak, in order to see the forest. Do you understand what all this means? the Fourth Gospel asks us. Do you really "get it," what all the sayings and signs, the cross and the empty tomb, signify? There are no angels in this Gospel—at least, they're not identified as such. There is no mention of Bethlehem or mangers or wise men or Nazareth. We don't even have here an actual account of Jesus' baptism, or breaking bread and pouring wine and passing them around the table at a last supper. We have, instead, an astounding statement that in Jesus, the Word of God became flesh and blood and walked this earth alongside us and voluntarily died for us, and that, by faith that he was the very God of very God, we can have life eternal and abundant beyond the limits of any biological definition, beyond any psychological profile, beyond any standards by which the world, locked in its chronologies and geographies, uses to measure. In every way that is significant, the person *Jesus* was God. There can be no better definition, there can be no fuller revelation, there can be no truer expression of who God is and what God is like and what God purposes and what God values. And so, Jesus is the way, the truth, and the life, and no one comes to the Father but through him for the very reason that he is the *Son*, *without* whom the *Father* would not *be* the Father. He is the very Word of God, God's will and God's agent which can no more be separated from *God* than our personality can be separated from *us*. And so, in everything that Jesus said, we hear God's own voice. In everything that Jesus did, we see God's own act. In everything that Jesus taught, we learn God's own command. In every instance of Jesus' forgiveness, we experience God's own mercy. In every case of Jesus' healing, we feel God's own touch. In every illustration of Jesus' friendship, we know the warmth of God's own love. If we have seen the *Son*, we have seen the *Father*. If we have heard the *Son*, we have heard the *Father*. And when we worship the *Son*, we worship the *Father*.

This is not simply a great teacher. This is not simply a gifted healer. This is not simply a noteworthy example. This is *God*, come to dwell among us, the light shining truth upon all creation, the bestower of grace inviting all people to become children of the most high. "No one has ever seen God" (1:18a). But we have seen God's perfect reflection, God's exact mirror image. "It is God the only Son, who is close to the Father's heart, who has made him known" (1:18b). In fact, we might say, Jesus is God's own heartbeat.

But didn't he look like one of *us*? Didn't he get hungry and tired, and have to eat and sleep? Didn't he bleed, when pierced in the side, and didn't he die, when nailed to the cross? There's the great wonder that Luke expressed in the story of a birth in a stall surrounded by shepherds, and Matthew expressed in the story of flight for safety into Egypt and then on to Nazareth. So totally human, this one who was the fullness of God. And so there is a hope that you and I, too, can have God as our Father and be called God's children, God's sons and daughters. For our being born of flesh and blood is no disqualification to being born anew, birthed by the Holy Spirit in the gushing waters of the baptismal font, nurtured for eternal life by the Holy Spirit in the eucharist which is our feeding on the bread of heaven, Jesus himself.

One of the early theologians of the church, Hilary, bishop of Poitiers, told what happened when he read the opening of the Gospel of John:

> Herein my soul, trembling and distressed, found a hope wider than it had imagined. First came its introduction to the knowledge of God the Father. Then it learnt that the eternity and infinity and beauty which, by the light of natural reason, it had attributed to its *Creator* belonged also to God the *Only-begotten* . . . [who] was revealed as having been in the beginning God with God. It saw also that there are very few who attain to the knowledge of this saving faith, though its reward be great, for even His *own* received Him *not*, though they who *receive* Him are promoted to be [children] of God by a birth, not of the *flesh* but of *faith*. . . . And lest this very truth that whosoever *will* may become a [child] of God should stagger the weakness of our faith . . . , God the Word became *flesh*, that through *His* Incarnation *our* flesh might attain to union with God the Word. And lest we should think that this incarnate Word was some *other* than God the Word, or that *His* flesh was of a body *different* from ours, He dwelt among us that by His *dwelling* He might be known as the *indwelling* God, and, by His dwelling among *us*,

known as God incarnate in no other flesh than our *own*, and moreover, though He had condescended to take our flesh, not destitute of his own attributes; for He, the Only-begotten of the Father, full of grace and truth, is fully possessed of His *own* attributes and truly endowed with *ours*.[1]

The language is archaic and the reasoning is complex, but the point is this: Because, in Jesus, the fullness of God lived among us in the flesh of our own humanity—we whose lives are but a speck on the cosmic timeline,—we, too, though flesh and blood, if we but have *faith* that Jesus is God's own Son, can *also* become children of God, adopted, by the power of the Holy Spirit, into the circle of love that bonds God the Father and God the Son, God and God's Word, God and Jesus, the identical reflection of God, the eternal creator of the entire universe. And *that* is a big deal!

---

1. Hilary of Poitiers, *On the Trinity*, 1:11 (emphasis added).

Epiphany of the Lord
Spanish Springs Presbyterian Church, Sparks, Nevada
January 6, 2011
ISAIAH 60:1–6
EPHESIANS 3:1–12
MATTHEW 2:1–12

"We, Too, Are God's Mighty Act"

SEVERAL YEARS AGO, A woman started coming to our church and did so steadily for a few weeks, and then abruptly stopped. I called her to ask if anything was wrong. She explained that she had told her mother she was attending worship services, and that her mother had become very upset with her, warning her not to get involved in a church. All she needed, her mother told her, was the Bible. A bit of further conversation convinced me that there was no point in any additional discussion. Her mother's judgment was more authoritative than anything I could say.

In our age of rampant individualism and easy dismissal of traditional authority, she was simply one of many people who claimed the Christian label for herself but saw no reason to participate in or make a commitment to a community of faith. As her mother had refused to do, so she would refuse to do. It was almost as if being a part of a church were somehow a sign that one's faith was not genuine, or was polluted. The woman said nothing about hypocrisy, about which *non*-church people often complain. She said nothing about always being asked to give money, about which *church* people sometimes complain. It was more an opinion that faith and the church had nothing to do with each other, had no relationship, leaving the Bible a sort of talisman or charm, a private possession that guarantees a personal salvation rather than God's gift entrusted to the church, without whose stewardship the scriptures would have passed into oblivion long ago.

That episode was not unique to Spanish Springs Presbyterian Church, nor to my experience. Just about any minister could relate the same story, and very likely many times over. The frustrating thing is that, from start to finish, the Bible, which this woman prized so highly, is about *community* and God calling to himself not just so many *individuals*, but a *people*. Its story reaches its climax in the experience of the church. And anyone who actually reads and thinks about Ephesians will surely see why it is often referred to as "the church's epistle." More than any other letter in the New Testament—most of which, by the way, are addressed explicitly to *churches*, that is, to organized congregations in communion with the band of believers in Jerusalem, not to *individuals*—Ephesians sets forth the absolute importance, the absolute *necessity*, of the church. So vitally important is the church in the opinion of the writer of Ephesians, in fact, that he attributes to it even a cosmic significance: ". . . so that through the church the wisdom of God in its rich variety might now be made known to the rulers and authorities in the heavenly places. This was in accordance with the eternal purpose that he has carried out in Christ Jesus our Lord" (Eph 3:10–11). The church is part and parcel of God's plan to set right even matters in heaven!

The erosion of denominational identification among many people who regard themselves as Christians has been accompanied by, perhaps *accelerated* by, a disregard of the church as an institution. "Ecclesiology" is the term that we use to refer to the place of the church in God's scheme for creation and God's hope for its redemption. But as "salvation" has become regarded by more and more people—both lay people and ministers, frankly—as either a commodity to be acquired or a personal status to be achieved, there has been less and less attention to the church as a creation of God, central to God's purpose from before the beginning of time.

Ephesians asserts that the world was created for the very purpose that has been realized in the church, which is the community of those who have been chosen by God, and that purpose is that *all* people, regardless of *race*, regardless of *nationality*, will come together, acknowledging God's authority and being *reconciled* to *God* through Jesus Christ as they are reconciled to *one another* through Jesus Christ. The church is no mere human invention. It was not constructed on a human blueprint. It is a heavenly reality, a mighty work of God just as impressive and just as important as God's act of creation itself, just as impressive and just as important as God's act of bringing forth a people from slavery through the parted waters of the sea and forging them into a nation that should declare his praise and show forth his glory to all of its neighbors so that they flock to the place where God is worshiped, bearing their treasures to make offering to God, laying on the altar all that glorifies God's name. "In former generations," Ephesians testifies, "this mystery was not made known to humankind, as it has now been revealed to his holy apostles and prophets by the Spirit: that is, the Gentiles have become fellow heirs, members of the same body, and sharers in the promise of Christ Jesus through the gospel" (3:5–6). So the church is not just a historical accident, an entity incidental to God's saving purpose, but the indispensable instrument, the appropriate vehicle, that God has chosen and through which God's saving purpose is to be realized. The church itself, multiracial, multinational, in which ethnic and cultural barriers are transcended and overcome, is critical to God's work of salvation, not merely a messenger, but an integral part of the truth that it communicates, not just a voice interchangeable with other voices, but itself the substance of what God has promised. What the church calls people to do and become, the church *itself* does and is—the community of the redeemed which is about the *business* of redemption, the very body of Christ, living *itself* in the *same* unity with God and with one another to which it summons every man, woman, and child. And so the church is both model and goal, the culmination of God's plan for the entire universe—the purpose that God has intended from all eternity.

Reading for our new midweek adult study a few weeks ago, I was reminded that, in the time of Jesus and the apostles, the term "Gentiles" would have raised some very definite images in the minds of Jews and Christians of Jewish background. In Old Testament times, of course, "Gentile" referred to anyone who wasn't a Jew, wasn't a member of the nation Israel. And while its meaning was still technically that broad during the first century, to most people, it would have more specifically meant "Romans." They were the principal foreigners with whom the Jews had to deal in those days. They were the specific foreigners who occupied their land, who had installed a puppet king to do Rome's bidding, who demanded taxes and imposed edicts, who sent Pontius Pilate as governor and whose soldiers nailed Jesus to the cross. When Paul advocated opening the church and its table to "Gentiles," his listeners would have been thinking not of foreigners in general, but of Romans in particular. And, as galling as it was for Jews to think of eating with and befriending their non-Jewish Near Eastern neighbors, it would have been *doubly* offensive to consider eating with, praying with, praying *for*, Romans. No wonder Paul ran into so much opposition from the Christians back in Jerusalem when he began fraternizing with non-Jews in Asia Minor! No wonder Peter was interrogated so thoroughly by his fellow apostles when he baptized Cornelius and his household! It wasn't nice, polite middle-class Americans like you and I that they were inviting into the church. It was the enemy of everything that every respectable Jew believed in and stood for! It was the foe that Jewish children had been taught to fear and hate! "In former generations," the writer of Ephesians declares, "this mystery was not made known to humankind, as it has now been revealed to his holy apostles and prophets by the Spirit: that is, the Gentiles"—substitute "Romans"—"have become fellow heirs, members of the same body, and sharers in the promise in Christ Jesus through the gospel" (3:5–6). Change "Romans" to any people that modern American Christians might consider the "enemy," people seemingly doing everything they can to distance themselves from God's grace—"North Koreans," "Al Qaida," you name it—and you will understand how *radical* was the prospect of including "Gentiles" in the church. And yet, Ephesians says, that is exactly what the church is for, that is exactly why God created it, that is exactly how the church is to function if it is to fulfill its essential role in God's scheme of salvation. And that is exactly why you and I must never disparage the church, must never abandon the church, must never take the church for granted.

The audience for which Matthew's Gospel was originally written was a group of believers in Jesus Christ who, because of their conviction that he was the Son of God, the Messiah long prophesied, had been expelled from their synagogues and now were in exile in Syria, a Gentile land under Roman rule. They still thought of themselves as Jews, under obligation to live according to the law of Moses. But there would have been little social support for living according to their faith. Observing holy days by making pilgrimage to the temple was impossible. Eating as the law prescribed was more difficult than it would have been back home in Israel. They had given up livelihoods and many of them, no doubt, were living in or near poverty. Their conviction that Jesus was their true king, the only one to whom they should pay homage and to whom alone they owed their highest allegiance, had turned their world upside down and earned them the status of refugees, as Jesus himself had been a refugee.

And then Matthew reminded them that, after all, it was not his own *Jewish* people who had recognized Jesus as the newborn king and honored him as such. It was some wise *Gentiles*, emissaries from foreign places such as the one in which they now found themselves living: "In the time of King Herod, after Jesus was born in Bethlehem of Judea, wise men from the East came to Jerusalem, asking, 'Where is the child who has been born king of the Jews? For we observed his star at its rising, and have come to pay him homage'" (Matt 2:1–2). From the time of his birth, Jesus, Matthew explained to his congregation, was not just for the *Jews*, but for the *Gentiles* as well. When they were informed that the scriptures identified the place of the Messiah's birth as Bethlehem, the wise men went there, led by a star until it stopped over the house where the infant was. "When they saw that the star had stopped, they were overwhelmed with joy. On entering the house, they saw the child with Mary its mother; and they knelt down and paid him homage. Then, opening their treasure chests, they offered him gifts of gold, frankincense, and myrrh" (2:10–11).

Might the Gentiles among whom the Christians were taking refuge in Syria *also* come to recognize Jesus as the Messiah, the Savior sent by God, fulfilling the prophecy of Isaiah, "Nations shall come to your light, and kings to the brightness of your dawn" (Isa 60:3)? Were they themselves, the church, to be the instrument through which God chose to achieve his eternal hope for creation by bringing to the Gentiles "the news of the boundless riches of Christ, and to make everyone see what is the plan of the mystery hidden for ages in God who created all things; so that through the church the wisdom of God in its rich variety might now be made known to the rulers and authorities" even in the *heavenly* places (Eph 3:8b–10)? And not only to *preach* such inclusion, but to *embody* it? To *be*, in *reality*, what it *proclaims*?

The birth of a messiah, formerly thought of as a privilege to which only the *Jews* were entitled, is now good news to *all* people. And the herald responsible for *communicating* that message is also the very agent through which that *happens*—the church, a people whom God has formed for himself and to whom, through Christ, he has entrusted its fulfillment. We, together, are God's creation, the welcoming keepers of the waters through which all people are brought out of slavery into the fullness of life that God has promised, the generous trustees of the bread which God provides as heavenly food to sustain the faithful on their earthly journey. We are what God has purposed from before time began to give testimony to the Word which became flesh in Jesus Christ, God's own Son, Savior of all. We are part of the entity *for* which the world *exists* and *through* which the world is being *redeemed*, not just the privileged *few*, but the *many* for whom Christ died. We are an integral part of God's work of salvation. We are the church. We, too, are God's mighty act.

Baptism of the Lord
Spanish Springs Presbyterian Church, Sparks, Nevada
January 13, 2002
ISAIAH 42:1–9
ACTS 10:34–43
MATTHEW 3:13–17

"Power to Be Meek"

OF ALL THE QUESTIONS about the Bible that I have been asked since I became a minister, I think the most frequent one is, "Why did Jesus have to be baptized?" A lot of people, when they think about baptism, remember that it has something to do with washing away sins, or, in Protestant understanding, that it *symbolizes* God's cleansing us of our sin. John the baptizer himself was offering baptism in connection with his call to repentance. Well, what did Jesus have to be repentant about? The amount of attention that question has attracted in commentaries on the various *accounts* of Jesus' baptism shows that it's not an easy question to explain away.

The question isn't just one that is asked by moderns. In Matthew, John *himself* protested Jesus' request to be baptized. "*I* need to be baptized by *you*," John said, "and do *you* come to *me*?" (Matt 3:14). John understood that Jesus had no need to be cleansed from sin, was not in *need* of a baptism of *repentance*. But John finally consented, after Jesus explained, "'Let it be so now; for it is proper for us in this way to fulfill all righteousness.' . . . And when Jesus had been baptized, just as he came up from the water, suddenly the heavens were opened to him and he saw the Spirit of God descending like a dove and alighting on him. And a voice from heaven said, 'This is my Son, the Beloved, with whom I am well pleased'" (3:15–17). And in the very *next* scene, Jesus is led by the Spirit out into the wilderness to be tested by the devil, and then, after he has *resisted* the devil's temptations, he begins his ministry in Galilee.

Actually, being a symbol of God's cleansing us of sin is only *one* of baptism's multifaceted meanings. And the sequence of these scenes in the early chapters of Matthew helps us to understand why it was that *Jesus* submitted to baptism by *John*. John regarded the ritual washing that he administered as sealing a person against the day of judgment—of preparing people for what they were going to be facing. When he saw Jesus approaching, perhaps standing in line with others waiting to kneel and have the water poured over his head, John *recognized* the *sinlessness* of the Christ who stood before him. It seems that Jesus had come all the way from Galilee seeking out John for just this purpose. It was important to Jesus to submit to John's ritual before entering upon his public work of forgiving people, of healing people, of feeding people, of restoring people to wholeness and blessing them with peace and offering them hope. And the result was that the Spirit of God came upon Jesus in a profound way at his baptism and a heavenly voice proclaimed him to be the beloved Son of God, pleasing to God, much like the way in which God introduced God's unnamed servant in the book of Isaiah: "I have put my spirit upon him," said God; "he will bring forth justice to the nations" (Isa 42:1b).

By right, Jesus, the Son of God, could have demanded that John and all the others gathered at the Jordan submit their sinful selves to be baptized by *him*, as *John* suggested would have been the *appropriate* thing to do. But Jesus did not parade his *sinlessness*, nor did he back away from the world's *sinfulness* and hold himself aloof from human imperfection. Instead, he *identified* with the sinners around him, shouldered their need for forgiveness and being put right with God, shared the shame and the pain of the human condition as he prepared for whatever commission God would lay upon him, obedient to God and loving of humankind. Jesus knew that righteousness without compassionate and self-sacrificing love is not righteousness at all. "Let it be so now," explained Jesus to his bewildered and embarrassed cousin, who was trembling, we may well suppose, at the realization that he was baptizing the Son of God; "for it is proper for us in this way to fulfill all righteousness" (Matt 3:15). And with the humility of an obedient servant, Jesus knelt in the muddy water and bowed his head, and he and John both proceeded to carry out God's work of *our* salvation.

Popular notions of *power* have more to do with swaggering bravado than with meekness. "By God, they're not going to kick us around," is a sentiment that sprang up on car and truck bumpers within hours of last September's tragedies. All of us probably envision first heroic action on the military battlefield when we think of courage and bravery, envision first missiles and bombers when we think of power and might. But the one who had all the power of God at his command—the power that brought the universe into being, that causes oceans to roar and mountains to crumble—apparently stood in line with common people who recognized just how weak they were to tame even their *own* instincts, to curb even their *own* appetites, to wrestle even their *own* desires, patiently waiting his turn to have a handful of water poured over his head, that all righteousness may be fulfilled. And in doing so, we see in Jesus the fulfillment of the prophecy that God's favor rests upon those who are willing to be powerless, willing to be submissive, willing to suffer, knowing that it is through such people that the Holy Spirit works to bring justice upon the earth. And in the light of the meekness of Christ, any spiritual arrogance that would *impose* its interpretation of God's will upon others, whether by military crusade or by crushing legalisms, is judged to be contrary to the ways of God.

"Righteousness" is doing all that God requires of us. In the Judaism of Jesus' time, and in the Old Testament, doing God's will was understood mainly as humbly accepting suffering. For Jesus to be *righteous* was not a matter of Jesus being *sinless*, but of Jesus being willing to suffer obediently according to God's will. The triumphalism that has so infected popular Christianity in the past couple of decades obscures, sometimes even denies, the Bible's testimony that the way of Christ is the way of meekness in a world that honors and admires power. Through the bestowal of the Spirit, God turned Jesus' baptism of repentance into Jesus' ordination for ministry, a preparation for the devil's temptations to power and prestige and promotion, a signaling of the way in which God's chosen one would be the servant of all people, even and especially sinners. He would break the tyranny of the *law* by identifying himself with those who had *no* chance of ever *fulfilling* it. He would bring about *our salvation* by allowing *himself* to be *sin's* most innocent and unjust *victim*. And along the way, not by full-page ads or entertaining extravaganzas, not by inducement of reward or threat of weapon, but by acts of kindness and words of sympathy, by compassionate deeds and sincere teachings, and above all by the assurance of forgiveness, Jesus brought many people to faith who felt themselves to be *powerless*, and empowered *them* by his own *love* to *endure* their sufferings and find a place of honor and welcome in the kingdom of heaven.

Early Christians saw, in the description of God's suffering servant in Isaiah, a foretelling of Jesus' own ministry and death and resurrection glory. The ancient Jews had already recognized in the suffering servant passages the description of anyone who would be righteous in God's sight, whether an individual or a group or an entire nation. Not in proud boastfulness, not in loud assertion of power and might, but in genuine service to others discharged in modesty—that is the way the righteously obedient live. Not by coercion or imposition of will, but by the persuasive example of loving sacrifice that approaches others not in condemnation but in sympathy—that is how the *purpose* of *God* triumphs. It is through the deeds of lowly servanthood that the wrongs of evildoers are neutralized and nullified. But the *ability* to *serve*, the *patience* to be God's true and effective *witness*, the *power* to be *meek*—these things are not *innate* to *any* human being, but are gifts bestowed by God's Spirit. And that is key to understanding why Jesus came to the Jordan to be baptized by John. And, therefore, it is central to the meaning of baptism in the name of the Father, Son, and Holy Spirit—so central, that it is right and proper that we baptize even tiny infants, still innocent, totally dependent on others, gentle in nature and powerless in the eyes of the world. And so the church from very early in its existence has encouraged all believing parents to bring their infant children for baptism, an early enlistment into the ranks of God's servants who are promised the equipment of the Holy Spirit for the work of endurance for the sake of God's saving purpose.

Notice a few things that the Isaiah passage says about being God's servant that Christians see fulfilled in Christ and that are characteristics of anyone who would regard him- or herself as a servant of God: "He will not cry or lift up his voice, or make it heard in the street" (Isa 42:2). The servant of God will undoubtedly have to endure many unpleasant things, wrongs, and injustices. That in no way *excuses* the wrongdoing or the injustice. But wrongs and injustices are to be endured as a part of servanthood and of our witness to Christ Jesus. We must not waste our time complaining about our lot or suggesting that we should somehow be exempt from all that Jesus endured. "A bruised reed he will not break, and a dimly burning wick he will not quench" (42:3a). Those who are just starting to respond to God in faith are to be *encouraged* in the faith they *have*, not *criticized* for not having *more* faith, and those who are just *beginning* to follow the ways of Jesus Christ are to be *commended* for their *strivings* rather than *condemned* for their *failures*, crushing their hopes with a burden of guilt and snuffing out their growing love of God with blasts of self-righteousness. That, I think, has some urgent implications for how the church today should go about dealing with issues that are making headlines and creating divisions in this and other denominations. And then there is this: "He will faithfully bring forth justice. He will not grow faint or be crushed until he has established justice in the earth; and the coastlands wait for his teaching" (42:3b–4). The faithful servant of God must not bemoan the injustices done to her or to him. But the faithful servant of God must speak out as an advocate on behalf of *others* who suffer injustice, those who are oppressed intentionally or unintentionally by individuals or by groups or by the very structure of society, those who risk being forgotten or overwhelmed or cast aside in the world's headlong rush toward wealth and fame and power.

And so Jesus submitted himself to the cruel injustice of the cross and told his followers that *they* must be willing to give up everything, even life itself, for the sake of giving witness to God's truth. And so Jesus honored and still honors and nurtures the first signs of faith with forgiveness and acceptance. And so Jesus exposed the ungodliness of greed and pride and lust by feeding the hungry and eating with sinners, by healing the socially unacceptable and embracing the untouchable, by seeking out the ones whom society (or, to contemporize a bit, the economy) regarded as expendable and whom the self-righteous pure regarded as unworthy, and Jesus calls *us* to do the *same*. And so Jesus fulfilled, and through those who are obedient to him, *still* fulfills, the role of God's servant, as "a light to the nations, to open the eyes that are blind, to bring out the prisoners from the dungeon, from the prison those who sit in darkness" (42:6d–7). The community called and upheld by God, through its faithful discharge of the patient witness of a servant, becomes the instrument through which the *whole world* shall be drawn into the covenant relationship whose identifying characteristic is the reign of God's justice. It is not through the exercise of *worldly power* that Jesus wins all people to himself, but through the loving obedience that identifies him as God's suffering servant, and identifies those who *follow* him as God's suffering servants, too.

Jesus came to John to be baptized, to identify with the plight of sinful humankind, and to receive from the Holy Spirit the power to be meek. "'Let it be so now,'" he testified; "'for it is proper for us in this way to fulfill all righteousness.' . . . And when Jesus had been baptized, just as he came up from the water, suddenly the heavens were opened to him and he saw the Spirit of God descending like a dove and alighting on him. And a voice from heaven said, 'This is my Son, the Beloved, with whom I am well pleased'" (Matt 3:15–17). So you and I come to the waters of baptism and find here the promise of our own equipment for obedient servanthood, the power to be meek. "For it is proper for us in this way to fulfill all righteousness" (3:15).

Second Sunday in Ordinary Time
First Presbyterian Church, Dodge City, Kansas
January 14, 1996
ISAIAH 49:1–7
1 CORINTHIANS 1:1–9
JOHN 1:29–42

"God's Promotion Policy"

THIS PAST FALL, SOME of us met on Wednesday evenings for a class that examined the Old Testament prophets' understanding of God. Among the things that we noticed was the fact that the prophets were not particularly successful people. The prophetic writings—almost a third of the entire Old Testament, not counting even the stories of the prophets in the *historical* books of the Bible—came from individuals whose delivery of God's word apparently made no impression on God's people. By and large, the people of Israel continued to violate God's will and to ignore God's purpose, to disobey God's commands and to doubt God's promises. With the notable exception of Jonah, who ended up sulking in the shade of a bush when the wicked people of Nineveh actually responded to his message of God's judgment by repenting and changing their ways, the Bible gives virtually no indication that the word of God that the prophets proclaimed changed people from stubborn to receptive or from complacent to zealous. And yet, people of faith have, for centuries, revered the prophetic writings of the Old Testament, recognizing in them God's word not only to men and women of ancient *Israel*, but to God's people of *every* age.

I had never really thought about it before our Wednesday evening class, but that is really quite an irony. By all contemporary standards, the Old Testament prophets were failures. Their messages of repentance did not avert God's judgment upon Israel by invasion and exile. Their messages of hope seldom rallied Israel to faithful reliance on God's strength and defiance of worldly threats. The events of history happened pretty much as they would have happened even *without* the prophets' pronouncements. And yet, there the prophets' writings are, in the Bible, still read in public and in private many hundreds of years later.

In some cases, we perceive that the prophets were well aware that people were not responding to the message that was being delivered. Where we see that perhaps most *clearly* is in this morning's Old Testament reading from the forty-ninth chapter of Isaiah. The prophet or his disciples had strongly sensed a call to serve God by speaking on God's behalf to the people of Israel a message of importance not only to Israel, but to all nations.

> Listen to me, O coastlands,
> > pay attention, you peoples from far away!
>
> The LORD called me before I was born,
> > while I was in my mother's womb he named me.
>
> He made my mouth like a sharp sword,
> > in the shadow of his hand he hid me;
>
> he made me a polished arrow,
> > in his quiver he hid me away. (Isa 49:1–2)

God's intent was that the words of the prophet's mouth spoken on God's behalf would *pierce* the people's hearts and open them to *obey* the Lord, that they would *massage* the people's hearts and warm them to *hope* in the Lord. "To bring Jacob back to him, and that Israel might be gathered to him" (49:5b)—*that* is why God formed the prophet in his mother's womb in the first place. For individuals with such a tremendous sense of God's calling and purpose in their lives, it must have been deeply distressing to feel that they had let God down. It seemed that their words had fallen on deaf ears and produced no perceptible change in behavior among the people to whom God had sent them. If there had been country and western music around in those days, I can imagine that there would have been a song titled "Mamas, Don't Let Your Children Grow Up to Be Prophets." For there was little glory in it, and certainly no fortune. God's truth has never been popular. And God's prophets who *speak* the truth have never been popular. The lament of the *servant* must *echo* the feelings of all of us who have ever tried to be faithfully obedient to God and found our words and deeds answered with insult or indifference: "I have labored in vain, I have spent my strength for nothing and vanity" (49:4a).

This servant's work on God's behalf, it seemed to him, had been without any result or value. Faithful in spite of his discouragement, though, he gave us testimony to the trustworthiness of the Lord: "Yet surely my cause is with the Lord, and my reward with my God" (49:4b). The prophet knew that his failure was not *God's* failing; God could not be faulted, and, ultimately, the servant could count on God to look upon the purity of his heart and reward it in *some* way, even if he had *not* been successful in awakening people to God. But his expectation of a *future blessing* did not ease the overwhelming sense that, because the people had not responded, *he* had *failed*. What had he done wrong? What had he said poorly? Why had he not made a positive difference? Had he perhaps made things *worse*, turning people *away* from God rather than bringing them *closer*?

Worldly standards of success are always a temptation when it comes to the things of God. I was reminded in some reading this week that getting exercised over numbers is not the way to be faithful to the Christian calling. We can be forgiven our sensitivity to worldly success, I suppose, when even the writer of Acts was impressed with numbers of people who were being baptized. I recall, though, a sermon in which the pastor of our church in Richmond, Virginia, reminded his listeners that the great commission of Jesus to his followers was not simply to go and make *converts*, but to go and make *disciples*—not necessarily the same thing, and something that requires much time and patience. Unfortunately, not everyone who is in the church is a disciple, and the task of making disciples of professing Christians is at least as difficult a task as first introducing people to Christ. On the other hand, some of us probably cannot remember *ever* having made a convert, but an awful lot of us over the years *have* been engaged in making *disciples*—by teaching, by preaching, by praying, by studying, by making an offering which provided the funds for church school curriculum, by transporting youth to a camp or a retreat or a mission project.

The prophet in today's reading made the common mistake of confusing faithfulness to his calling with results from his efforts. The Bible makes no such correlation, and the reward which God promises is not based on any statistics that we can produce. The reward is based on faithful obedience in the work. Jesus told the parable of the talents to followers who were asking him about the signs of his coming and of the end of the age. You remember the story, in which a wealthy man preparing to go on a journey had left various amounts of money with his slaves, and how they invested the money and doubled the amounts—except for the slave to whom only *one* talent had been given; *he* decided to keep it *safe*, and so it had no chance to produce anything more. "Well done, good and trustworthy slave," said the master to each servant who had invested the money; "you have been trustworthy in a few things, I will put you in charge of many things" (Matt 25:21, 23). We miss the point of the master's rebuke of the slave who did not invest the money entrusted to him if we suppose it is because he did not turn a profit. The faithlessness of the slave who did *not* invest was *not* his *failure* to *make* money, but his *failure* to *try*. His fault was not in his *results*, but in his choosing not to *risk*, in his choosing *not* to do what he was *commissioned* to do.

Imagine the shock and dismay of the servant prophet when God answered his lament about the poor results of his labors with the words,

> "It is too light a thing that you should be my servant
> > to raise up the tribes of Jacob
> > and to restore the survivors of Israel;
> I will give you as a light to the nations,
> > that my salvation may reach to the end of the earth." (Isa 49:6)

God knew all about the prophet's year-end report, but God had a great mission that needed to be accomplished—spreading salvation even to the ends of the earth. Impressed with a servant who had shown such faithful dedication to his appointed task, God promoted him to a commission of even greater responsibility. What God desires and what God rewards is *faithfulness*. That hardly fits human notions of success.

There is an obvious lesson here for ministers and church officers and church school teachers and circle leaders. But there is an important lesson here, too, for *every* Christian. Having finally mustered the courage to turn to your seatmate on a long airplane flight and share what Jesus Christ means in your life; having finally mustered the courage to confront your spouse about how his or her drinking is destroying the family and ruining God's good gifts of life and marriage; having finally found the courage to confront a wayward child about friends and lifestyle that are turning him or her away from attention to the health of the spirit; having finally found the courage to walk down whatever fearful dark alley you have felt Christ has been leading you, only to be met with rebuke or ridicule or resentment or rejection, the natural reaction is to think the effort a failure that does not warrant repeating. You did it in good faith that God would use you to produce some great and positive results, and you don't *discern* any great and positive results. But God credits your effort to be faithful and values it over any particular result. And the *results* are in *God's* hands *anyway*.

Think of Jesus, the Lamb of God who takes away the *sin* of the world! Think of Jesus, who won to himself, what?—kings and princes, and captains of industry and media personalities and all manner of impressive folk? No—a handful of fishermen and a tax collector, some beggars and prostitutes, and one who eventually betrayed him to the authorities. And of those who sometimes came to hear, many must have turned against him in the end, or what seemed the end. Resented, reviled, rejected—not unlike the servant prophet, certainly no success by any standard that the *world* uses. Resented, reviled, rejected—and resurrected to glory by the God to whom he was ever faithful.

As followers of Christ, our task—yours and mine—is to be faithful to our commission to make disciples, giving our best efforts, trusting the results to God, recognizing that *God* is ultimately the *only* accurate judge of the heart, and the only true assessor of our efforts. Do not be discouraged by what may seem a failure. God answers faithfulness to the calling by promotion to responsibility for even *greater* faithfulness. First, consider honestly and prayerfully where Christ is calling you to give witness to God's love and compassion and healing and justice and forgiveness, recognizing that it may *well be* some place *you* would rather not *go*, some situation in which *you* would rather not be *involved*. Then take courage in the *promises* of God, go and discharge your commission in faithful dedication. Having been faithful in *that*, you will be in line for a promotion!

Third Sunday in Ordinary Time
Spanish Springs Presbyterian Church, Sparks, Nevada
January 24, 1999
ISAIAH 9:1–4
1 CORINTHIANS 1:10–18
MATTHEW 4:12–23

"Won to Be One"

THE NINETEENTH CENTURY WITNESSED a tremendous explosion of Christian mission activity throughout the world. As trade routes and communications networks reached Asia, Africa, and the South Pacific, and as these places came under the influence or control of nations in western Europe and North America, Christian evangelists and preachers, doctors and teachers came to win converts to the faith and to minister to the sick and the abused and the unlearned. The message preached was the testimony that there is but one true God, and that it is God's will that *all* people be joined together in faith through his Son, believing in Christ, and looking solely to him as their pattern for living.

It was not long before many of these Asian and African and Pacific lands had missionaries representing many different denominations, each witnessing in a somewhat different way to the one true God. Missionaries from the Protestant churches of Europe found themselves for perhaps the first time in an atmosphere of denominational competition. Missionaries from North America, where denominations were already an accepted fact of religious life, might have hoped to leave sectarian differences at home. But they soon found that they could not escape the embarrassment of contradictory doctrines and the confusion of variant forms of worship and church government even in the remote jungles of Africa or on the exotic islands of the Pacific. For some thoughtful missionaries, the divisions between Christian denominations, startlingly apparent in virgin fields like Korea and India, were *more* than a source of *embarrassment* and *confusion*. To them, the divisions seemed an appalling display of human sinfulness, a tearing to pieces the one body of Christ. Far from summoning people to prepare for the coming of the kingdom of God by being reconciled to one another, the introduction of Christianity to the native populations was creating walls between peoples where there had been none before, making a mockery of Christ's prayer that all of his followers might be one. For what sort of faith had the native peoples been evangelized?—one of disharmony and rivalry? To what purpose had the converts been won?—the perpetuation of ancient feuds rooted in the *impossibility* of expressing divine mysteries in human words? What sort of witness was being made to the natives by vying creeds and competing liturgies?

Among the denominations with large mission operations in India in the late 1800s were the Presbyterians, the Reformed Church, and the Congregationalists, all sharing a common heritage of Reformed theology, and the Anglicans and British Methodists. Grieved by their divided witness to Jesus Christ, the Presbyterians, Reformed, and Congregational missions to India joined in 1908 to form the South India United Church. After considerable discussion, these three denominations were able to overcome differences in church government that had been transplanted to foreign shores. They found it possible to *unite* their voice of praise and witness to Jesus Christ, the Lord of *India* as well as the Lord of England and America.

Soon, the Methodists and Anglicans in India became involved in negotiations to unite with the new South India United Church, but longstanding differences in the way they viewed communion and ordination caused the discussions to drag on for years. Eventually, an agreement was reached that paved the way for a more comprehensive union in which the Anglicans and Methodists could *also* participate. The final problem had been the question of who could ordain ministers and the nature of the authority of the bishop. The solution: *all* ministers at the time of union would be accepted with *equal* rights and status in the new church, *however* they had been ordained. Then, for an interval of thirty years, all ordinations of *new* ministers would be performed by bishops with the assistance of elders. Finally, in 1947, the *Church of South India* came into being with the reelection of five Anglican bishops and the election and consecration of nine new bishops. A million Indian Christians were brought together into one independent, indigenous communion. Neither

Presbyterian, Congregational, Methodist, nor Anglican, the Christian witness in a Hindu land became a *united* one, and one that suited the needs of the Indian Christians. In subsequent years, the *Lutheran* mission in south India joined the new church as well. Each of the constituent denominations had given up a tradition to which it had held fast for centuries. But important as they were, *none* of these traditions could be deemed *more important* than Christ's prayer that *all* his followers might be *one*.

With good reason, modern ecumenicists look with *hope* upon the achievements of the Church of South India and similar experiences of denominational merger in parts of Africa, in Canada and Australia, and even in the United States, such as the formation of the United Church of Christ in 1957. More recently, there have been reunions of alienated branches of the same denomination, including our own Presbyterian Church (USA) reunion in 1983 that healed a division dating to the Civil War. And there have been mergers of denominations separated more by obsolete ethnic traditions than by vital theological distinctions—unions such as the establishment of the Evangelical Lutheran Church in America.

At the same time, modern ecumenicists find it more and more *incomprehensible* that *some* denominations and congregations *perpetuate* ancient divisions and cast *suspicion* upon ecumenical organizations. Some churches do not permit their members even to worship with other Christians. Perhaps saddest of all, certain denominations and even individual congregations close the communion table—the most important symbol of reconciliation in Christ—to all but their own members, assuming for *themselves* the authority to restrict access to the *Lord's* table among those who confess faith in Jesus Christ, placing *human* conditions upon the channels of *God's* free grace.

In the first century, of course, there *were* no Presbyterians or Methodists or Baptists or Roman Catholics or Lutherans, although each of these groups finds warrant for its specific doctrine and distinctive practice in the pattern of the New Testament church. But the fact is, that in the first few generations of believers, thankful response to the good news of Jesus Christ was much more important than theological hairsplitting. Uniformity of worship or even church government was neither expected nor particularly encouraged. The relationship between Father, Son, and Holy Spirit was more *experienced* than *debated*. The mystery of Christ's presence in bread and wine was something to be *celebrated* rather than *explained*. The form of church government was considered a way of *accomplishing the mission* rather than an *article of faith*.

The New Testament word for "church" is the Greek term "ekklesia," which means "coming together." No congregation thought of itself as "independent." Now, in our own time, the radical individualization of faith and internalization of authority threatens to render each Christian a church unto him- or herself, and that jeopardizes the very *meaning* of the church.

But humankind being what *it* is, and the sinful tendencies of disharmony and disunity being what *they* are, even some of the *earliest* Christians apparently could not resist making distinctions and asserting inequalities. It was the apostle Paul who first brought the Christian message to Corinth. So it must have been especially painful to him to hear of the internal problems which beset that young congregation. Chief among them seems to have been a divisiveness which, to Paul, was the very *opposite* of the Christian love that the church *should* model. Paul wrote to the Corinthians from Ephesus: "Now I appeal to you, brothers and sisters, by the name of our Lord Jesus Christ, that all of you be in *agreement* and that there be *no divisions* among you, but that you be united in the *same* mind and the *same* purpose" (1 Cor 1:10). In the days before his conversion on the road to Damascus, Paul *himself* had been one to draw distinctions between people. His entire upbringing and training as a Pharisee had been based on *differentiating* between the *holy* and the *profane*, on *preserving* the *purity* of doctrine and practice, on *maintaining* strict *segregation* between people of the *covenant* and *other* women and men.

What a major triumph of faith it had been for this Jew among Jews to realize that there is no ultimate distinction between Jew and Gentile! What a total change for him to become the strongest advocate for extending the Christian gospel *beyond* the children of Abraham to include people who hungered for good news in Syria and Greece and throughout the known world! Paul had matured in his vision to discern that *unity*—true unity—is based not on matters of race or nationality, gender or economic status, not even on maintaining the law, but rather on the person of Jesus Christ. Christ is the catalyst for all people to be united in those things that matter the most, and so the church of Jesus Christ as a whole and in each of its separate congregations must be a microcosm of what all humankind is destined to become—a new creation reconciled with God and reconciled with each other, *one* in praise and *one* in service, singing to one God and serving one Lord, all people together becoming more and more conformed to the life of Christ and showing him forth in their own life together. *Christ* is our ultimate model—he and no other, not even Paul. For it is none other than Christ who was crucified for all of humanity, and it is into *his* life and death that *we* are baptized as *his* followers and *his* church. And any loyalty which distracts our attention from that truth—any particularity of church government that stands in the way of *fulfilling* Christ's mission, any detail of theological explanation that has the effect of excluding some from the promise of God's grace—is a snag that tugs at the seamless robe of Christ and obscures the light of the gospel. Paul perceived that the Christian communities scattered in the midst of an unbelieving world were to be the leaven that would bring about the subjection of all things to Christ's lordship, and their example would anticipate and give testimony to the *unity* of the faith until, as Revelation puts it, "The kingdom of the world has become the kingdom of our Lord and of his Christ, and he shall reign for ever and ever" (Rev 11:15b RSV).

How do we create this unity? How do we make it happen? "We" *can't*. Paul teaches that our unity in *Christ* is not something that *we* can bring about. Our unity in Christ is something that *already exists*; it is *already* a *fact* by virtue of our incorporation *into* Christ through our *baptism*. The *whole church* is Christ's body; that's not *our* doing, but *his*. Christian unity only waits to be demonstrated in our attitudes and our prayers and our actions. We can choose to *ignore* it; we can erect walls of exclusion at the hazard of opposing God's will. We can try to *deny* it; we can refuse to commune with those of other denominations at the risk of blaspheming the Holy Spirit. As Christians of a particular tradition, we can dwell on the *differences* between denominations that result from historical circumstance and the limitations of human expression; we can assert that *our* experience of Christ is different from and better than *their* experience of Christ, that *our* understanding of Christ is different from and better than *their* experience of Christ. Or we can point to what we already have in common—Jesus Christ himself; we can witness to our transforming oneness in him, practicing humble forbearance with each other, gratefully celebrating our faith that the *whole church* is *his* body, and praying daily that all divisions will end, that sectarian violence will be replaced by faithfulness to the Prince of Peace as seems finally to be happening in Northern Ireland, that angry shouting between people of differing theological perspectives will give way to respectful dialogue, that distrust between and within the denominations will yield to earnest confession and mutual forgiveness.

Our Lord did not die on the cross for the purpose of plunging us into factional contention; we were not won to the faith to give witness to a *divided* Christ. He died that the broken relationship between humankind and God might be *repaired* and that people might be *reconciled* with each other; he won us to himself that *we* might be *one* with *him*. *Everyone* who professes faith in Jesus Christ is due our respect, our welcome, our hospitality, our prayers, our acceptance as a brother or sister. *Uniformity* is not essential and is not the goal. *Unanimity* of *opinion* is not required and not even desirable. Only complete faith in the one Lord Jesus Christ, who died for us, in whose name we were all baptized, and whose body we are.

Fourth Sunday in Ordinary Time
First Presbyterian Church, Dodge City, Kansas
January 28, 1996
MICAH 6:1–8
1 CORINTHIANS 1:18–31
MATTHEW 5:1–12

"Blessed Are You"

THIS MORNING'S SCRIPTURE READINGS include two of the most beloved and most memorized passages of the Bible, and rightly so. Our Old Testament lesson from Micah is a capsule summary of the whole teaching of scripture about what God wants from the human beings that God has created. Our Gospel lesson is a sort of inaugural address by Jesus setting forth what his ministry and teaching would be all about. The passages are comforting in times of trouble and encouraging in periods of discouragement. Many a person of faith has recited one or both in anxious moments when despair threatened to overwhelm.

But as justly famous and as frequently quoted as these passages are, it seems that we have a very hard time accepting them as true in our day-to-day living. Both passages claim a reality that is *contrary* to the wisdom by which the *world* seems to operate, and *opposite* to the way that *we* seem to think most of the time. For all the pious talk of "Christian values" that has invaded our political discourse in the past few years, we see relatively little witness being made around us to the wisdom of humility and meekness, to the practice of kindness and justice, to the blessedness of poverty and mourning. Aren't people who try to be peacemakers simply opening themselves up to criticism by all sides as unpatriotic bleeding-hearts or idealistic busybodies? And isn't persecution something that any right-thinking person tries to avoid at all cost? No wonder the lectionary committee recommended for reading with the Beatitudes and the Micah passage these lines from 1 Corinthians: "We proclaim Christ crucified, a stumbling block to Jews and foolishness to Gentiles, but to those who are called, both Jews and Greeks, Christ the power of God and the wisdom of God. For God's foolishness is wiser than human wisdom, and God's weakness is stronger than human strength" (1 Cor 1:23–25). By the standards of wisdom under which the *world* teaches us to operate—the standards of profit, the standards of self-assertion, the standards of comfort, the standards of self-esteem—the Beatitudes are absolute foolishness and Micah's passage is the sentimental souvenir of a bygone era. Surely, in an age whose ethics are being dictated by the proverbial "bottom line" and that counts success almost solely in terms of business acumen, the teachings of the prophet and the teachings of Jesus are far too idealistic for any individual to take seriously as a blueprint for his or her life. And surely, common sense tells us that any organization that espouses such a program for its members isn't going to be around very long in today's market.

But the Beatitudes are not a product of human wisdom; they are a statement of divine reality. They are not a proposition; they are straightforward statements about the ways of God. They are not negotiable; they are the word of the Lord. Jesus did not offer the Beatitudes as ideals to be striven for in the future. Jesus declared the Beatitudes as statements of present fact and certain hope *now* for those who follow him and for the church they comprise. Jesus did not say that the poor in spirit, the mournful, the meek, the merciful and all the rest should be patient in their suffering *now* in order to be blessed *later*. Jesus said that such people are *already* blessed because of what God promises them. Jesus did not command that his followers adopt poverty and start mourning and seek out persecution in order to get a *reward*, heavenly or earthly. Jesus said that his followers, who are *already* poor in spirit and in mourning and meek and longing for righteousness and engaged in the risky and thankless task of making peace, are blessed *now*, in those very circumstances. They already have a special relationship with God, and the kingdom is their inheritance.

In ancient Palestine, health and wealth and reputation were commonly considered to be indications of God's favor. In such a culture, Jesus' teaching was a radical rebuke of what everybody thought they knew to be true. Even Matthew's change from Luke's "the poor" to "the poor in spirit" yields an implausible result: surely the kingdom of heaven must belong not to the spiritually needy, but to the spiritually full?—especially if, as one modern interpreter puts it, the word traditionally translated as "blessed" could be rendered by the contemporary colloquialism "okay,"[1] as in, "It's okay to be poor in spirit, because the kingdom of heaven is yours"? But it is not only the wisdom of the *ancient* world that makes the Beatitudes seem foolish; they are foolish according to the wisdom of the *modern* world as well, and in the past several years, *worldly* wisdom has been flooding the church, threatening to make Christianity a business and to make Jesus a mascot.

Being "poor in spirit" means understanding life as a gracious gift, something unearned and undeserved, a stewardship, something to be used in gratitude and with a constant mindfulness of our total dependence upon God and not upon savings accounts and insurance policies and academic degrees and cleverness and beauty and charm. Quite likely, it will be those who have few material comforts who will *best understand* that everything we have comes to us without our having done anything to earn it. But that understanding is not beyond the reach of those of us who are *affluent*, *if* we are humble enough to remember to thank God. In either case—poor or affluent,—those who acknowledge the graciousness of God in all things already *have* a great blessing. And having recognized that all things are from God in *this* world, God will give them all things in the world to come.

"Those who mourn" are not just the ones who are bereaved, but all who sorrow for the world, for the lack of justice for the poor and the devastation worked by human greed and lust for power; Jesus is echoing here the prophet Isaiah who was grieving over the destruction of Jerusalem. The mournful *lament* that God's will is not yet accomplished in the world, that sin is *still* rampant and that arrogance *still* blocks godliness. They are already blessed with a vision of God and with the dedication to stand by God in his sorrow at human sinfulness. To them, Jesus gives his assurance that the last word is not yet written, that *God's* purpose shall triumph, that all who sorrow *now* will one day rejoice in God's *reversal* of the world's injustices. So they do not *resign* themselves to the condition of the world.

"The meek" are not "the weak." They are not push-overs, but they are not violent; they are humble and gentle in dealing with others, having humbled themselves before the greatness of God. But in that is their strength. Having renounced the ways of worldly power, of slander and of

---

1. Boring, "Gospel of Matthew," 176.

force and of envy and of greed, they are already blessed in being imitators of Christ himself, whose power was in truth and righteousness, and who, having died ignominiously on the cross, God raised to glory. "The wicked shall be cut off," promised the psalmist, "but those who wait for the Lord shall inherit the land. . . . The meek shall inherit the land, and delight themselves in abundant prosperity" (Ps 37:9, 11).

"Those who hunger and thirst for righteousness" are the people who long for the coming of God's kingdom and God's vindication of right. They are the people who crave more than anything else to see the will of God done in the world. They are blessed with God's own yearning that people be motivated by something more Christlike than hunger for a larger piece of the pie and something more worthy than thirst for power and privilege. And Jesus promises that *their* hunger and thirst—the hunger and thirst for righteousness in the world—shall be satisfied.

"The merciful" are people who *do* mercy; they do not simply feel sympathetic, they are actively engaged in merciful deeds that demonstrate the love and compassion and forgiveness and acceptance of Jesus Christ. The truly merciful will likely be reviled and criticized, just as Christ was reviled and criticized for *his* deeds of mercy, but the followers of Christ are blessed to identify with the Lord's *suffering* as well as the Lord's *joy*. They are assured of God's *own* mercy at the judgment.

"The pure in heart" are those who are single-mindedly devoted to God and God's Son, who never allow the distractions of consumerism or security or entertainment to divert their attention from seeking the heart of God and the mind of Christ. Surely that is a blessing beyond anything that we can buy, beyond anything that human invention can concoct. And Jesus promises that the pure in heart shall enjoy in the last day what their heart has been so set on—complete fellowship with God.

To be a "peacemaker" is to be actively *risking* oneself for peace. We deceive ourselves if we think that we can accomplish *God's* purpose with the *devil's* weapons. We deceive ourselves, too, if we think that we can help bring about the wholeness for which Christ gave his life without a readiness to humble our pride and practice forbearance and forswear the worldly habits of retribution and revenge and prejudice and self-deceit. Christ said to turn the other cheek, to forgive an unlimited amount, to welcome back joyfully the prodigal. The promise is the highest honor God can grant: to be received as God's own children, and to inherit all that God has to bestow.

Any and all such people can expect the same sort of persecution that Jesus endured. But if we trust Jesus—and all of this rests upon nothing greater and nothing less than Jesus' own word,—all the world's cynicism and doubt and ridicule and rejection cannot shake our conviction of the truth that *blessedness* is the state of the poor, the mournful, the meek, the seekers of righteousness, the merciful, the pure in heart, and the peacemakers, and that God reckons such people worthy to inherit the kingdom. Now, which is the sheer folly and which is the genuine wisdom?

"Blessed are you. . . ." Is Jesus talking about *you* when he says, "Blessed are the poor in spirit, for theirs is the kingdom of heaven. Blessed are those who mourn, for they will be comforted" (Matt 5:3–4)? Is Jesus talking about *your* church when he says, "Blessed are the meek, for they will inherit the earth. Blessed are those who hunger and thirst for righteousness, for they will be filled" (5:5–6)? Is Jesus talking about *your* family when he says, "Blessed are the merciful, for they will receive mercy. Blessed are the pure in heart, for they will see God" (5:7–8)? Is Jesus talking about *your* nation and its leaders when he says, "Blessed are the peacemakers, for they will be called children of God. Blessed are those who are persecuted for righteousness' sake, for theirs is the kingdom of heaven" (5:9–10)? Jesus speaks in Matthew's Gospel not only to a group of people gathered on a hillside in Palestine almost two thousand years ago, but to you and me sitting here this morning in Dodge City, and to the members of his church in every age and place. "Blessed are you when people revile you and persecute you and utter all kinds of evil against you falsely on my account. Rejoice and be glad, for your reward is great in heaven, for in the same way they persecuted the prophets who were before you" (5:11–12) The Beatitudes are a call from Jesus to you and to me and to this entire congregation and to the whole Christian church to act *now* in accord with the coming kingdom of God, not to sit in isolated devotion lost in pious thoughts, but together to walk humbly with God. Is *your* life a daily and constant demonstration of the truth of that sort of wisdom? Blessed are you.

Fifth Sunday in Ordinary Time
First Presbyterian Church, Norfolk, Nebraska
February 4, 1990
ISAIAH 58:3–9a
1 CORINTHIANS 2:1–11
MATTHEW 5:13–16

"Uncovering the Light"

WILLIAM GLADSTONE, THREE TIMES the prime minister of Great Britain in the late 1800s, once wrote that we are daily, in a thousand subtle ways, tempted to let religion spoil our morality.[1] He was reflecting upon how many of the devout are careful to fulfill the formal commands of their religion, observing the sabbath, praying regularly, quoting the Commandments, and yet in all their scrupulous attention to matters of individual piety, neglecting entirely to do those things in their public lives to which a genuine faith should direct them. Three centuries earlier, Martin Luther had been troubled by much the same thing. He wrote that, as a result of the many fast days of the church, and the priests' insistence on their observance, Christians of his day had come to a point where they regarded it as a greater sin to eat butter on a fast day than to lie, swear, or commit fornication.[2] So enormous was concern for personal salvation in the life hereafter that it overshadowed the teachings of Jesus about ethics in *this* life. Fear of what might happen at death had diverted all attention away from the goal of living responsibly in communion with God *now*.

Following the fall of Jerusalem in 587 BC, the Jewish people exiled in Babylon had observed a series of annual fasts as a way of mourning the

---

1. John Morely, *William Ewart Gladstone* (London: Macmillan, 1903), II, 185, quoted at Kilpatrick, "Book of Isaiah, Exposition," 678.

2. Luther, *Appeal to the Christian Nobility*, quoted in Rauschenbusch, *Theology for the Social Gospel*, 36.

destruction of the holy city and repenting of the sins that had invited the divine judgment. So far as we can tell, there were four such fast days, one on the anniversary of the beginning of the Babylonian siege of Jerusalem, one to commemorate the capture of the city, one to mark its destruction, and one to remember the murder of Gedaliah, the Babylonian governor of Judah. By the time the exiles were allowed to return to Jerusalem, forty years after its fall, the fasts had become a mere *form* for most people. Any real sense of repentance had dissolved into an attitude of religious *quid pro quo*—a bargaining with God: if we observe a fast as God has directed, then God will certainly restore Judah to its former wealth and glory.

Shortly after their return from exile, the people began to be troubled and disillusioned. Their fasts had not resulted in the divine favor they expected. The rebuilding of Jerusalem was progressing slowly. They detected no promise of a renewal of Judah's great power and wealth. In our Old Testament reading from the book of Isaiah, they appealed to the prophet, asking why their conspicuous religiosity seemed to be of no avail, why their situation was yet unchanged. They questioned God through the prophet:

> Why have we fasted, and thou seest it not?
> Why have we humbled ourselves, and thou takest no knowledge of it?
> (Isa 58:3a–b RSV)

Why were their very proper religious observances not winning God's favor?

According to the law, fasting called for a complete cessation of labor. But in fact, while the wealthy fasted, they required their employees to keep the shops and mills operating; not even religious rituals could interrupt the transaction of business. Dreams of individual profit and visions of personal gain crowded out true prayer. Rather than a reverent expression of repentance and intercession by all of the people together, irrespective of family name and station in life, the public fast had become a vainglorious display of false piety by the affluent and the comfortable. And the wealthy no longer fasted in a spirit of true repentance, but only to satisfy themselves of their own righteousness, doing what was expected by their fellows and what was deemed necessary to hold God to his part of the bargain.

The prophet clearly detected the selfish element in Israel's relations with God; the people worshiped God so that God would reward them, not out of that pure love which seeks nothing in return. When their fasts did not yield the anticipated result, they complained that God was not living up to his part of the contract. Did their devotion not merit God's gratitude? Had they not earned God's material blessing? God answered them:

> Behold, in the day of your fast you seek your own pleasure,
>   and oppress all your workers.
> Behold, you fast only to quarrel and to fight
>   and to hit with wicked fist.
> Fasting like yours this day
>   will not make your voice to be heard on high. (58:3b–4 RSV)

Their religion had become a self-indulgent excuse to delight in their own emotions. They regarded the fasts as a magical formula to compel God to give them what *they wanted*. From their selfish approach to religion, a God who *refused* to be *manipulated* was an *unreliable* God. In response to their rituals and their abuse of the working class, God thundered,

> Will you call *this* a *fast*,
> and a day *acceptable* to the LORD? (58:5c RSV)

God was clearly not impressed.

> Is *this* not the fast that *I* choose:
>   to loose the bonds of wickedness,
>   to undo the thongs of the yoke,
> to let the oppressed go free,
>   and to break every yoke?
> Is it not to share your bread with the hungry,
>   and bring the homeless poor into your house;
> when you see the naked, to cover him,
>   and not to hide yourself from your own flesh [that is, your own countrymen and women]? (58:6–7 RSV)

The actions that are of supreme importance to God, the things that manifest true repentance and genuine devotion, are those which demonstrate concern for human beings, and especially for the poor and the oppressed. The God of Israel was a God of liberation who had brought the people up out of bondage in Egypt and had returned them from exile in Babylon, who fed them with manna and refreshed them with water in the desert. The behavior specially pleasing to God is not a fast that mortifies the flesh, but deeds that restore freedom and satisfy human needs—the loosing from bonds and the setting free the captive, the feeding of the hungry and the support of the afflicted. Men and women and children are of more importance to God than any religious ritual, any pious talk. And the faithful will be rewarded not with wealth and ease, not with affluence and comfort, but with true communion with God, the blessings of his own presence.

> If you pour yourself out for the hungry
> and satisfy the desire of the afflicted,
> then shall your light rise in the darkness
> and your gloom be as the noonday.
> And the LORD will guide you continually,
> and satisfy your desire with good things,
> and make your bones strong;
> and you shall be like a watered garden,
> like a spring of water,
> whose waters fail not.
> And your ancient ruins shall be rebuilt;
> you shall raise up the foundations of many generations. (58:10-12a RSV)

> Then shall your light break forth like the dawn,
> and your healing shall spring up speedily;
> your righteousness shall go before you,
> the glory of the LORD shall be your rear guard.
> Then you shall call, and the LORD will answer;
> you shall cry, and he will say, Here I am. (58:8-9a RSV)

During the late 1800s, American Christianity was strongly influenced by revivalism, with the emphasis on personal salvation. In the early years of the twentieth century, there was a reaction among some theologians who were alarmed by the resulting unprecedented neglect of the social dimensions of Christianity, the interpersonal characteristic that had always been fundamental to the faith. These theologians preached the need to take seriously the words of the prophets and the teachings of Jesus about how people of faith are to conduct themselves in society. Their emphasis came to be known as the "Social Gospel Movement," and although people who regarded personal salvation as the only legitimate interest of the church maligned it as an innovation, the movement sought to remind Christians of the historic role of the church in public life. They based their message on the biblical image of the kingdom of God of which Jesus so frequently spoke—a realm in which God's will is acknowledged as supreme, one in which our relations with other people are governed by love, one in which God's command is our pleasure. The chief representative of the Social Gospel Movement was the Baptist preacher, seminary professor, and prolific writer, Walter Rauschenbusch. As pastor of the Second German Baptist Church on the edge of the New York City slum known as Hell's Kitchen, he had come face to face with the horrors of poverty. He had discovered that the pious philanthropy of individual Christians, well-meaning though it was, could make no fundamental change in the conditions that produce hunger and homelessness. The church must speak out for social responsibility. The welfare of humankind, including attacking the roots of poverty, must become every Christian's concern. In explanation of the Social Gospel Movement, and as an illustration of the sort of thing that Gladstone meant by saying that we are tempted to let our religion spoil our morality, Rauschenbusch wrote in one of his books:

> A health officer of Toronto told me a story. . . . If milk is found [to be] too dirty, the cans are emptied and marked with large red labels. This hits the farmer where he lives. He may not care about the health of Toronto, but he does care for the good opinion of his own neighbourhood, and when he drives to the station and finds his friends chuckling over the red labels on his [milk] cans, it acts as a moral irritant. One day a Mennonite farmer found his cans labeled and he swore a worldly oath. The Mennonites are a devout people who take the teachings of Christ seriously and refuse to swear, even in lawcourts. This man was brought before his church and excluded. But, mark well, not for introducing cow dung into the intestines of babies, but for expressing his belief in the damnation of the wicked in a non-theological way.[3]

You see, his swearing was deemed a spiritual offense grave enough to have him excluded from the church, while the church ignored the fact that his unsanitary practices threatened the lives of his fellow citizens. Rauschenbusch believed that the more appropriate response of the church would have been to say: "'Our brother was angry and used the name of God profanely in his anger; we urge him to settle this alone with God. But he has also defiled the milk supply by unclean methods. Having the life and health of young children in his keeping, he has failed in his trust. Voted, that he be excluded until he has proved his lasting repentance.' The result would be the same, but the sense of sin would do

---

3. Rauschenbusch, *Theology for the Social Gospel*, 35.

its work more intelligently."[4] Condemning the farmer for swearing, while ignoring the public health hazard created by contaminating the milk, is the spiritual equivalent of not being able to see the forest for the trees. Sometimes, we become so preoccupied with taking the spiritual temperature and monitoring the spiritual pulse of the sinner that we ignore the effect of sin upon God's beloved creation.

The Social Gospel Movement was condemned by some people for distracting attention from personal salvation. But can our hope for personal salvation ever be separated from social responsibility? Can it be a proper excuse for failing to heed God's command and Jesus' commission to feed the hungry, to heal the sick, to relieve the oppressed, to share our wealth with the poor? Rauschenbusch observed that the fact we are too respectable to get drunk or to swear is no proof of our righteousness. Our moral and religious quality is measured by the degree to which we merge our lives and will in the divine purpose of the kingdom of God. On the other hand, human sinfulness stands out in its true proportion not when we are tripped up by ill-temper or when we wander into paths of personal shame, but when we try to establish private little kingdoms of self-interest, thwarting peace and justice and the welfare of others because we perceive that our neighbors' well-being jeopardizes our own privileges, our own wealth, our own power over the disadvantaged.

The Social Gospel Movement had a lot to do with the enactment of child labor laws and the closing of sweat shops in America and England. And the united voice of Christians around the world may finally be helping to bring an end to the sin of apartheid in South Africa today. "The more we approach pure Christianity," wrote Rauschenbusch, "the more will the Christian signify [someone] who loves [hu]mankind with a religious passion and excludes none. The feeling which Jesus had when he said, 'I am the hungry, the naked, the lonely,' will be in the emotional consciousness of all holy [people] in the coming days. The sense of solidarity [with all people] is one of the distinctive marks of the true followers of Jesus."[5]

To be a disciple of Jesus Christ is to be a person who lives for *others*, just as *he* lived for others. We do not have a choice in the matter; Jesus said that we *are* the salt of the earth, we *are* the light of the world. But what is of less use than tasteless salt, or a light hidden under a basket? What

---

4. Rauschenbusch, *Theology for the Social Gospel*, 35–36.
5. Rauschenbusch, *Theology for the Social Gospel*, 108–9.

is more unthinkable than a disciple who is concerned with maintaining his own privileges in society or is preoccupied with assuring her own status of affluence? What is of less significance than a follower of Christ who will not declare the truth of God's liberating purpose to a world that is bound in chains of hunger and affliction and fear? The Christian is called upon to uncover the light that already shines within. "Let your light so shine before [others], that they may *see* your *good works* and give glory to your Father who is in heaven" (Matt 5:16 RSV). The light shines through the lives of the righteous, lives lived in commitment to neighbors near and far, lives producing good works of passionate caring for the well-being of *others*, *all* others, excluding not a *single one*, because God has declared and Jesus has demonstrated the divine love for *each* person, the divine love which each of us is to imitate every moment of our lives. Lifting the yoke of the debtor, freeing the oppressed, giving our bread to the hungry, sharing our homes with those who have none, clothing the naked—this is the sign of genuine repentance and pious devotion that is pleasing to God. This is the way that the light of Jesus Christ breaks forth like the dawn into the whole world, that all people might be blessed by the blessing we have received, and that God might be glorified in us.

Sixth Sunday in Ordinary Time
First Presbyterian Church, Ponca City, Oklahoma
February 16, 2014
DEUTERONOMY 30:15–20
1 CORINTHIANS 3:1–9
MATTHEW 5:17–26

"First Be Reconciled"

"To live in love with saints above, O that would be glory! But here below, with saints we know, well, that's a different story." So goes the anonymous saying about life in the church. Believers in Jesus Christ declare that they look forward to a glorious and blissful existence in the life to come. Meanwhile, they find that it tries their Christian patience to live among fellow Christians, those whom scripture refers to as "saints"—both the saintly ones and the unsaintly ones.

Anyone who has been very long in the church, almost any church, has probably had ample cause to wonder how Christians can sometimes behave in such an un-Christlike manner toward each other. The very institution that the Master called to model for the world the kingdom of God, to be a witness for peace and an agency of reconciliation demonstrating compassion and mercy, composed of individuals called to be ambassadors for our Lord, too often seems to be the very *last* place one would go to be tutored in the ways of Christ.

This is why the apostle Paul was so greatly troubled about the contentious condition of the Corinthian church. We can only speculate about the circumstances that had led to the factions in the congregation at Corinth—how it came about that one group declared Paul to be *its* authority, another Apollos, another Cephas—but it is clear that the precise *cause* of disunity was not the question upper-most in Paul's mind when he wrote his first letter to that church. His concern was that there was factionalism *at all*, that there was discord and hard feeling among *any* members of the church. Paul was keenly aware that the spread of the gospel depended upon demonstrating to the world the change that the indwelling spirit of Christ can make in a person. So he was greatly alarmed at the sort of witness the Corinthian Christians were offering on behalf of the faith. What kind of ambassadors for Christ did they make, habitually arguing with each other, making insinuations, questioning motives? Obviously, these new Christians had not taken fully to heart the apostles' teachings about the faith. Obviously, these Greeks who were accustomed to debating philosophical propositions were approaching Christianity as just another matter of speculation, and not as the truth that demands total commitment—the truth that can and must change a person's entire life.

Evidently, some of the Corinthians, sophisticated in worldly wisdom, had complained that Paul, when he had been among them, had not taught them with impressive depth, had not preached to them in any great detail. In answer to their complaint, Paul responded that, due to the circumstances, he had chosen to witness to them only of "Jesus Christ, and him crucified" (1 Cor 2:2b). He was unable to speak any more profoundly than he did, because his pupils had not yet reached the degree of spiritual maturity that would permit them to comprehend. "I . . . could not speak to you as spiritual people, but rather as people of the flesh, as infants in Christ. I fed you with milk, not solid food, for you were not ready for solid food. Even now you are still not ready, for you are still of the flesh" (3:1–3a).

The very fact that they were quarreling among themselves, that they had plainly not yet digested even the "milk," as Paul called it, proved their unreadiness for "solid food," the more advanced teaching for which they thought themselves so eminently qualified. They were yet too earthly minded, valuing too much the things that the world esteems, considering too much their own prestige, behaving too much out of pride and self-interest; they lacked the simple moral qualities of kind consideration, mutual forbearance, sincerity, and humility. They were yet immature, spiritually, and showed few signs of growing up; their partisanship demonstrated a serious deficiency of Christian fellowship and love and faith and service. The way they talked to and about each other, the way they hung on to old grudges and perpetuated petty feuds, made their congregation the very opposite of a fellowship of Christian love. Their bickering rivalry erased the very characteristics that should distinguish the Christian community from the culture around it.

In every respect, the conduct of the Christian should be such as to reveal the fruits of the Spirit. There must be that about us which will enable anyone who meets us to identify instantly that we are empowered by none other than Christ; and that isn't simply the *words* we *speak*, but the *way* we *live*. The Corinthians aspired to be spiritual, but their behavior was no *different*, and perhaps even *worse*, than the behavior of the world outside the church door. "For as long as there is jealousy and quarreling among you, are you not of the flesh, and behaving according to human inclinations?" (3:3b).

It grieves me deeply whenever I hear people, some of whom are quite dear to me, say that they choose not to belong to any congregation, because their past experiences in the church have been so painful. I think of one family in particular, family friends when I was growing up in Denver, who used to come listen to me preach on occasion when I was still in seminary, and who one day confided to my mother, "I suppose you wonder why we don't belong to a church or worship regularly. We used to, when we lived in another city. In fact, we were quite active in the church. But we just don't want to be hurt like that again. We've dropped out of church life, because we just can't take the fighting anymore."

That family, I fear, is far from unique. It is reported that the ancient Romans used to remark in wonder, "See those Christians, how they love each other!"[1] Clearly, that is the sort of witness that Paul envisioned for the churches he established. But in the history of Christianity, there have been far too many congregations like the one in Corinth, where that exclamation is said not in admiration but in sarcasm, "See those Christians, how they love each other!" That should not only shame us. It should cut us to the quick and drive us to our knees in prayers of confession and petition.

Shortly before the people of Israel entered the promised land, and just before his own death, Moses called them together, laying out before them the commands of God and the way that they must behave in order to fulfill their covenant relationship with God. Our Old Testament reading this morning is a summary of all that Moses said to the people, and it is striking in its demand for a definite, concrete decision on the people's part. The Corinthians, many centuries later, assumed that they could

---

1. See Tertullian, *Apology*, ch. 39.

respond to God's truth in the fashion of dilettantes, rounding out their intellectual diet by spooning a dab of Christianity on their plates from the philosophical smorgasbord.

But Moses had made it clear to the people of Israel coming out of the wilderness that God accepts from those who would identify themselves as his own nothing less than an absolute commitment. The decision that Moses put before the people was not one that admitted of *occasional* devotion or *conditional* dedication. There could be no intermediate position of "maybe" or "sometimes." One chooses either to obey God's commandments or not, and the sharpness of the distinction can be dulled neither by appealing to philosophy or psychology, nor to social convention or popular wisdom.

> See, I have set before you today life and prosperity, death and adversity. If you obey the commandments of the Lord your God that I am commanding you today, by loving the Lord your God, walking in his ways, and observing his commandments, decrees, and ordinances, then you shall live and become numerous, and the Lord your God will bless you in the land that you are entering to possess. But if your heart turns away and you do not hear, but are led astray to bow down to other gods and serve them, I declare to you today that you shall perish; you shall not live long in the land that you are crossing the Jordan to enter and possess. I call heaven and earth to witness against you today that I have set before you life and death, blessings and curses. Choose life so that you and your descendants may live, loving the Lord your God, obeying him, and holding fast to him. (Deut 30:15–20a)

To obey any other voice, to choose any other path, is idolatry; the choice is either for God or for idols. Moses' word was God's word. To heed what he said, and obey, was *life*; to disregard it, and disobey, was *death*.

Matthew wanted us to know that Jesus is our new Moses, fulfilling the law and the prophets, surpassing them with a more excellent way. The Sermon on the Mount gives us our way of life, no longer just "Thou shalt not," but "Blessed are those who." Love's imperative applies now to enemies as well as friends and family, to non-Jews and not just people of the covenant. God is interested not just in *what* we do, but the motive *behind* it. Few enough people can really obey the old law. The scribes and the Pharisees of old, perhaps, could fulfill it technically. But Jesus commanded an even greater righteousness than that. "Do not think that I have come to abolish the law or the prophets; I have come not abolish but to fulfill. . . . For I tell you, unless your righteousness exceeds that of the scribes and Pharisees, you will never enter the kingdom of heaven" (Matt 5:17, 20). And Jesus gave them an example of the measure of righteousness God requires:

> "You have heard that it was said to those of ancient times, 'You shall not murder'; and 'whoever murders shall be liable to judgment.' But I say to you that if you are angry with a brother or sister, you will be liable to judgment; and if you insult a brother or sister, you will be liable to the council; and if you say, 'You fool,' you will be liable to the hell of fire. So when you are offering your gift at the altar, if you remember that your brother or sister has something against you, leave your gift there before the altar and go; first be reconciled to your brother or sister, and *then* come and offer your gift." (Matt 5:21–24)

Recognizing God's design *behind* the law, Jesus understood that murder is not only done with stones and knives, but with contemptuous sneers and idle gossip and vicious insult and even casual indifference. Looking behind the act to its motive and thought, Jesus perceived that anger and contempt are murder, every bit as much as a gunshot. They are poison to the very soul.

Why is it, then, that in so many churches, folks feel free to criticize their neighbor, to comment on other people's business, to stake out turf and spend their energies defending it, to harbor grudges, even to indoctrinate their children so that succeeding generations may be cursed with the same destructive anger and dissension? Building issues are particularly fruitful occasions for dissension in churches. But I know of churches where deep lines of division within the congregation go back to the grandparents' fight over Sunday school curriculum or even something as incidental to the kingdom of God as the color of the carpet. There have been instances where business rivalries and family squabbles have invaded a church and metastasized to the point that the entire congregation was divided into alliances with this person or that. And some congregations owe their very existence to a split in some *other* congregation; think of it—a church founded not on the love of God in Jesus Christ, but on anger and dissension. So the *Corinthians* were tending, witnesses *not* to spiritual excellence, but to the habits of the flesh, walking *not* in the ways of the Lord by keeping his commandments and his statutes and his ordinances, but turning their hearts away, serving the idols of pride and jealousy and discord.

It is pointless for us to try to maintain right relations with *God* if we are not at peace with our *neighbor*; it is not the *indignant* who are blessed, but the *peacemakers*. It is spurious for us come to worship if our heart is either closed in upon itself or nursing hatred; God demands to be worshiped in spirit and truth. Better, Jesus said, to leave the sanctuary at the most sacred moment of worship than to delay one instant doing whatever is necessary to heal estrangement or remove anger. The duty of *reconciliation* takes *priority* even over bringing our offering to God. Disciples are not only *forbidden* to be *angry*. We are obligated to *seek reconciliation*, both with those who have offended *us*, and with whomever *we* have offended. It is not a question of who's in the right and who's in the wrong—objections such as that glorify our own pride rather than our humble Savior. It is not a question of reciprocity or self-defense—objections such as that usurp judgment from our merciful Lord. Pride and rivalry must be cast aside. Jesus knew that a heart congested by grudges cannot open itself in adoration to God.

As long as there is any jealousy and strife among us, we are of the flesh, and behaving like unbelievers. For then we have not opened our hearts to the spirit of Christ Jesus. Then we have not accepted his call to true righteousness. If the forgiveness which is ours in Christ does not move us to reject the maxim of an eye for an eye, does not prompt us to forswear gossip and innuendo, does not compel us to seek out the sister or brother who has wronged us or whom we have wronged, then we have undervalued the cost of our salvation. But when we practice the ways of mutual forbearance and communal harmony, when we discipline ourselves to look only for the best in others, when we demonstrate to the world the peace of our Lord, then all people will know that we are followers of Jesus Christ, and we will be effective ambassadors of his gospel.

Come, people of faith, let us bring our offering and worship our God. But first, let us be reconciled to one another.

Seventh Sunday in Ordinary Time
First Presbyterian Church, Norfolk, Nebraska
February 25, 1990
ISAIAH 49:8-13
1 CORINTHIANS 3:10-11, 16-23
MATTHEW 5:27-37

"To Pluck Out an Eye, to Cut Off a Hand"

YOU MAY HAVE HEARD people joke about the fine line between "preaching" and "meddling." I suppose that we all have our own sense of where the boundary lies between sermons which are so general and uncontroversial as to be simply "preaching," and those applications of scripture to specific life situations which constitute "meddling." Lest you wonder, this sermon clearly falls under the category of "meddling," and unapologetically so. It is based on a passage that probably causes each of us to wish that it were not in the Bible, because it makes us—you and me—so uncomfortable. At least, in my meddling, I find myself in good company—with people like the Old Testament prophets, and the apostle Paul, and Jesus.

"You have heard that it was said, 'You shall not commit adultery.' But I say to you that every one who looks at a woman lustfully has already committed adultery with her in his heart. If your right eye causes you to sin, pluck it out and throw it away; it is better that you lose one of your members than that your whole body be thrown into hell. . . .

"It was also said, 'Whoever divorces his wife, let him give her a certificate of divorce.' But I say to you that every one who divorces his wife, except on the ground of unchastity, makes her an adulteress; and whoever marries a divorced woman commits adultery.

"Again you have heard that it was said to the men of old, 'You shall not swear falsely, but shall perform to the Lord what you have sworn.' But I say to you, Do not swear at all, either by heaven, for it is the throne of God, or by the earth, for it is his footstool, or by Jerusalem, for it is the city of the great King. And do not swear by your head, for you cannot make one hair white or black. Let what you say be simply 'Yes' or 'No'; anything more than this comes from evil." (Matt 5:27–29, 31–37 RSV)

As we sit here this morning, observers of and contributors to American culture in the late twentieth century, this discourse of Jesus sounds singularly antiquated in both outlook and expression. Not only is the behavior that Jesus condemned becoming more and more accepted as commonplace, but the remedies he prescribed are excessive by the standards of any civilized legal system. When we read this passage, we may even begin to question: Where is the forgiveness that we thought was at the heart of the gospel? Where is the grace? Where is the live-and-let-live ethic of a tolerant and pluralistic society? Our minds conjure up images of the bizarre reports that we sometimes hear of people who follow this scripture passage to the letter and actually mutilate an eye or cut off a hand. "Kooks," we say to ourselves. "Masochists." "Hopeless literalists." "Fanatics." Nobody in their right mind, we think, would actually do what Jesus counsels here. Surely he did not mean for his words to be taken at face value. And in the process of subduing the radical remedies recommended here, we tend to reduce also the severity of God's judgment upon the sins of which Jesus spoke. Many of us give little concern to much of what Jesus condemned, especially thoughts which never ripen into act. Looking lustfully at a woman (or a man)—do you remember how Jimmy Carter was ridiculed for his confession about "lusting in his heart"? Surely nobody seriously calls such things "sin" anymore. Psychologists even claim that unfulfilled lust is unhealthy. They camouflage its real nature, perhaps, by replacing the term "lust" with the word "fantasy."

Every week, we as a congregation pray that God will deliver us from temptation. But do we think seriously about delivering *ourselves* from temptation?—by refusing to watch movies or television shows or listen to music that we know in our heart of hearts are meant to produce unwholesome thoughts, by refusing to expose ourselves to media messages that prompt us to do that which we ought not to do and to leave undone that which we ought to do. Or do we ignore our puritanical instincts for the more base? Most human beings are, as it were, addicted to sin, and we pleasure in nurturing our habit. A recovered alcoholic recognizes that he or she must never take another drink, or the enslavement to liquor will start all over again. In a very real sense, she or he is performing the equivalent of cutting off the right hand or plucking out the right eye by abstaining from that which tempts to ruin. But how many among *us* take so seriously the consequences of sin that we voluntarily remove ourselves from its seductive reach? How many among us really take these teachings of Jesus to heart?

Jesus Christ is all about forgiveness and new beginnings. Not only did he restore sight to the blind, heal the sick, and call forth the lame to walk, but he also forgave sinners. His death on a cross was for the purpose of making a sufficient sacrifice, once for all, for our sins, that we might be forgiven by God and our lives redeemed from the pit. Yet many of us forget the full message of Jesus to the woman caught in adultery. He said not only, "Neither do I condemn you," but also, "Do not sin again" (John 8:11 RSV). While it is a fundamental belief of our faith that Jesus forgave freely, no Christian church can ever claim that sin is of no consequence. The apostolic witness is that Jesus Christ died to save us from our sin. To suggest that sin is a trivial matter is to declare that God's sacrifice in Christ Jesus was trivial, too. While many Christian churches declare that they accept people where they are, no true church teaches that it is God's purpose to *leave* them there.

It seems that Jesus himself was misunderstood on this score. He was so frequently heard to forgive sinners and to condemn those who pursued the letter of the law, that he was finally moved to correct any false impressions that sin is not serious and that the commandments are irrelevant. Recall these words from our Gospel reading last Sunday: "Think not that I have come to abolish the law and the prophets; I have come not to abolish them but to fulfill them. For truly, I say to you, till heaven and earth pass away, not an iota, not a dot, will pass from the law until all is accomplished" (Matt 5:17–18 RSV).

We do not know what became of the adulterous woman after her encounter with Jesus. My own hope is that she went, as Jesus had directed, and sinned no more. Out of her gratitude for the only kindness she had probably ever known, and the most important message ever declared to her—"Your sins are forgiven,"—I think that she truly repented—turned her life around, spurned temptation, and cleaved to virtue the rest of her days. We may presume that she had never before heard words of forgiveness. We hear them often from the pulpit and read them in the Bible. Perhaps they tend to blend with the deceptive teaching of our culture about indifference to sin, so that the two become confused. But there was nothing cheap about the grace that Jesus offered to the adulterous woman. It was granted freely, but with a command that demonstrated the measure of her need and tested the sincerity of her purpose: "Go, and do not sin again" (John 8:11 RSV).

The New Testament indicates clearly that forgiveness and repentance are inextricably related; if a person is truly grateful for forgiveness, repentance is the inevitable result. And repentance assumes a comprehension of the reality of sin. Jesus' words are enlightening for anyone who considers sin to be a quaint concept, one which is socially and psychologically irrelevant, or who regards God's forgiveness as his or her "due." "I have come not to abolish [the law and the prophets]," said Jesus, "but to fulfill them. . . . Whoever then relaxes one of the least of these commandments and teaches men so, shall be called least in the kingdom of heaven. . . . For I tell you, unless your righteousness exceeds that of the scribes and Pharisees, you will never enter the kingdom of heaven" (5:17b, 19 RSV).

The scribes and Pharisees were nothing if not conspicuously righteous. Suddenly, Jesus' recommendation to pluck out the eye that looks at another lustfully, or to cut off the hand that causes one to sin, is no longer just a case of exaggeration, common to Near Eastern rhetoric, but deadly serious teaching. For, says Jesus, anyone who looks at a woman lustfully has in fact *already* committed adultery; it is better that you lose one of your members than that your whole body be thrown into hell.

As a minister of the gospel, seeking to be responsible to my charge, I do not counsel *anyone* to pluck out an eye or cut off a hand. I *do* advocate taking seriously the *gravity* with which Jesus speaks of sin, and our absolute need of avoiding impurity. We may suppose that our thoughts and private deeds involve no one but ourselves. We may think that if no sinful act follows upon our sinful thought, then no harm has been done. That was the Jewish understanding of morality that Jesus overturned. He teaches us to thrust our temptations away. Even if the eye should not be plucked out or the hand amputated, the lustful book should be left closed, the unwholesome amusement should not attract our interest or our dollars, the destructive friendship should be terminated. They might be as dear to us as our own eye or hand, but they should be cut off ere they become a cancer that eats away at our soul.

Is there protest that all things are lawful to the Christian? Then remember that a Christian surrenders what is *lawful* for the sake of being a faithful disciple of Jesus Christ and a grateful child of God. We may feel deprived by turning off the lewd recording or walking out of a scandalous movie or by quitting a job where we are tempted to dishonesty, public harm, or private lust. Yet it is much better to be deprived of these than to keep ourselves from abundant life in Christ, or to miss the entrance to the kingdom of God. If we begin to resent the sharpness of the pruning hook, we should remember that it is wielded in order to produce wholesome fruit.

As great a contrast as Jesus' words about plucking out the eye and cutting off the hand are to the casual standards of our culture, his teaching on divorce and swearing is even more at variance with modern practice. Regarding divorce, Jesus shows that it is not the statute books that define the marriage relationship. The civil law concerns itself with the legal steps necessary to effect marriage and divorce, but the legal forms are of little significance for the Christian. Marriage is not something to be entered into lightly, and certainly not with the attitude that it can be terminated if it does not work out to the immediate and total satisfaction of the parties. It is a relationship of deep moral importance—so much importance, in fact, that once entered into, it should have primacy over questions of career, over pastimes, over other interests with which it might interfere. It is a sacramental act, reflecting the love between God and humankind. It is established as a foretaste of the kingdom. That is the basis upon which God ordained it, and the standard by which marriage or its disruption is judged. It may be that the relationship between a particular husband and wife has become so destructive and so contrary to God's purpose for marriage that divorce is the lesser evil, but Jesus makes clear in this passage that anything that contributes to the instability of marriage (including, it seems, the ease with which one may legally terminate it) or anything that frustrates the purpose for which marriage was ordained, is a sin and God will judge it as such.

Jesus also attacked the untruthfulness of his generation by telling his followers, "Do not swear at all" (5:34 RSV). The only reason for oaths was that falsehood had become so common in society. Although *others* may be presumed not to tell the truth unless they are *compelled* to do so, the followers of Jesus are to be completely truthful at all times. A simple assertion should be sufficient for those who call themselves his disciples. "Let what you say be simply 'Yes' or 'No'; anything more than this comes from evil" (5:37 RSV) or, as some biblical texts read, "from the evil one."

How much Jesus demands of his followers! How seriously he takes sin, this man who seemed to forgive so freely! How insistent he is that his followers be pure, these same ones whom he had gathered about him from the fishing docks, from the tax collector's office, from the brothels. Someone has commented that the great need for modern men and women is not to be told that they are sinners, for they already know that, but to assure them that they are forgiven. But as the popular media reinforces the gospel of the "me generation" now entering adulthood, it may be time to reaffirm, as the neo-orthodox theologians did half a century and more ago, the reality of sin, and the magnitude of its offense. It is not difficult for us to imagine the pain inflicted upon a faithful husband or wife by an adulterous spouse, or the pain that a parent feels from an ungrateful child. The injuries can be read in the victim's face—the sense of alienation, rejection, incomprehension of how his or her faithful love could be so discounted. The promise of God's forgiveness may sometimes have the effect of blinding us to the fact that each sinful thought, word, action, or inaction affects God in the same way. Jesus spoke of God as being like the father of a son who has left home and squandered his inheritance which the father worked a lifetime to accumulate. Our confessions speak of how sin violates God's justice. But how often do we ponder the *pain* which our sin must cause God—the tears and anguish of the one who created us from no other motive than his love?

Paul's words in our 1 Corinthians passage today speak of the obligation of those who teach in the church to be faithful to the task of building with sound materials upon the only sure foundation, which is Christ Jesus. Materials of lesser quality will not survive the test. Doctrines that offer cheap grace, that preach forgiveness without repentance, or that fail to credit Jesus' hard words, compromise the gospel. It is the task of the preacher sometimes to meddle, and the obligation of all Christians to encourage each other to faithfulness in Christ Jesus.

We are not called to judge others, but to love others; to warn against the hazards to the soul which sin invites, and to proclaim God's precious forgiveness. The Christian who acknowledges him- or herself to be a sinner can hardly become a judge of others. But anyone who knows the joy of forgiveness that has moved him or her to turn life around can testify that true gratitude toward God is a mighty motivation for a life of faithful obedience, avoiding any temptation to sin that would stab at the heart of the God who forgives us, and who calls us to forgive each other.

Transfiguration of the Lord
Spanish Springs Presbyterian Church, Sparks, Nevada
February 6, 2005
EXODUS 24:12–18
2 PETER 1:16–21
MATTHEW 17:1–9

"The Meaning of Messiah"

PETER MIGHT HAVE WONDERED why Jesus seemed still to hold him in special confidence after his stunning rebuke just a few days earlier. Surely, his Lord's words must yet have stung in Peter's memory. It had all started positively enough. "'You are the Messiah, the Son of the living God'" (Matt 16:16), Peter had boldly said at long last, after months of being with Jesus. None of the other disciples had *dared* to *utter* such a startling thing. Perhaps none of the others had realized that *truth* about Jesus, their companion and teacher and friend. But Jesus had seemed to acquiesce in Peter's pronouncement when Jesus ordered the disciples—sternly, Matthew says—not to tell anyone the truth of what Peter had proclaimed: that Jesus was indeed the Messiah. But it was *then* that Jesus had *also* begun to talk to the disciples about the *suffering* that he must undergo at the hands of the elders and chief priests and scribes, and be killed. Peter had told him to stop saying such things, or to take precautions that they would never come about. "'Get behind me, Satan!'" said Jesus. "'You are a stumbling block to me'" (16:23). Those words must have hurt Peter deeply. "Then Jesus told his disciples, 'If any want to become my followers, let them deny themselves and take up their cross and follow me. For those who want to save their life will lose it, and those who lose their life for my sake will find it'" (16:24–25). And "six days later, Jesus took with him Peter and James and his brother John and led them up a high mountain" (17:1). Peter may have been dim-witted, but his heart was good, and the same stubbornness that first resisted the truth Jesus was telling him about the need to suffer and die would cause Peter to defend that truth of the crucifixion once he finally understood. So, once again, Jesus invited Peter on a special expedition, and once again, Peter followed obediently.

Just what it was that had finally opened Peter's eyes to realize that Jesus was the Messiah, the Son of the living God, scripture doesn't say—only that it was God's own doing, not an intelligence that came about through *human* channels. Indeed, flesh and blood would have reached a much *different* conclusion about what the Messiah would be like—a great king on a great throne with a great army at his command, like David of old, surely not someone who spent his time with the leprous and the blind, feeding ne'er-do-wells and blessing spendthrifts, forgiving prostitutes and promoting vagrancy. So, Peter must have been given some divine insight to confess that Jesus *was* the Messiah, but insight that still left him *short* of the knowledge that Jesus must suffer and die. Peter had not been listening carefully enough to what Jesus was teaching, had not been thinking through the implications of what Jesus was demonstrating in his ministry of feeding and healing and encouraging and forgiving. Peter did not yet know the meaning of "Messiah," as he had made clear by trying to hold Jesus back from his fatal journey to Jerusalem. And it is quite likely that Peter did not know what it meant to be a *follower* of the Messiah, who insisted that his *disciples* must deny *them*selves—their own interests and their own desires—and, instead, walk under the shadow of their own execution. In fact, some years *after Jesus'* crucifixion, Peter would know full well the truth of Jesus' words about discipleship—Peter himself would be crucified for the crime of being faithful to Jesus.

There, on the mountain, something wondrous happened. Peter and the others saw Jesus' face shine like the sun, and his clothes became dazzling white. And suddenly, Moses and Elijah were there—the great prophets of the past, standing and talking with Jesus. Again, Peter missed the point. He certainly meant no harm, but just the opposite, when he suggested building three tabernacles to commemorate the miraculous event. But even before he could finish his pious proposal, a bright cloud appeared overhead, and a voice from the cloud thundered, "This is my Son, the Beloved; with him I am well pleased; listen to him!" (17:5b) And Peter and the disciples fell to the ground in fear. And then it was over. Jesus came and touched them. They looked up, and all they saw was Jesus. And Jesus led them back down the mountain to where people pressed him again with requests for healing, and where he again told the disciples that he was about to be killed.

The story of the transfiguration is one of the strangest episodes in all of scripture, and the strangeness is even more accentuated by its seemingly random appearance among stories of miraculous healings and miraculous feedings and predictions of the crucifixion. It reminds us of Moses on Mount Sinai and the words that came from heaven when Jesus was baptized, but it is not just a repetition of those things. Closer examination of the context and the content and the role of Peter disclose that it was not really a *random* event at *all*. Matthew very much meant for his readers to remember that these *very same words* came from heaven at Jesus' baptism by John the Baptist, who, by now, had been beheaded for *his* faithfulness, and that God had engulfed another mountain with a cloud when he spoke to *Moses*. In the midst of the details of ministry and the busy-ness of traveling hither and yon caring for those in need, Jesus took Peter and the other two up high above the mundane level of their activity to gain a perspective on what it was all about, and to understand what *Jesus* was all about—to understand what it meant that *Jesus* was the *Messiah*, as Peter had proclaimed, and to hear for themselves that God *approved* of his ministry and *confirmed* his Sonship and commanded *them* to take his teachings to heart and to understand that obedience to God requires even the willingness to suffer and die.

Transfiguration Sunday is a fitting close to the season of the Epiphany, in which the church celebrates the glory of God revealed in Christ, and a fitting preparation for Lent, in which the church remembers the suffering *servanthood* of Christ in obedience to God. Just so, the transfiguration itself happened just after Peter, mulling over the miracles and teachings of Jesus, had discerned that Jesus was the Messiah, and just before Jesus' fateful turn toward Jerusalem. Matthew invites us to ponder, as Peter was made to consider, just what it means that *Jesus* is the Messiah.

That question is with Christians in every age. On one important level, I think that is the root of the great and growing cleavage in Christianity today—whether Christianity should be a religion of the mountaintop, commemorating a glory high above the plains of human struggle with a Savior who is dazzling white, or whether Christianity shall be a religion of the valley, where Jesus is seen in muddy garments and the followers of the Savior offer *themselves* in suffering servanthood to victims of every disease and injustice. Peter stands for *all* disciples, including *us*, in wanting to build monuments to Christ the Messiah as he certainly deserves, there, far removed from the wretchedness and despair of political oppression and malnutrition and AIDS. But the voice from the cloud speaks to *us* as well as to *Peter* when it says, "This is my Son, the beloved; with him I am well pleased; listen to him!" (17:5b)—listen to this person who was born in humble surroundings, who was a child refugee, who learned the carpenter's trade in exile, this person who devotes himself to healing the sick and feeding the hungry and blessing the poor, this person who preaches forgiveness and acceptance and love of enemies, this person who commands turning the other cheek and giving both coat and cloak and offering what we have to those who are in need and trusting only to God's goodness, this person who says that it is necessary for us to walk into the very headquarters of the evildoers who are out to destroy him and who *will* destroy him, this person who says that anyone who would follow *him* must do the same, this person who came and touched the disciples who had fallen to the ground and were overcome by fear and said to them, "Get up and do not be afraid" (17:7b). This is the Messiah whom Peter identified, without even knowing the meaning of what he had announced. "This is my Son, the Beloved," said the voice from heaven; "with him I am well pleased; listen to him!" (17:5b)

In an age dedicated to convenience and comfort and entertainment and profit and me-ism, will Christianity *continue* to be a cross-bearing religion? Will Christians follow the Messiah back down off the mountain to minister to the sick, hungry, homeless masses? Or will Christianity be a religion that grants the privilege of *escaping* the press of the crowd and *remaining* on the mountain to bask in the glow of Jesus' radiance, unmoved by the sorrows of the world? It depends, I think, upon what we understand the meaning of "Messiah" to be, and, if we decide that "Messiah" has something to do with servanthood and being willing to obey even to the point of surrendering everything, then there is the question of taking the teachings of *that* sort of Messiah *truly* to *heart*. Are we impressed by the transfiguration mainly because of the spectacular *vision*, or because of the authoritative *command*? As far as its value for disciples, the transfiguration is important only if it convinces *us* to *attend obediently* to Jesus' teachings in word and deed as God's direction to *us*. The climax of the transfiguration was when, having heard the divine confirmation that *Jesus is* the Son of God, the Messiah, the disciples followed Jesus back down from the mountaintop and ministered to the sick and the hungry and the sin-ridden, which drew them closer and closer to Jerusalem.

There has been a strange silence in response to the invasion by the health-and-wealth gospel into the church during the 1980s and 1990s. Where is the testimony of those who believe that Jesus is to be taken at his word when he says, "If any want to become my followers, let them deny themselves and take up their cross and follow me. For those who want to *save* their life will *lose* it, and those who lose their life for *my* sake will *find* it" (16:24–25)? There has been a strange silence in response to charges by those who benefit from the status quo that the mainline churches are too cozy with the world. Where is the testimony of Christians who take seriously the need to wade out courageously into the social discussions of the day giving witness to Jesus, who welcomes to his table the despised and the rejected, foreigners and all manner of folk who were considered unclean? There has been a strange silence in response to complaints that socially active Christians are ignoring the imperatives of the Bible. Where is the testimony of those who take literally the prophetic witness of God's concern for the poor and the gospel witness of Jesus' ministry to the poor, and the witness of scripture from front to back that people of faith are to elevate the needs of the destitute above the desires bred by our own self-interested affluence? It is time for the church to declare again that what Jesus said and what Jesus did are the very word and act of God, and that the command "Listen to him!" means for Christians to be attentive and active in overcoming selfishness and complacency and greed. Will we be a servant people following a servant Lord down from the Mount of the Transfiguration through the valley of human need and up the hill of Calvary? Or will we stay firmly at ease in our tents? The issue is joined today in a manner that tests the very roots of our faith.

Years after the strange event on the mountaintop, Peter, or someone writing in his name, testified in scripture that it was *Jesus Christ*, the minister to the poor and blind and hungry and lame and despised and diseased who "received honor and glory from God the Father when that voice was conveyed to him by the Majestic Glory, saying, 'This is my Son, my Beloved, with whom I am well pleased'" (2 Pet 1:17). The transfiguration was God's confirmation that Jesus is the promised Messiah, the Son of the living God—Jesus, who told his disciples and tells *us*, "If any want to become my followers, let them deny themselves and take up their cross and follow me" (Matt 16:24).

Ash Wednesday
Spanish Springs Presbyterian Church, Sparks, Nevada
February 13, 2002
ISAIAH 58:1–12
2 CORINTHIANS 5:20b—6:10
MATTHEW 6:1–6, 16–21

"A Proper Lent"

WE ARE GATHERED HERE tonight to worship God as we begin the season of Lent. Traditionally, Lent is a time of reflection; and penitence—of considering how far we have fallen short of God's expectations, and for seeking to make amends. By the Middle Ages, the church had developed an elaborate system of calculating the punishment one would receive after death for various sins, and particular deeds that sinners could perform in *this* life to reduce the length of punishment in the *next*. You and I are spiritual heirs of church reformers who *rejected* such tallies and remedies. Martin Luther and John Calvin and Martin Bucer and others saw no biblical rationale for practices of that kind. They found nothing in scripture that supports the notion that we can in *any* way earn God's approval by *works*, or, to put it more bluntly, that we can escape purgatory by masses and pilgrimages and reciting phrases and paying money.

We are saved not by anything that *we* can *do*, you and I. We do not deserve, and can never earn, God's saving mercy. God's forgiveness is based not on what *we* do, but on what *God* has *already done*, sacrificing his own Son on the cross. And, because we recognize that, we are freed from any need to draw attention to our own goodness by praying longer and more loudly than other people do, or by giving more money, and more publicly, than other people do, or by fasting more severely and more often than other people do. But for forty days—reminiscent of Jesus' retreat in the wilderness and his facing down temptation, reminiscent of the Israelites' wandering in the desert and learning to trust and obey God, reminiscent of Noah's journey on the ark and making a new start for this creation that God loves—we are still invited, through the message of the scripture readings, through the mood of the music, through the extra opportunities for study and prayer, to consider soberly and honestly the ways in which we have been unfaithful to God and disloyal to Christ and unresponsive to the Holy Spirit.

There is nothing in scripture that requires self-flagellation, either spiritually or physically. But it is appropriate, as we approach Good Friday, to reflect, to consider, to adopt disciplines that can help us grow more aware of God in our lives and in the world around us, can help us draw closer to Jesus Christ as our Lord and our friend, can make us more sensitive to the leading of the Holy Spirit in our vocations, in our home life, in our civic responsibilities, in our neighborhoods, in our church. And as Easter nears, when the church each year celebrates the joyous news of Christ's resurrection, it is appropriate for us to ponder what Christ's being our risen and living Lord means as a practical matter—to examine whether, in our thoughts and our words and our actions, we truly *believe* that Christ is risen, we truly *behave* as if Christ is still living, we truly give *Christ* our loyal allegiance as Lord of our lives.

In ancient Israel, people thought of piety in terms of giving alms and praying and fasting. Perhaps these are some of the things that come to mind when you and I think of Lent. Undoubtedly, for some people, Lent is an introduction to prayer and fasting and giving alms. When I was a child, living in the heavily Roman Catholic city of El Paso, it was quite obvious that Lent, for a lot of people, was a time of year (and, perhaps for some people, the *only* time of year) for fasting and praying and giving financially. I came to think of such things as "Catholic," something that Protestants don't do. I wasn't yet so familiar with the Gospel according to Matthew. Did you listen carefully to what Jesus said in our Gospel reading this evening? Jesus seems to have taken for granted that his followers would naturally do things like pray and fast and give alms. In the Sermon on the Mount, he didn't say, "*if* you give alms"; he said, "*when* you give alms" (Matt 6:3). He didn't say, "*if* you pray"; he said, "*whenever* you pray" (6:6). He didn't say, "*if* you fast"; he said, "*when* you fast" (6:17). These things aren't the exclusive property of Roman Catholicism. These are things that *Protestants* should do, too. These are things that people of faith in God were doing even before the birth of Jesus.

Jesus, of course, and the prophets before him, too, objected to doing *anything* for the purpose of drawing attention to *ourselves*, criticized rituals that made no change in the condition of the human heart, dismissed as pointless much that popularly is referred to as "religious." Anything that the worshiper might do to put the emphasis on herself or himself missed entirely the *real point* of worship, and the *true nature* of faith. To do something in order to be admired by one's fellows wins just that—human approval. But Jesus went even further than criticizing things done to impress *others*. He said that to do some pious act in order to impress *ourselves* is to have a *prideful* motive for praying, for fasting, for giving an offering. "When *you* give alms, do not let your left hand know what your right hand is doing, so that your alms may be done in secret; and your Father who *sees* in secret will reward you" (6:3–4). Jesus was saying that we should give not out of a calculating spirit, but freely and spontaneously and thankfully. We should not only avoid lifting ourselves up in the eyes of the people *around* us, but avoid lifting ourselves up in our *own* eyes. For *either* of those motives says that we are doing the thing for our own gratification and our own promotion, to feed *our pride* rather than to respond to *God's love*. Undoubtedly, that is one reason that the Reformers regarded Lent as not very useful and even detrimental to one's spiritual well-being. So a lot of us in the Protestant tradition have grown up hardly noticing Lent at all, realizing, perhaps, that we should live faithfully in *all* seasons, but never really taking the opportunity to think deeply about what that means. There is wisdom to the traditional Christian calendar, and those who follow it—not slavishly, but as an aid to memory and understanding—find that they begin to *share* the *rhythm* of Christ's own life.

But to become more deeply entwined in *Christ's* own life is to become more profoundly open to the joys and sorrows of *others*. Truly to draw nearer to *Christ* is to become more sensitive to the needs of the *world*. To be grateful that God has bridged the gap that our sin creates between God and us by sacrificing Jesus on the cross is to commit *ourselves* to bridging the gap that our *mutual* sin creates between us and our fellow men and women. The apostle Paul was deeply grieved to know that he and several members of the church in Corinth were estranged from one another. He had been instrumental in the establishment and growth of the church at Corinth. But party strife and religious faction there had created division and alienation, rivalry and contention that had no place in the life of Christ's church. Did those who were bickering and backbiting not know that Christ died for their sisters and their brothers whom they were slandering, whom they were shunning, whom they were treating with contempt? Did they not understand that Christ was all about reconciling people to God, and that meant reconciling people to one another? There could be no righteousness apart from doing right by each other. There could be no salvation outside of the saving community of the church. There could be no treasure in heaven if they were trying to deny their brothers and sisters the riches of God's grace.

Salvation is not a finish line that anyone arrives at by pushing others out of the way. And, in our epistle lesson this evening, Paul catalogued a list of ways in which he had denied himself and put others first in his discipleship—living the Lenten life even before there *was* a season of Lent, fasting not by design but by virtue of sometimes simply not having anything to eat, because he had given up his livelihood for the sake of the gospel; praying not because the calendar commanded it but because he cared deeply about the people whom Christ had called him to serve; giving everything he had not as a way of buying his entrance into heaven but because Jesus his Lord had given up everything, even his life, for Paul. "As servants of God, we have commended ourselves in every way: through great endurance, in afflictions, hardships, calamities, beatings, imprisonments, riots, labors, sleepless nights, hunger; by purity, knowledge, patience, kindness, holiness of spirit, genuine love, truthful speech, and the power of God; with the weapons of righteousness for the right hand and for the left; in honor and dishonor; in ill repute and good repute" (2 Cor 6:4–8a). It was not a matter of personal pride or selfish gain for Paul. It was all about his love for Jesus Christ that compelled deeds of love for others, including the Christians at Corinth. But nothing that Paul could give up for the sake of preaching and doing the good news of Jesus Christ could be more than what God had already given Paul. "We are treated as impostors, and yet are true; as unknown, and yet are well known; as dying, and see—we are alive; as punished, and yet not killed; as sorrowful, yet always rejoicing; as poor, yet making many rich; as having nothing, and yet possessing everything" (6:8b–10).

Fasting, praying, giving alms, and all the other things that have been associated with Lent from time to time and that you and I might consider extraordinary and sometimes deem contrived—they're of no avail if piety ends there. "Look," God said through the prophet Isaiah, "you serve your own interest on your fast day, and oppress all your workers" (Isa 58:3b). Those who ate very well the other days of the week, those who could afford to take a day off from work to attend religious ceremonies while insisting that their employees toil in their absence, those who enjoyed the attention their sackcloth and ashes and their ritual dishevelment attracted to their religiosity, God *condemned* rather than *applauded*. "Look, *you* fast only to quarrel and to fight and to strike with a wicked fist. Such fasting as you do today will not make your voice heard on high" (58:4). They weren't practicing humility. They were stoking their own pride. "Is such the fast that I choose, a day to humble oneself? Is it to bow down the head like a bulrush, and to lie in sackcloth and ashes? Will you call this a fast, a day acceptable to the Lord?" (58:5). To seek God's favor by drawing distinctions between one's righteous self and *others' sinfulness* doesn't impress God in the least. Holiness is not measured by an annual gesture of self-righteousness, but in daily actions of freeing others from the bondage of poverty and sickness and oppression and despair, from the burden of guilt and loneliness and injustice and shame. "Is not *this* the fast that *I* choose: to loose the bonds of injustice, to undo the thongs of the yoke, to let the oppressed go free, and to break every yoke? Is it not to share your bread with the hungry, and bring the homeless poor into your house; when you see the naked, to cover them, and not to hide yourself from your own kin?" (58:6–7). *That* is what will get God's attention more than any practiced ceremony or prescribed ritual. *That* is what constitutes a *proper* Lent—one that makes love a habit and sacrifice a joy and forgiveness a well that is never exhausted. "Then you shall call, and the Lord will answer; you shall cry for help, and he will say, Here I am" (58:9a).

Receive the smudge of ashes not as a sign that you have become *better* than others, but as a sign that you recognize your role in the common sin of humankind, *and* your role in God's purpose of redemption. *When* you fast during this Lenten season, do so out of commitment that others may eat who otherwise would be hungry. *When* you pray over these next forty days, do so out of gratitude for the salvation that has already been won for you by Christ's death on the cross and that compels you to be infinitely forbearing and generously forgiving of others. *When* you give of your material wealth for the sake of the poor and of the poor in spirit as, together, we draw closer to the cross on which our Savior died, remember that Christ died also for the person to the right of you and the person to the left of you and the person who speaks a different language, whose skin is a different color, who may even confess a different creed. So, you will grow in your compassion and sympathy for others, you will increase in the wonderment of your own salvation, you will feast richly at the table our Lord spreads before us now in anticipation of the feast that awaits us all in the kingdom of heaven. To do so, dear ones, is to observe a proper Lent.

First Sunday in Lent
Spanish Springs Presbyterian Church, Sparks, Nevada
February 17, 2002
Genesis 2:4b–9, 15–17, 25—3:7
Romans 5:12–19
Matthew 4:1–11

"Who Do You Trust?"

There is probably no part of the Bible that has been so often quoted and so often misunderstood as the story of the garden in Eden. For many centuries, and especially within the Protestant tradition of the Christian church, it has been misused to justify the subjugation of women, it has been misused to create an aura of taboo and shame around sex and sexuality, it has been misused to decipher the reason that people die, it has been misused to explain the pervasiveness of sin, it has been misused to warrant the pollution of the planet and the destruction of wildlife habitat and the elimination of whole species, it has been misused to characterize God's creation as bad and therefore something that we should denigrate in life and look forward to escaping from in death.

Actually, the garden in Eden story stands for *none* of these things. To the degree that we *use* it for these purposes, we have *misread* it and, regrettably, we are *missing* the *true* point that it makes. The *woman* was no less important to God's purpose than the *man*. There is nothing inherently shameful about the sexual activity that *God*, in fact, *commanded*. People were *already* made of dust and subject to degeneration and death and decay from the moment they were first created, and as it turned out, eating the forbidden fruit *didn't* cause them to die. Genesis doesn't say that we are born *in* or *with sin*. God's command was to *preserve* and *take care of* creation and promote the natural capacities that God had ordained. God had already, in the previous chapter, pronounced "good" everything that God had created, including humankind, and it's really not appropriate to accuse God of being a liar.

But something very significant *did* happen in the garden in Eden story that is fundamental to our proper understanding about God and about humankind—a test that our very first ancestors *failed*, and that you and I face daily. It has to do with the fact that God has an intention and purpose and design for creation. It has to do with the fact that God has *communicated* that intention and purpose and design to the only creatures who have a moral self-consciousness. It has to do with the fact that God created human beings with the ability to make choices. It has to do with fear. And it has to do with trust.

At first, there *was* no issue of trust in the garden. God made human beings, as God had made other creatures, and provided for their needs. God gave them a vocation—to till the garden and keep it, to name the creatures that had no names for themselves, to become one flesh, suggesting sexual union. God invited them to feast on every fruit the garden produced except only the fruit that came from one lone tree. They had remarkable freedom and remarkably few questions. They took as *true* what God said, and they took at *face value* God's promise to take care of them and their needs, and God's *ability* to take care of them and their needs. All was paradise.

But then an element of *doubt* about God's goodness was introduced, and with it, fear and anxiety came into the world that God had created to be peaceful and secure. We all know about the conversation between the woman and the serpent. Notice that the woman seemed to have no *fear* of the serpent, and, by the way, seems not to have regarded it as unusual that animals could talk. "Did God say, 'You shall not . . . ?'" (Gen 3:1). And immediately, and for the first time, the focus shifted from God's providence and permission to God's reservation and restriction. And when the serpent said, "You will not die" (3:4), there was introduced the possibility that God had lied—there was introduced the possibility that there was some *other* authority about how to live in the world than *God* who *made* the world. And when the serpent said, "[God] knows that when you eat of it your eyes will be opened, and you will be like God, knowing good and evil" (3:5), the trustworthiness of God's motives became an issue, centered on the *very* question that has *ever after* been the chief source of fear and anxiety for humankind—death.

The man and the woman in the story hadn't had to think about that before—they had simply trusted God to take care of them, to meet their needs, to continue providing what was good for them in life *or* in death. Now, the matter of trust was joined intimately to fear—the fear of death—and the suspicion that God was withholding something that was necessary to their best interests, wasn't telling them the whole story, was being dishonest with them, was manipulating them. That suspicion came to dominate the relationship between man, woman, and God; the serpent's suggestion in fact *poisoned* the relationship between man, woman, and God with the venom of distrust at life's most sensitive point. And those who had been made for each other became ashamed to be looked upon by the other, and by God who made them, and they were afraid, and they hid.

When the one condition established by God in their lease agreement for the garden in Eden came to be scrutinized as an *option*, their entire existence became controlled by distrust, and the result was constant and pervasive anxiety. When they chose to *question* God's promise, when they came to *doubt* God's providential care, when they decided that they must take their future into their *own* hands, they became *enemies* of each other, preoccupied with achieving some *advantage* one over the other and *concealing* their *true* selves and they became *alienated* from God, supposing that they were all alone in a dangerous world that God had *actually* created for fellowship and community and had pronounced *good*. Even *God*, they now interpreted as a *threat*. Their vocation, they neglected. Their peace, they rejected. Their whole consciousness, they now focused completely on their own selves. And they were afraid. Their new agenda of seeking their *own* good brought with it only *terror*—a way of life vastly different from all the good things God desired for them, a destiny that God had not envisioned for any of us.

Commentators disagree about exactly what the tree of the knowledge of good and evil represents. I think it has to do with reaching for something that is not properly within our grasp—the desire to choose for *ourselves* how the world should be. But we must not be overly occupied with identifying exactly what sort of "knowledge" the "knowledge of good and evil" is. The *real* issue is trusting the word of God, which means, ultimately, trusting God as our highest authority, trusting that *God's* wisdom is greater than ours, including God's establishment of *limits*, trusting that God wants only what is *best* for us. By the way, as a Latin major, I know the difference between subject and object, and that today's sermon should properly be titled "*Whom* Do You Trust?," but some of us are old enough to remember that Johnny Carson, before he became the star of the Tonight Show, was the emcee of a television game show called "Who Do You Trust?" Of course, it was intended purely as entertainment. But the show's title, perhaps inadvertently, raises what is the most profoundly crucial question that you and I face in life. Psychologists tell us that trust is *the* major issue of human development, starting in infancy and early childhood. In the infancy of the world and childhood of human experience, the wrong choice set *awry* God's heartfelt hope for creation, and introduced the emotions of fear and anxiety. And although our first ancestors did not immediately suffer *physical* death, their confidence in God died, and, perhaps, their spirits.

It is important for us to be clear that the temptation of the serpent was *not* to do something that looked at all *wicked*. The temptation was to become like *God*. What aspiration, on the face of it, could be more *pleasing* to God? It would be rather like being able to feed hungry people, or enlisting God's power to keep people from harm, or establishing a government of love and goodness over all the nations of the earth. The serpent was not suggesting murder or rape or grand larceny. Nor did the devil tempt Jesus with anything morally offensive in the wilderness. Quite to the contrary, turning rocks into loaves of bread to feed hungry people would be a wonderful thing, wouldn't it, with the added benefit that Jesus could feed himself since he was famished after forty days and nights of fasting? Demonstrating God's ability to safeguard from harm would certainly make a lot of people sit up and take notice that there *is* a God, besides confirming that God would respond at Jesus' beck and call. Think what Jesus could accomplish as the emperor of the world, replacing all of those selfish and narrow-minded despots on their pretentious thrones; surely worshiping Satan would be a small price to pay for world peace and prosperity!

"Away with you, Satan!" said Jesus, "for it is written, 'Worship the Lord your God, and serve only him'" (Matt 4:10). Even results that seem to *comport* with God's *purpose* cannot justify putting our trust in some authority *other* than God. Do we inhabit the earth that God has given us for our home on *God's* terms, or do we become distrusting of God when the timetable of peace becomes too slow, when the supply of food becomes too uncertain, when the length of life seems too short, when the fact of death itself leads us to think that we are being cheated by God? Do we creatures think that *we* are in a better position to know how creation should have been designed than the great cosmic *designer*? "You will not die," said the serpent, more crafty than any other wild animal that the Lord God had made; "for God knows that when you eat of it your eyes will be opened, and you will be like God, knowing good and evil" (Gen 3:4b–5). And right there, at the very beginning of the Bible, is the fundamental issue with which you and I and every human being have to grapple: Who do you trust? Will it be God, who brought us and everything that *is* into being, and who also, for whatever reason that is a product of divine wisdom, says there are some things that we must *not* do? Or will it be ourselves, who think that if being godlike is good for *God*, being godlike must be good for *us*, too, and we will choose to *ignore* whatever boundaries seem to stand between us and *im*mortality. Query: with all of our technological advances in genetics and data retrieval and analysis and electrical power grids and nuclear weaponry, how much less anxious and fearful are we than our ancestors were?

But the story of the garden in Eden is not a condemnation of science or technology or the quest for knowledge. It is a story about trusting God. It is often said, with regard to Eden, that we can't go back. But "the fall," as it is called, is more *John Milton's* description than the *Bible's*. Our dangerous games of trying to *deny* our mortality by amassing fortunes, by seeking fame, by conquering nations, by promoting ourselves as "number one" and turning all of life into a competition, all stem from our fear and anxiety that God's purpose is *not* good, that God's commands are *not* true, that God's promises are *not* dependable, that God *hasn't* been *honest* with us—that we need to grab and assert and domineer and guarantee for *ourselves* what we can't trust *God* to do *for* us—give some meaning to our existence that outlasts our conscious and bodily experience in this world. But the result is always the same. "So when the woman saw that the tree was good for food, and that it was a delight to the eyes, and that the tree was to be desired to make one wise, she took of its fruit and ate; and she also gave some to her husband, who was with her, and he ate" (3:6)—that is, the *man*, to whom God *first* pronounced the prohibition about eating the fruit of the tree. "Then the eyes of both were opened, and they knew that they were naked; and they sewed fig leaves together and made loincloths for themselves" (3:7). And when God came walking in the garden that evening, the man and the woman *hid* themselves, and "the Lord God called to the man, and said to him, 'Where are you?' [The man] said, 'I heard the sound of you in the garden, and I was afraid'" (3:10).

There are voices out there tempting us to try to create our own immortality—to find our security in spending our resources on weapons; to establish an immortal *reputation*, if not immortality *itself*, by how much we have and whom we control; to build our *own* paradise by gobbling up *today*, in *our* lifetime, what God gave as a heritage for *all* generations. They are voices that prey on our fears, and end up only magnifying our anxiety. When all is said and done, it comes down to the same question that Jesus answered by humbly and obediently submitting to the public shame and apparent failure of the cross—and finding in that humble obedience the *genuine* path to *eternal life*: The question, Who do *you* trust?

Second Sunday in Lent
Spanish Springs Presbyterian Church, Sparks, Nevada
February 24, 2002
GENESIS 12:1–4a
ROMANS 4:1–5, 13–17
JOHN 3:1–17

"Called to Be a Blessing"

THE TESTIMONY OF SCRIPTURE reaches out to us from the mist of ancient human memory and announces the first act in the saving history of God that culminates with the cross and the empty tomb: "Now the LORD said to Abram, 'Go from your country and your kindred and your father's house to the land that I will show you. I will make of you a great nation, and I will bless you, and make your name great, so that you will be a blessing. I will bless those who bless you, and the one who curses you I will curse; and in *you* all the families of the earth shall be blessed'" (Gen 12:1–3). Without any hint of why or how God chose Abraham, without any background information about Abraham's personality or character and very little about his circumstances, the Bible tersely records, "Now the LORD said to Abram, 'Go . . .'" (12:1a). And the Bible tells us just as simply and with as little description, "So Abram went . . ." (12:4a). And thus begins the *second* page of God's dealing with the world—a world in which creation had proved itself to be wayward, incapable, it seems, of righting itself, having tasted first of forbidden fruit, and then of blood.

But the point of the passage, and the importance of Abraham for people of faith ever since, in fact lies in that very sparsity of detail; no elaboration is required, for the essence of the matter is just this: the Lord spoke, and Abraham obeyed. There was no interlude required for thought, no balancing of pro's and con's before Abraham took the dramatic step of cutting himself off from home and family—a thing virtually unheard of in Semitic culture ancient or modern—solely on the strength of a fantastic promise—"I will ... make your name great" (12:2)—all the *more* fantastic because his wife, Sarah, was *barren*. Such a promise as God gave was beyond all human reason, but, then, so was such a response as Abraham made: "So Abram went, as the LORD had told him" (12:4a). It lies beyond logic, it precludes debate. It was, quite simply, the response of pure faith. God took a *chance* on Abraham, without any proof of his worthiness or certainty of his suitable obedience, so far as scripture tells us. And *Abraham* responded by taking a chance on *God*, without any negotiation with God or consultation with his family and without any demand for guarantee. Off Abraham went into the unknown, turning his back on the familiar and the friendly, obeying God's call and trusting in God's promise, scarcely conscious, we suppose, that the redemption of the entire race hinged on his faithfulness.

Walter Brueggemann, an Old Testament scholar who has done much to provide fresh perspective on the ancient stories in Genesis, points out the hopeless situation into which God's word of promise had come.[1] In the world in which Abraham and Sarah lived, her barrenness was the very opposite of promise. Humanly speaking, Abraham's family had no prospects at all, so central was *progeny* to one's being. Far from feeling "blessed," a couple that had no children would have been presumed to be "cursed" by God, and yet God promised blessing to Abraham whom he was calling to begin a pilgrimage, to abandon and renounce everything that he had known and to set out for he-knew-not-where. One thing was certain—to remain in the safety of the *familiar* and the *known* was to *remain barren*, and without any possibility of *changing* that circumstance; to *relinquish* safety and to *risk* setting out for the *unknown* was to act out *hope*. Abraham believed the promise. He asked no questions. He simply obeyed the call of God without any tangible guarantees or visible evidence. And as a result, this pioneer of faith, this prototype for every disciple who ever forsook everything and followed the leading of God, did indeed become what God *called* him to be—a blessing to all the families of the earth.

Some moderns might object that Abraham had nothing to lose by obeying God's call to leave home and journey into the unknown—unlike those of us today who have houses to care for and mortgage payments to make, careers in which we have invested considerable time and money

---

1. Brueggemann, *Genesis*, 117.

and *for* which we have developed impressive knowledge and skills, children whom we hope to send to the best colleges, and the need to amass financial provision for ourselves in our old age. Why should Abraham *not* have struck his tent and set out on an odyssey, simply for the sheer adventure of it? But such a question just proves the arrogance of our age. In fact, by hoisting his sail to catch God's breath which blows where it chooses, Abraham risked no less than *we* would. Responding to God's call *always* involves risk and requires willingness to abandon oneself to uncertainty, removing oneself from *old securities* and placing oneself in the situation where genuine *faith* may develop. In Abraham's time, travel was difficult, and journeying beyond the territories of one's own kinfolk was dangerous. Would there be food for his household? Would there be water for his stock? Would he and his entourage be greeted by strangers offering hospitality, or threatening hostility? Abraham could not have known the answer to any of these questions beforehand, and uncertainty as to any *one* of them would have been enough to keep many a twenty-first-century sophisticate from venturing reliance on God's promise. But only by a ready willingness to *leave* the comfortable security of *home* could the hopeless barrenness of Abraham's quiet existence be transformed into a fruitful life through which all the families of the earth would be blessed.

Faith is the capacity to embrace with such passion and courage and confidence the future that God has proclaimed that we willingly relinquish the comfortable securities of the present. And what the very terseness of scripture's description of God's call and Abraham's response attests is the faithfulness of Abraham. His life in Haran was not ideal, but it was familiar. Although he must have been troubled by not having an heir, there would have been a sense of security in the routine of his daily duties. There were probably times that he regarded his responsibilities within the family as a sacred obligation, moments in which what had always *been* must have suggested to him that so it always *should* be. But then came the call of God to *abandon* what had always been, to rise to a *new* responsibility of *cosmic* significance, to trust God as he had likely never had to trust anyone before, and so, to *allow* God to make of him a great nation, so that *he* would be a blessing.

According to John's Gospel, there was a Pharisee, a learned leader of the Jews, who came to Jesus, having been impressed with the divine nature of the signs that Jesus had performed. But the poor man was hobbled by the fetters of conventional wisdom and stale expectations. Like so many of *us* in the twenty-first century, this man was high on literalism and low on imagination; his soul had been so tutored in the prosaic that his mind could not understand the profound truth that only *poetry* can convey. And so he missed entirely Jesus' meaning when, having perceived the man's unspoken question, Jesus told him that no one can see the kingdom of God without being born from above. "How can anyone be born after having grown old?" the man objected. "Can one enter a second time into the mother's womb and be born?" (John 3:4). He had not the faith to venture out from his old perceptions of reality; although a teacher of Israel, he had not the trust in God's promise long given in the prophets to believe that God was calling him, Nicodemus, from earth-bound horizons to eternal life. And so, although he grew in respect for Jesus, and defended Jesus against critics, and even defied the authorities by going to pay respects to the dead body of Jesus after the crucifixion, Nicodemus never became a *disciple* of Jesus.

He could not; for *admiring* Jesus, even *quoting* Jesus, falls short of having *faith* in Jesus, falls short of *obeying* Jesus, falls short of being the Spirit's own progeny so that will and intellect may yield to unquestioning obedience to the divine call to risk and abandon. *"Only he who believes is obedient,"* wrote one of the twentieth century's most influential Christian theologians, *"and only he who is obedient believes. . . .* For faith is only real when there is obedience, never without it, and faith only becomes faith in the act of obedience."[2] And without risking the old self—the old securities, the old expectations, the old assumptions, the old hopelessness,—there is no learning the meaning of faith, and there can be no birth from above, and so, someone very much in need of being blessed through us must perhaps go *without* such a blessing. Abraham could not have known how critical *his* role would be in God's working the salvation of the world; he was merely answering the call of God to leave his old life behind and set out trustingly into the unknown which God was preparing. And yet, not "merely," for see how much depended upon his being faithful! It is not *ours* to judge how God will use our faithfulness, as it was not *Abraham's* to judge, as indeed it was not *Jesus'* role to judge how God would use *his* faithfulness on the cross. Nor is it ours to demand safety in the doing or to be guaranteed of successful results. No call of God is void of God's purpose. No purpose of God is insignificant. No one who *responds* to God's call can *fail* to be a blessing.

---

2. Bonhoeffer, *Cost of Discipleship*, 69 (emphasis original).

To what adventure of faith may God in Jesus Christ be calling *you*? Is it to *remain* in some hopeless situation of barrenness? Is it to *rest* in the assumption that God wants nothing more *from* you than you have already given, and nothing more *of* you than you already are? Or is it to risk setting out on a pilgrimage without any earthly guarantee of reward and without any tangible proof of success, but which is needful to further God's purpose of redeeming creation? To what adventure of faith may God in Jesus Christ be calling this church? We wouldn't be here in a new church if we thought that God wanted us to *remain* in the comfort of the familiar, the proven, the secure. Less than three and half years old, we can't rest content with what *has* been, under the assumption that nothing more ever *can* be. Surely you and I recognize the need boldly and imaginatively to commit our energies and our resources to mission and ministry both here in Spanish Springs and around the world in response to the call that God places before us in scripture and in headlines, whether the opportunity presents itself in the form of a denominational appeal received in the mail from Louisville or in the form of an indigent sojourner who knocks at or door. It requires courage to risk journeying into the unknown. It requires faith. The children of *Nicodemus* protect themselves from the risk of God's unknown by objecting to the cost of venturing out, to the impracticality of venturing out, to the discomfort of venturing out. Captive to worldly concerns, they never act in faith. The children of *Abraham* neither debate the merits of God's call nor ponder the inconvenience of it nor ignore it in hope that the opportunity for faithful obedience will pass unnoticed. Born from above, they simply hear the call of God, and obey, and they become a blessing.

"Now the Lord said to Abram, 'Go . . .'" (Gen 12:1a). "So Abram went . . ." (12:4a). That is faith. And that is what people *do* who answer the call to be a blessing.

Third Sunday in Lent
First Presbyterian Church, Dodge City, Kansas
March 7, 1993
EXODUS 17:1-7
ROMANS 5:1-11
JOHN 4:5-42

"Life in the Wilderness"

THE HEBREWS WERE WANDERING somewhere in the wilderness between the Red Sea and Canaan, between promise and fulfillment. God had shown with a mighty miracle that they were not to remain in the hopeless occupation of slavery, and had tapped Moses as the one through whom God would bring them up out of Egypt and deliver them to a land of their own where they could thrive and prosper in freedom. But in between, there was that vast empty space of mountains and deserts and threatening armies, devoid of anything like civilization, lacking even in food and water, to all appearances.

This generation, of course, had never seen Canaan, the land of their ancestors Abraham and Isaac and Jacob. Their journey was based solely on hope. Egypt, they *knew*—the harshness of their taskmasters, but also the predictability of bread to eat and water to drink. They had been glad enough to leave, but their destination was so far beyond the horizon that after a few days or a few weeks or a few months, they began to doubt, and then to complain, and then to accuse. First, they complained about the lack of food: "If only we had died by the hand of the Lord in the land of Egypt, when we sat by the fleshpots and ate our fill of bread; for you have brought us out into this wilderness to kill this whole assembly with hunger" (Exod 16:3). Then, in this morning's reading, they complained about the lack of water: "Why did you bring us out of Egypt, to kill us and our children and livestock with thirst?" (17:3b).

Now, food and water are not unreasonable requests. And we have to be a little astounded to realize that, so far as the Bible is concerned, neither Moses nor God had thought about the people's need to eat and drink on their journey. An oversight in planning? Moses was pretty exercised about the situation. "So Moses cried out to the LORD, 'What shall I *do* with this people? They are almost ready to *stone* me'" (17:4). And God responded, in the first instance with a fine flaky bread that came with the morning dew and the sudden appearance of quails in the camp at evening, and, in the second instance, with a flow of water that sprang from a rock at the base of Mount Horeb when Moses struck the stone with his staff—the same staff that Moses used to turn the Nile to blood, poisoning the river of Egypt, and then to dry up a path through the sea for the Israelites' way of escape.

It is important to the point of the story that God did not turn the wilderness miraculously into a garden—God did not create a ribbon of green across the center of the Sinai for the people, where they and anyone could simply progress from one oasis to the next one visible just a few miles away. The wilderness *remained* a wilderness. The desert *remained* a desert. The barrenness *remained*, to the *eye*, just *that*. But when the people cried out, when Moses appealed for help, God provided whatever was needed, and did so for what turned out to be a long, long journey. And the Israelites, after they finally came into Canaan, remembered those forty years in the desert as a golden age of faith, in which they learned who God *was*, and came to *trust* God, and found God *reliable*. It had not been *easy*, had not been *pleasant*, but it *had* been *needful*. And every time the people were in danger of *forgetting* the importance of reliance on God, of obedience to God, of the faithfulness of God, there arose a prophet to remind them of the time that God brought their ancestors up out of the misery of slavery in Egypt and sustained them miraculously across the wilderness that offered no obvious means of survival, but in which God nevertheless was present and answered their cries and satisfied their needs. The people had feared *death* in the wilderness. But it was in the *wilderness* that God in fact gave them *life*.

Modern geologists and hydrologists say that, indeed, there is quite a lot of water in the Sinai, locked in an aquifer that can be penetrated by today's drilling equipment. But you certainly wouldn't know it to look across the landscape. Perhaps if there *had* been an oasis early along their way, the Israelites would have been content to settle down *there*, far short of the destination God had reserved for them, far short of fulfilling the destiny God had in mind for them—the destiny of being a blessing to all the families of the earth, as we read last Sunday. But this was supposed to be a community on the move from a past that was intolerable for them and unsatisfactory to God, to a future of blessing not only for themselves but for all of creation. In between, they must pass through the wilderness, a space of seeming chaos and incompleteness, of yearning and unsettledness, but also a place of hope in which their well-being required that they have faith in the God who had proclaimed the promise and through whom alone it could and would be fulfilled.

It is difficult, sometimes, to recognize the hopeless situations in which we exist if we have become accustomed to them. For the Israelites, slavery must have become normal. They got up in the morning, ate their ration of gruel, went out to sweat in the sun all day making bricks and building buildings that did not belong to them and that they would never enjoy, and then went back to their quarters at night for another ration of gruel and then sleep so they could get up the next day and do it all over again. It sounds like the routine of a lot of folks even *today* who aren't slaves in the *technical* sense, but still see no possibility for anything different. Or it may be a marriage in which there is no intimacy or shared dream. Or it may be a public mindset that has created and now accepts as normal an order based on fear and requires that we always have an enemy in order to insure, for those who benefit from it, the continuation of the status quo. It isn't that that sort of life is *good*, or good for *us*, but we have *adapted* to it, even though it has meant remaining in bondage.

And then something happens—some word of challenge, some glimmer of hope, some promise of freedom—that coaxes us out of the familiar box. Some impossibility suddenly crumbles and a way is opened before us—some Red Sea is miraculously parted—and we timidly venture forth, and then are daunted to discover that we have to traverse a trackless wilderness landscape before entering the promised land. The territory lacks the landmarks to which we've grown accustomed. We're suddenly responsible for having to choose which clocks and whistles we will answer. The gruel isn't plopped down on schedule on a table in front of us. And we wonder why we ever left our familiar, if oppressive, past. And we fear that we will die of hunger and thirst before we get to where we're going.

The story of Israel's existence in the Sinai is a testimony that God gives *life* in the wilderness—both that there *is* such life, and that God is the *source* of it. Moses did not, God did not, bring the Israelites out of

Egypt to kill them and their children and their livestock with either hunger or thirst. But God *did* bring them into the wilderness to develop *faith*. And there was manna in the morning and quails in the evening and water from the hardest and driest of rocks. When the need was food and water, God did not answer Moses' desperate plea with advice about how to deal with the people's complaining, how to be a better leader, how to find an easier road. God provided the food that was needed and the water that was required, right there in the forbidding wilderness, just where one would least expect it. Bread from heaven. Water from stone. The people were still in the wilderness. But, they learned, so was God.

A woman of Samaria was locked into a routine that boded no possibility of change, no expectation of newness. Every day was pretty much the same as the one before, a burden of gossip, a chore at the well. Very likely, no one had ever spoken to her words promising anything better, or different. The common interpretation of her marital history was that she had found all of her meaning in promiscuity; that may be the case, or maybe she never seemed able to please her husbands, and so she was successively divorced and remarried (remember, a *woman's* ability to initiate a divorce was pretty limited in those days). As likely as not, she had been battered and abused. The fact that she had been married so many times suggests that she had become accustomed to the basic situation, even though the faces of the men kept changing. At any rate, she encountered a liberator one day as she was going about her normal routine. She "came to draw water, and Jesus said to her, 'Give *me* a drink, . . . The Samaritan woman said to him, 'How is it that you, a Jew, ask a drink of me, a woman of Samaria?' (Jews do not share things in common with Samaritans)" (John 4:7, 9). The literal translation of that would be, "Jews do not use vessels in common with Samaritans"—like buckets or ladles. So she was surprised that a *Jew* would even *consider* receiving a drink of water from a *Samaritan*. "Jesus answered her, 'If you knew the gift of God, and who it is that is saying to you, "Give me a drink," *you* would have asked *him*, and *he* would have given you *living* water'" (4:10).

Jesus, at this point, was inviting the woman to step out of her life that was enmeshed in repeated disappointment and constant rumor and endless routine and into a life of freedom and self-respect and fulfillment, whatever specific shape it would take. She would have to cast aside habitual assumptions and her ordinary way of looking at things, which meant, for her, entering a wilderness. Referring to the well, "Jesus said to her, 'Everyone who drinks of this water will be thirsty again, but those who drink of the water that *I* will give them will *never* be thirsty. The water that *I* will give will become in them a spring of water gushing up to eternal life.' The woman said to him, 'Sir, give me this water, so that I may never be thirsty or have to keep coming here to draw water'" (4:13–15). She entered the wilderness, the region of risk devoid of the familiar landmarks and the accustomed abuses. She affirmed that she had heard of a promised land: "The woman said to [Jesus], 'I know that Messiah is coming' (who is called Christ)" (4:25a). And Jesus confirmed just how close she had come to it: "Jesus said to her, 'I am he, the one who is speaking to you'" (4:26). And she left her water jar behind and went back to the city telling everyone to come out and see a man who had told her everything she had ever done. She was not quite to the promised land yet—she still was not completely certain that *this* was the person she and her people had been waiting for,—but she was pretty close. She entered the wilderness by stepping across the prescribed boundaries of behavior—talking to a Jewish man who happened to be at the well one day—and found life there. "'Those who drink of the water that I will give them will never be thirsty,'" Jesus told her. "'The water that I will give will become in them a spring of water gushing up to eternal life'" (4:14).

A wilderness always lies between where we are and where God calls us to be—as individuals, as a society, as a church. And the wilderness sometimes looks so forbidding that it causes us to give up any possibility of crossing it; the promise sounds good, but better not venture getting stuck out there without food and without water, so we stay in the old bondage to which we have become accustomed, even though we may hate it, even though we sense that it is far less than the freedom for which we yearn and for which we were created. But the wilderness is the place where faith is learned—where we can see no oasis anywhere around us but only hard, dry rock, and so we turn, as we must, to God, and suddenly there flows out what we need for abundant, and eternal, life.

Fourth Sunday in Lent
Spanish Springs Presbyterian Church, Sparks, Nevada
March 6, 2005
1 SAMUEL 16:1–13
EPHESIANS 5:8–14
JOHN 9:1–41

"Sight Restored"

AS A MINISTER, I have often been asked, "What was wrong with those people that they didn't understand who Jesus was?" And a close second is the corollary, "Why didn't they do what he said?" In my own mind, that immediately raises the question, "Why don't those of *us* who *know* who Jesus was do what he said?"

We frequently tend to hold the people of the *Bible* up to a standard of Christian behavior that we *modern* Christians fail to achieve. And that raises the further question about *us*: Don't *we* understand who Jesus was? And that's not just a question for the newer Christians among us, or the younger ones, but even and more especially those who have been Christians for many years, who have grown up and perhaps grown old with the reading and hearing of the gospel. For what is true of people in *general* is just as true of *Christians*: the more we *think* we know—perhaps the more we *tell* people how much we know,—the *more*, it is likely, we have to *learn*. And the more *dogmatic* and *self-righteous* our attitude about our faith, the more certain it is that we have missed the meaning of Jesus. That, after all, was the problem with the *Pharisees*—they knew all about the scriptures, they knew all about the law, but they were so absolute in what they *thought* they knew, they couldn't perceive that Jesus was the Son of God. What was *wrong* with those people? Frankly, they were too much like *us*.

No story in the Gospels makes the point better than the incident of the man born blind. As usual, it is important to look at the context of the passage—what comes *before* and what comes *after*. In the chapters leading up to this episode, the Pharisees and the temple authorities and the other leaders of the Jews have been complaining about Jesus, and some have even sought to have him arrested. In the chapter immediately before this one, Jesus shames those who are about to stone a woman caught in adultery, which the law commanded as punishment for such an act, and then he declares himself to be "'the light of the world'" (John 8:12). Some of the Jews ask him point blank, "'Who are you?'" (8:25), and accuse him of being possessed by a demon, and *then* try to stone *him*. It is then that John shows Jesus walking along and coming across a man born blind. Jesus quickly disposes of the disciples' question about whether it was the *man* or his *parents* who had sinned so that his blindness was a punishment—he was not born blind as a punishment for anyone's sin, Jesus says, but so that God's work might be made manifest. And then Jesus spits on the ground and makes mud and smears it on the man's eyes and tells him to go wash in the waters of Siloam. Now, Siloam is the very pool from which the water was drawn for the rituals of the Feast of Tabernacles, and it was on the occasion of the Feast of Tabernacles that Jesus had declared, "'Let anyone who is thirsty come to me, and let the one who believes in me drink'" (7:37b–38a). John helpfully informs us that "Siloam" means "sent," and John all the way through his Gospel has been referring to Jesus as "he who was sent." So John signals, in many ways, that this episode of curing the man who had been born blind is a manifestation of the identity of Jesus, providing a frank *answer* to the Jews' question, "'Who are you?'"

If that were all there was to it, the Pharisees might have been jealous of Jesus, but they would have had no grounds for criticizing him. The problem comes in the innocent-sounding little verse, "Now it was a *sabbath* day when Jesus made the mud and opened his eyes" (9:14). The issue wasn't that Jesus had performed a *miracle*; *that* wasn't what precipitated the crisis in the council of the Pharisees that led to the man being interrogated, and the man's *parents* being interrogated, and then the man *himself* a *second* time, and finally his being expelled from the synagogue. At least officially, the objection was that Jesus had made clay on the *sabbath*. The act of kneading either dough or clay was one of the thirty-nine things specifically forbidden to be done on the sabbath under the law. And it was *that*, the *very* sort of slip-up for which the Pharisees had been *watching*, that led them to *pounce*. It wasn't the man who had been *healed* that they were really after—it was *Jesus*. But when the man ridiculed their pompous and self-righteous claims to all religious knowledge, they threw him out of the synagogue.

The Pharisees, in their self-assurance of their wisdom and their self-righteousness of their purity and their self-proclamation of their authority on the matters of God, knew for a fact that anyone who broke God's *law* could *not* have been *sent* by God. "'This man is not from God,'" they snorted, "'for he does not observe the sabbath'" (9:16a). Proof positive. Point made. Case closed, as far as they were concerned. And if we think that such simplistic litmus-testing is confined to the past, consider for just a moment some of the tests being applied *today* in judging who is and who isn't a real Christian, or who is and who isn't a person of God, or who is and who isn't worthy of God's merciful love. At least, we ought to be aware enough of our own tendency to make such judgments to begin to comprehend "why those people don't understand who Jesus was"—Jesus, who seemed to violate, in fact *did* violate, the laws that they knew by heart were the rules by which God wanted all good people to live. "Some of the Pharisees said, 'This man is not from God, for he does not observe the sabbath'" (9:16a).

Your test and mine might not be whether a person makes clay on the sabbath, but you and I very likely have some similarly simple standards by which we judge whether a person is *godly* or not, whether a person is a *Christian* or not. "But others," John tells us, "said, 'How can a man who is a *sinner* perform such *signs*?'" (9:16b). And the man who had been healed said himself of Jesus, when interrogated by the keepers and interpreters of the law, "'I do not know whether he is a sinner. One thing I *do* know, that though I was *blind*, now I *see*. . . . Never since the world began has it been heard that anyone opened the eyes of a person born blind. If this man were not from God, he could do nothing'" (9:25, 32–33). "'As long as I am in the world,'" Jesus had said when he first saw the man born blind, "'I am the light of the world'" (9:5). And he said to his disciples, to those who were his followers, "'We must work the works of him who sent me while it is day'" (9:4a)—"'*we* must work the works of him who sent me.'"

The man had been blind all of his life. He did not *ask* to have his sight restored. Indeed, he had never had use of his eyes—he didn't know what it *was* to see, and so he was probably long past grieving his lack of eyesight. He and Jesus didn't even have a conversation about it—Jesus just slathered the mud on his eyes and told him to go wash. Except for another visit or two to Bethany, Jesus was *staying* in Jerusalem all that time—there was no new urgency, either from the man's condition or Jesus' itinerary, that required the miracle to be done on the *sabbath*; Jesus could just as easily have come back and found him the *next* day, and with a lot less criticism from the Pharisees. Apparently, the thought of the man being even one more day in darkness was too much for Jesus to abide. But the *theological* point, and the significance of this story for us, lies in Jesus' impetuous disregard of rational propriety and conventional behavior that is involved in his claim to be the light of the world, illumining common human assumptions with the reality of God's truth. Jesus the light pierces even the goodness of the sabbath observance. Jesus the Word of God preempts even the words of the law, and he enlists his followers to the same apparent disregard of proprieties and boundaries and taboos when anyone's ability to see clearly and truthfully is at stake. And suddenly, our judgments about who *is* and who *isn't* a *sinner* must be exploded and cast aside as being irrelevant if not downright sinful in themselves, lest we stand in the way of the miracles of God.

For even the most liberal-minded among us, that is a radical notion, even a threatening one. Is everything that we have ever been taught, everything we have ever considered to be right and wrong, to be turned on its head and tossed out the window? How can the world function if rules can be so easily ignored, if standards can be so casually neglected? So must even the most liberal-minded of the leaders of the Jews have thought when they heard what Jesus was doing. And they, like we, could only come to terms with it by accepting, on faith, that Jesus was sent by God ("Siloam"), and hear in the authority of his command the one voice that we have to follow in life. Immediately after the episode of the healing of the man born blind and Jesus' confrontation with the Pharisees over it, Jesus announces that he is the authentic gate for the sheep, the only way to salvation, and the good shepherd, whose commitment to the sheep is absolute even to the point of dying for them. Why didn't those people understand who Jesus was? We might as well ask, why do we not open our homes to the poor, why do we not forgive over and over those who wrong us over and over, why do we continue to wage war when Jesus commanded us to turn the other cheek? Don't we understand who Jesus is? Are the laws that we have inherited and the rules that we have invented, whether in society or in the church, more sacred than the commands of the living Lord Jesus Christ? Surely, all of our rationalizations must fall before the word of the one whom God has sent, and we must constantly examine our certainties to make sure that they are not obscuring the light of God which must dispel every blindness, including our own, we who may think that no one sees the will of God as clearly as *we* do!

Sometimes, to restore our own spiritual sight, it may take some such unwelcome and unsanitary exercise as Jesus smearing dirt and spittle on *our* eyes so that we have to go and wash them in the waters of the one whom God sent into the world, and rise from the waters to see anew or for the first time that no law or rule or custom, however ancient or however dear, can be allowed to stand in the way of God's redeeming love. "Jesus said, 'I came into this world for judgment so that those who do *not* see may *see*, and those who *do* see may become *blind*.' Some of the Pharisees near him heard this and said to him, 'Surely *we* are not blind, are we?' Jesus said to them, 'If you were *blind*, you would not have *sin*. But now that you say, "We *see*," your sin *remains*'" (9:39–41).

"Why couldn't those people back then understand who Jesus was? Were they blind?" Hopefully, it will not take us losing our eyesight and being reduced to the status of panhandlers to realize that each blind beggar is so important to God that no rule of convention or propriety excuses us from ministering to him or her, and from inviting him or her into our church, into our homes. And, of course, not just blind beggars. Jesus said to his disciples, "We must work the works of him who sent me" (9:4a). Sight must be restored, starting with our own.

Fifth Sunday in Lent
Spanish Springs Presbyterian Church, Sparks, Nevada
April 10, 2011
EZEKIEL 37:1–14
ROMANS 8:6–11
JOHN 11:1–45

"To Live Again"

EVELYN HEAVED A SIGH as she folded the last of Buzz's shirts. She sat back in the chair and looked at the plaid flannel, frayed at the points of the collar. It had been one of his favorite work shirts. Had she purchased it for him as a gift? She tried to remember. He had had it for a long time—so long, in fact, that she could not recall its ever not having hung in their closet. When was the last time she had seen him wear it? It was hard to say, it was such a familiar sight. Probably not since he had been ill—really ill, too ill to do any odd jobs around the house. His arms had grown too weak in his last few months even to nail up a picture hook—so unlike the vigorous man that he had been as recently as his sixty-fifth birthday. How cruel it seemed. How unfair. They had so looked forward to retirement—doing things together, traveling, enjoying the grandchildren. And then that wicked, relentless disease.... Her mind recalled the last Christmas they had put up a real Christmas tree; surely Buzz was wearing that old flannel shirt then, when they brought the tree into the house and set it up in the stand. Yes, yes, she was quite sure of it. And Mike and Connie were home that Christmas, and what joy filled the house.

Tears came to Evelyn's eyes, but she fought them back. No, no, she would not cry again. She must close the chapter, just as she would close the lid on the cardboard box that held Buzz's clothes. Mike had taken a few things after the funeral. These rest would go to the Salvation Army. She would close the lid; she *must* close the lid, just as the lid had been closed on the casket before the funeral, and remained closed. She knew the teachings of the Bible—she had known them all her life—and she truly believed that she and Buzz would one day be reunited in the presence of the Lord. But, in the meantime, the hurt was fresh and the wound in her heart seemed that it would never heal. With a strong dose of will, she folded over the cardboard flaps of the box and slipped them under each other. There, it was done.

She sat back in the chair and looked out through the window at the bare trees and brown grass of late winter, and the lumps of snow here and there that marked the places large drifts had been a few weeks earlier. Buzz loved spring—he always looked forward to yard work, to the earth coming to life again after months of short days and cold nights. That tree by the driveway—Evelyn remembered the spring day many years ago that she and Buzz had planted it, together, had watered it, had pruned it, and how it was now mature enough to shelter birds' nests and provide welcome shade in the heat of the summer. Another occasion on which Buzz had worn that flannel shirt, surely, perhaps with the sleeves rolled up as a sign that winter was over.

But it had been a long winter, this one—a winter of sickness and hopelessness. There could only be one outcome, Evelyn remembered the doctor saying. There might be a temporary arrest of the deterioration, but there could only be one outcome. But then, there is really only one ultimate outcome for *any* of us, she had told herself—it is the same whether you are healthy or sick; if you're not sick now, one day you *will* be. Evelyn remembered thinking that, when the minister had first come to see Buzz in the hospital. Cynicism had crept into her soul these past several months. She never before would have considered each day of living just a delay in the inevitable. But now, the "inevitable" had come to pass for Buzz, and she was alone. There were decisions to be made, which she had no interest in making. There were documents to be signed, which she had no energy for signing. There were thank-you notes to be written, which she had no eagerness to write. She no longer felt at home in the world, or even in her own house; her discipline of routine had withered with the waning strength of Buzz's body.

Evelyn had become numb to the expressions of sympathy that acquaintances offered. She knew that people were trying to be helpful. Nice words, she thought, not one of which will bring Buzz back. Why hadn't people been as vocal to *Buzz* about how much he meant to them during his *illness* as they had been to *her* after his *death*? And now he was gone, and she felt utterly empty. She was not a bitter woman by nature, but perhaps her very lack of experience with bitter feelings was making it more difficult for her to rally out of her bitterness now. Never before had she had such difficulty sleeping as the last several nights, nor such trouble getting out of bed in the morning. A friend had said something about depression being a stage of grief, and about bitterness, too, but it had not seemed worth looking into. Of *course* she was depressed, and she had every *right* to be, didn't she? The truth was, she felt as dead as her husband. Nothing seemed pleasurable to her anymore. No effort she might make seemed worthwhile.

She missed him terribly—after forty-two years of marriage, that was natural. They were not all perfect, of course—forty-two years of washing his dishes and washing his clothes were hardly romantic. Yet, now that there was no one whose dishes and clothes needed washing.... It had been a good marriage. They had grown close in a thousand ways that young starry-eyed lovers never consider. If only she could have had another year with him, another day with him. If only there had been a cure. Why were we put on this earth to live and love and die? She had always believed in the goodness of God and in the resurrection—had taught this to her children and to her Sunday school children—but her belief had never been so tested. She could still say the words, but her prayers for understanding seemed to go unanswered.

The telephone rang. Evelyn got up and walked across the bedroom to the nightstand and picked up the receiver. "Hello," she said weakly.

"Evelyn?"

"Yes."

"This is Judy Hudson. I'm sorry to bother you at a time like this."

"No, that's all right. Thank you for coming to the funeral."

"Well, I wanted to be there. You know, Buzz was such a wonderful person, always so cheerful and pleasant and kind. We will certainly miss him at the church."

"Yes, he was all those things," Evelyn agreed.

"Well, if this is something that you don't feel up to doing just now, please feel free to say so."

"What is it?" Evelyn asked apprehensively.

"Well, you know that we both ended up on the funeral dinner committee of the women's association this year."

"Yes."

"I'm afraid that we've had another death in the congregation. The family has asked if we could provide a meal at the church. Again, if you don't feel up to it now—"

"Well, I'm not sure that I do, really."

"I certainly understand, Evelyn. I know that it has been a difficult time for you. It is so hard to lose someone who has been so close to us. We are certainly praying for you, and for Mike and Connie, too. Please let me know if there's anything that I can be doing for you."

"Thank you," said Evelyn.

"Bye now," said Judy.

Evelyn hung up the receiver. She and Buzz had always been moderately active in the church. They had done their share, up until the time that Buzz became ill. She just wasn't up to this now. They ought to know that at the church. She hoped that they understood. There were others who could and should be doing the work now, anyway. Evelyn was feeling old today. Judy was a nice person, a woman in early middle age who seemed sincere in her sympathy at the funeral and afterward, when she had brought a casserole by the house and had put her arm around Evelyn's shoulder and offered a brief prayer. She should have told her again that she appreciated her kindness, Evelyn thought. Perhaps a little note to her—yes, she ought to write a note to her while she was thinking about it.

Evelyn went to the kitchen and reached up above the desk for some stationery and the church directory to look up Judy's address. As she did, a copy of Buzz's funeral worship order fell from the shelf down onto the desk. On the cover was a picture of the sun breaking out from behind a cloud, and a Bible verse was printed in script in the bottom part of the picture. Evelyn picked it up and looked at it. Had she noticed the words earlier? Surely, she must have read them at the funeral, perhaps over and over. But just now, she could not remember ever having seen the words before. "Blessed be the God and Father of our Lord Jesus Christ," the scripture read, "the Father of mercies and God of all comfort, who comforts us in all *our* affliction, so that we may be able to comfort those who are in *any* affliction, with the comfort with which we ourselves are comforted by God" (2 Cor 1:3–4 RSV).

"So that *we* may be able to comfort," Evelyn said the words slowly to herself. "Who comforts us in all our affliction, so that we may be able to comfort" (1:4a RSV).

Suddenly, it dawned on Evelyn that she had not even asked whose family the meal was for. She felt a flash of embarrassment, but it gave way to a genuine desire to know who in the congregation had died, and who, like herself, was now grieving the loss of someone whom they had loved. She opened the church directory and found Judy Hudson's telephone number. "Judy," she said when a woman answered at the other end of the line. "This is Evelyn. I'm sorry, I didn't think to thank you just now for being so kind to me these past couple of weeks."

"Oh, it's not necessary to thank me. That's what it means to be a church family."

"And I didn't even think to ask who it was that died."

"Philip Martinez. Did you know him? They are fairly new in the church—a young couple with a baby girl. His wife's name is Clarissa."

"No, I don't think that—wait a minute. You mean that young couple who have been sitting up near the front? And that adorable little baby?"

"Yes, they're the ones. They started coming back about Christmastime, and joined in January. Their baby was baptized last Sunday—I guess you weren't in church, it being so soon after Buzz's death."

"Oh no, oh no," said Evelyn, suddenly forgetting everything but the picture of the young family in her mind. "Oh no. What happened?"

"It was an industrial accident at the place where he worked. Yesterday afternoon."

"No, no, no. They couldn't have been married but a few years. They had so much to look forward to."

"I know," Judy agreed.

Compassion flooded Evelyn's soul, extinguishing every concern except for the grieving young widow. Perhaps Evelyn's own recent loss made her more sensitive to the pain that this young mother must be experiencing, but it was a real concern for Mrs. Martinez and not any projection of her own grief that now prompted Evelyn to ask, "Judy, do you have their address?"

"Yes, I think that I wrote it down when I saw it in the last newsletter. Just a minute." There was a rustling of papers at the other end of the telephone. "Here it is—2716 Birchmount Avenue, Apartment 308."

"Thank you, Judy," Evelyn said as she scribbled the address on the back of Buzz's funeral order. "Oh, and, please, I *do* want to help with the meal."

"I'll put you down and I'll be back in touch," said Judy.

"Good-bye," said Evelyn.

She had not been out of the house in days. She glanced quickly in the hall mirror now as she opened the closet door to get her coat and scarf. Her dress was not exactly what she would have chosen if she had *planned* to go out, but she felt an urgency about her task that would not permit her time to change. On her way out the door to the garage, she picked up her purse. She opened the garage door, got into the car, turned on the ignition, and backed out of the driveway. "2716 Birchmount," she said aloud to herself, committing the address to memory. So intent was Evelyn on thinking of the fastest route to Birchmount Avenue that she did not notice the buds on the tree alongside the driveway, and how one of them had sprouted a new green leaf.

Palm/Passion Sunday
Spanish Springs Presbyterian Church, Sparks, Nevada
April 17, 2011
ISAIAH 50:4–9a
PHILIPPIANS 2:5–11
MATTHEW 21:1–11

"What Shall We Do with Jesus?"

> Now at the festival the governor was accustomed to release a prisoner for the crowd, anyone whom they wanted. At that time they had a notorious prisoner, called Jesus Barabbas. So after they had gathered, Pilate said to them, "Whom do you want me to release for you, Jesus Barabbas or Jesus who is called the Messiah?" For he realized that it was out of jealousy that they had handed him over. . . . Now the chief priests and the elders persuaded the crowds to ask for Barabbas and to have Jesus killed. The governor again said to them, "Which of the two do you want me to release for you?" And they said, "Barabbas." Pilate said to them, "Then what should I do with Jesus who is called the Messiah?" (Matt 27:15–18, 20–22a)

THE QUESTION THAT PILATE asked is the most important question that confronts any person. What shall I do with Jesus? And it confronts the church as well. What shall *we* do with Jesus? Our answer has real consequences not only for us individually, but for all of God's creation. We cannot escape the question, not even by ignoring it, for even such silence disguises an answer. We cannot be noncommittal. There is no doubt of the fact that Jesus was a real person who lived in human history. There is no doubt of the fact that he went around Palestine healing and teaching and preaching the kingdom of God. There is no doubt of the fact that he was charged by the Jewish religious leaders with blasphemy and by the Roman government with treason, that he was condemned to a punishment that the Romans reserved for rebels and slaves and criminals of the lowest class, and that he died on a cross outside the city walls of Jerusalem. We know from the Bible what the Jewish and Roman *authorities* did with Jesus. But Pilate's question echoes through the long centuries since then and within the confines of every human heart and in the midst of every church council. And the question must be answered anew in the church by every succeeding generation that reads of how Jesus was brought before the crowd at the praetorium, and it must be answered individually by every person who hears the proclamation of the gospel.

Simply referring to ourselves as "Christians," either individually or as a nation or culture, does not really provide a full answer to the question. Nor, for that matter, does replying that we are church members. Whether we have merely a passing acquaintance with Jesus or know him intimately, whether we are familiar with little more than his birth in a stable and his death on a cross or whether we have diligently searched the scriptures to study about him in depth, whether we worship him only at Christmas and Easter or come faithfully and joyfully to praise him and offer him our thanksgiving on each Lord's Day, the ultimate question remains for each of us separately and for all of us together: What shall we do with Jesus? And I am not sure that the answer that is given within our society, and even within the church, is consistently different from the response that the crowd gave in the streets of ancient Jerusalem on that first Good Friday.

In many churches, the Sunday before Easter has come to be dominated by the story of Jesus' entry into the holy city a few days before the Passover. But it is also *Passion* Sunday, with the focus on Christ's arrest and trial and crucifixion. The triumphal entry and the passion—what greater contrast could be imagined? In the one scene, Jesus is surrounded by a great multitude that has followed him from Jericho, spreading their garments and tree branches on the road before him, and joyfully shouting, "Hosanna to the Son of David! Blessed is the one who comes in the name of the Lord! Hosanna in the highest heaven" (21:9b)! What do *they* do with Jesus? At least for the moment, they hail him as King and Savior. It is a festive mood, one in which Jesus finally seems to be getting the acclaim that a great healer and teacher might expect, and that the Son of God deserves. The fame of Jesus had spread from the villages of Galilee to the great holy city itself. "When he entered Jerusalem, the whole city was in turmoil, asking, 'Who is this?' The crowds were saying, 'This is the prophet Jesus from Nazareth in Galilee'" (21:10–11). He was greeted as the Son of David, the legitimate heir to the throne of the great king.

But in the other scene, the crowds of the holy city stand in the square before the Roman governor, angrily shouting, "Let him be crucified! . . . Let him be crucified!" (27:22, 23) The mood is no longer festive, but ugly. The people who had waited long for the coming of the Messiah, the people who had expected God to send them a great king, rejected Jesus in favor of a false messiah and a hero-of-the-moment. It seems that they had been impressed with this new teacher and miracle-worker from Nazareth for a little while, but now their interest had waned. Apparently, the crowd that had followed him from Jericho had deserted him; even the disciples had abandoned him, and he stood alone facing the mob. What do *they* do with Jesus? They put him on trial—they presume to pass judgment upon God himself, in human form—and they condemn him and sentence him to death.

Certainly, much of the moral blame for the crucifixion of Jesus must fall on Pilate and the Roman forces occupying Palestine. According to Matthew's Gospel, Pilate realized that Jesus was innocent of any real crime, and that the chief priests and elders had delivered him up because they were envious of him. Even Pilate's wife, we are told, was convinced that Jesus was a righteous man, and she had a dream that the governor should take no action against him. But the real villains in Matthew's account are the chief priests and the elders, and the crowd that was so easily persuaded to save Barabbas and to destroy Jesus. Do you sense the cruel irony? The very people who were supposed to know the most about the promise of a king, the very people who claimed to worship the only true God, the very people who *should* have known what to do with God's Messiah when he finally came, who *should* have given him their absolute allegiance and unequivocal loyalty, turned against Jesus in an instant. He wasn't the sort of messiah they expected. He wasn't the kind of king that they wanted. And at once we are confronted with the faithlessness of the human creature as Matthew contrasts the acclaim for Jesus at the gates of the city with the bloodthirsty designs of the mob calling for his condemnation and death.

After many months of doing good works and showing compassion and teaching the will of God on the hillsides and along the seashore and in the homes of Galilee, Jesus had come to Jerusalem, fulfilling the prophecies. He entered the city a celebrity, a friend to those who sensed the weight of their sin and to any who existed on the margins of society.

Surely the crowd had heard the reports that Jesus healed the sick, fed the hungry, freed those who were possessed by demons, pronounced God's forgiveness, even restored life to the dead. And by chasing the money changers and merchants from the temple, he perhaps even added to his stature in the eyes of the common folk who hoped for the inauguration of a new order, for they had no love for the abuses that took place daily in the house of God.

But the people had even *less* love for the *Romans*, and they were easily swayed by the winds of opinion. While Jesus seemed occupied with criticizing the perverters of religion, another man was willing to deal aggressively with the foreign army that occupied their land. Barabbas, so we are told in Mark and Luke, had given bloody vent to Israel's thirst for vengeance. His gospel of hatred was far more popular than an ethic of turning the other cheek. Meanwhile, the chief priests and elders perceived that Jesus posed a serious threat to their prestige and privilege. They recognized in the crowd's excitement for the insurrectionist Barabbas an opportunity to be rid of this Jesus called the Messiah who had disrupted the lucrative peace of the temple and had stirred the resentment of the common people. And in the moral weakness of Pontius Pilate and the changeable allegiances of the human heart, they found the effective means to their end. Scripture records the rest.

The annual rehearsal of Christ's passion reminds us of the costly sacrifice that God made for our salvation, and the awful reality of sin so grotesque that it is even capable of crucifying the Son of God. The full dimension of sin has not diminished since Jesus' time. It is not so difficult for us to understand what happened on the streets of Jerusalem. In our own time, we have seen mobs whipped to emotional irrationality by the venom of hate-filled speech. We know what crowds can do, how they can be manipulated so that the darkest evil can seem the highest virtue, how the pure of heart can be attacked and beaten to death as the mob cheers on the assailants, how the voices of mercy and compassion can be intimidated into silence. We know how public opinion can change so radically from saluting someone as a great liberator one day to vilifying him as a threat to the established order the next, and, conversely, how an unprincipled blackguard can become a folk-hero overnight. In our heart of hearts, we *understand* how a fickle crowd two thousand years ago in a strange Near Eastern land was persuaded to choose Barabbas over the Son of God. For we know *ourselves*. One commentator observed that Pilate had *reason* to recognize the envy of the chief priests and elders when he saw it, for he harbored envy in his *own* breast *as well*.[1] The emotions of the crowd are not foreign to us, are they?

But still Pilate's question dogs us—it follows us to the grocery store and the dinner table, to the movie theater and the magazine rack, to the voting booth and the town forum, to the boardroom and the workshop, to the club meeting and the locker room. The question comes to us in all of these settings: What shall we do with Jesus? Why, you and I tell ourselves, we shall *worship* him, of course! After all, we're *Christians*; we have *faith* in him. We *know* the gospel story; we *believe*. *We* would never reject him. *We* could never condemn him to the cross. *We* fit with the *Palm Sunday* crowd, not with that ignorant and sinful bunch on *Good Friday*. And maybe we even *believe* it. Surely, no Christian would nail Jesus to a cross. I doubt that even the most emphatic *non*-Christian would be so inhuman. For he committed no crime. But what of the more subtle forms of rejecting Jesus—of rationalizing the comfort and privilege that we enjoy at others' expense, of excusing our susceptibility to lust and our inclination to prejudice, of justifying our resentment of neighbor and our silence in the face of oppression? And simply trying to *ignore* Jesus is to reject him as *well*.

What *shall* we do with Jesus—we as individuals and we as the church? Shall we temper his words and actions so that they do not seem such a nuisance? Shall we assume that he did not quite mean what he said about forgiving others and feeding the hungry and refraining from sin? Shall we decide that his talk about loving our neighbors and even our enemies is a nice ideal that we should keep in mind but that he never expected us to attain? Shall we rationalize the frankness out of his teachings about the love of possessions and spiritualize the power out of his commands to free those who are bound? At least the *Good Friday* crowd was *honest* about *their* rejection. *Or* shall we hail him as Lord of creation and King of our lives indeed, taking him into our hearts without reservation, recognizing that his life and death and resurrection were the turning point for the history of the world and the critical event for each of our lives, accepting his forthright teachings as our marching orders and his humble servanthood as our pattern of living, adopting his command to love even the unlovely not simply as a pleasant philosophical proposition but as our very motive for being, giving of ourselves in every way in boundless gratitude to the one who gave up his very life for our

---

1. Buttrick, "Gospel according to St. Matthew, Exposition," 595.

salvation, acknowledging Christ's claim over our time and our talents and our money, and seeking to return to him not the *smallest possible* portion but the very *greatest*, confessing his lordship over the church and rededicating the church to serving as his uncompromising prophetic and loving instrument for redeeming a needy and broken world?

What shall we do with Jesus? The apostle Paul wrote to the Christians at Philippi almost two thousand years ago, encouraging them in the proper way to respond to the Son of God, and to pattern one's own behavior:

> Let the same mind be in you that was in Christ Jesus,
> who, though he was in the form of God,
>> did not regard equality with God
>> as something to be exploited,
> but emptied himself,
>> taking the form of a slave,
>> being born in human likeness.
> And being found in human form,
>> he humbled himself
>> and became obedient to the point of death—
>> even death on a cross.
> Therefore God also highly exalted him
>> and gave him the name
>> that is above every name,
> so that at the name of Jesus
>> every knee should bend,
>> in heaven and on earth and under the earth,
> and every tongue should confess
>> that Jesus Christ is Lord,
>> to the glory of God the Father. (Phil 2:5–11)

The crowd that greeted him as Savior and King was right. Members and friends of Spanish Springs Presbyterian Church, what shall *we* do with Jesus?

Maundy Thursday
Spanish Springs Presbyterian Church, Sparks, Nevada
March 28, 2002
EXODUS 12:1–4, 11–14
1 CORINTHIANS 11:23–26
JOHN 13:1–17, 31b–35

"Testimonial Dinner"

AS THE WINDS OF Reformation blew through Europe in the sixteenth century, one of the places it visited and transformed was the city of Zurich, in Switzerland. The zealous reformer of the church there was a man named Huldreich Zwingli, one of the spiritual forebears of believers who today are part of the Reformed tradition of Christian faith, including the Presbyterians. But we are also the children of John Calvin and John Knox, who strongly disagreed with Zwingli on at least one cardinal tenet of the faith.

They all criticized Roman Catholic theology and medieval Roman Catholic practices, including the teaching that, in the hands of a priest, the bread and wine of the Lord's Supper become the actual flesh and blood of Jesus. But when Zwingli said that the Lord's Supper is therefore nothing but a *memorial* of Christ's *death*, Calvin and Knox protested that he had badly missed what the sacrament means. Jesus said, "Do this in remembrance of me" (1 Cor 11:24b). And so we do. But Jesus *also* said, "Where two or three are gathered in my name, I am there *among* them" (Matt 18:20). The supper of bread and wine is the oldest and the central act of Christian worship. And every time we come to the Lord's table, every time we participate in the sacrament that Christ instituted the night before his crucifixion, it is *not* a *memorial* service. It is a *meal*, hosted and attended by the Lord Jesus Christ. Zwingli seems not to have realized that you can't have a *memorial* for someone who is *alive* and *present* in our *midst*. You can't mourn someone who is still at work in the world and acting through us to bring peace and wholeness and forgiveness to all people. The testimony of the Christian gospel is that Jesus Christ was *raised* from the dead. Jesus Christ is not just a *memory*. Jesus Christ is our *living Lord*. When we come to the Lord's table, it is to feast with Christ, at his invitation. The point of observing the sacrament of the *Lord's* Supper is *not* to remind us that the *Last* Supper happened once upon a time *long ago*, but to *share in Christ's life today*—to join him in fellowship and in ministry and in devotion and in friendship—to live with him, to die with him, to rise with him, not with sad tears of recollecting the injustice of the *crucifixion*, but with joyful testimony to the miracle of the *resurrection*.

Long before the time of Jesus, the Jews were enslaved in Egypt. God heard their cries of anguish, saw their suffering, grieved at the hardships laid upon the people specially chosen to give witness to God's will of freedom from want, freedom from fear, freedom from sin, freedom from bondage. And so God acted, through the obedient words and deeds of Moses, to prepare them for the end of their slavery. And even before the events of that final night in Egypt, when God promised to convince Pharaoh to let the Hebrews go by striking down the firstborn of all the Egyptians, he told Moses to have his people smear blood on their doorposts and eat their dinner hurriedly and be prepared to travel on a moment's notice, their loins girded, their sandals on their feet, their staff in their hands, and to repeat that *same* meal generation after generation as a perpetual reminder of God's faithful salvation from slavery. The Passover is a time of joyous thanksgiving for a miracle that the Bible celebrates over and over. But God's salvation from slavery isn't just a *memory*. The annual reminder is not to be just a lesson in long-ago history. It was and remains a constant testimony to God's faithfulness, to God's justice, to God's love, to God's purpose of liberation in *every* age, including today, and to show that God's people are *ready* for it, that they have *faith* in it, that they are *participants* in it, still, now, even thousands of years after the exodus through the waters of the Red Sea, through the wilderness of Sinai, into the promised land of peace and justice, prosperity and hope.

The book of Exodus, and *all* the Old Testament, is *our* book, *too*— yours and mine, Christians everywhere. Passover is your festival and mine, a large piece of our memory of the *past* and our identity in the *present*. Not just Jews, but Christians, as well, are children of hurried bread, celebrants of the great festival of urgent departure, people whose destiny is *not* enslavement to the empires of *this* world, but freedom to live as

God intended, not as subjects of the world's tyrants and despots, but as God's own people, beyond the claims and threats of this world's powers and principalities, beyond its cynicism and its skepticism, beyond its prejudices and its injustices, beyond even the terrors of death. We, too, are children of the marked doorposts—God's sign of redemption in the night-times of chaos and crying. We, too, are ready to set out on the journey God directs—a pilgrimage to the certainty of a world transformed by the power of truth and the wisdom of forgiveness and the methods of love. And as the Passover is a continuing testimony to God's saving activity in the *present*, not just a reminder of God's saving act once upon a time in the *past*, so the Lord's Supper is a testimony to the lordship of the living Jesus Christ right now, in the year 2002, not just a memorial of his death on the cross of Calvary, long ago and far away. The Hebrews of old did not end their days in chains in Egypt. And the cross, the empire's way of threat and hatred and fear, was not the end of Jesus, nor of God's miracles of life and salvation. We do not *mourn* God's *defeat*. We *testify* to God's *victory*. And we do it every time we take the bread and the cup from the table where Christ joins us, gathered together, just as he promised.

It can't have been easy for the Hebrews to respond to Moses' strange directions with gestures of confident hope. There was not a mightier empire in the world at that time than Egypt. The pharaohs were thought to be gods. Even in death, they loomed large—the pyramids are monuments to their claims of a dynasty that would last as long as earth itself. It didn't, of course, and Egypt, in *its* turn, was conquered by *other* empires that had the *same* aspirations to power without limits. And, eventually, *they* were conquered, too. But, for the Hebrews quarrying stone and baking bricks and erecting towering monuments to untamed egos and storehouses of imperial monopolies, it must have seemed that the chief and only facts of life were the taskmaster's lash on one's back and the food ration in one's bowl—that is, until someone reminded them that they didn't *belong* to *Pharaoh*, *they* belonged to *God*. And there must have been plenty of scoffers when Moses told them to slaughter a lamb and smear its blood on the doorpost and eat the roasted lamb as they were standing, dressed for travel and just waiting the signal for God to open the door out of their misery. What a foolish little footnote of history it would have been, if God had not been faithful to work their salvation by opening a way through the sea. But the God of justice and righteousness and dignity and peace, the God of love and hope and salvation and life, did just *that*—piled up the waters and made a path for the Hebrews to walk to freedom on dry ground, saved not just for their *own* sake, but for the sake of giving testimony ever after to the loving and liberating ways of God, God's purpose of wholeness and redemption, for all people, even Gentiles, even the Egyptians and Pharaoh their ruler, not a god after all, but powerless, the Egyptians discovered, to stop the steadfast march of men and women and children that the one and only true God had put into motion—the march toward *God's* kingdom of peace and justice, hope fulfilled and salvation accomplished. "This day shall be a day of remembrance for you," God told Moses. "You shall celebrate it as a festival to the Lord; throughout your generations you shall observe it as a perpetual ordinance. . . . You shall observe the festival of unleavened bread, for on this very day I brought your companies out of the land of Egypt" (Exod 12:14, 17a).

"The Lord Jesus on the night when he was betrayed took a loaf of bread, and when he had given thanks, he broke it and said, 'This is my body that is for you. Do this in remembrance of me.' In the same way he took the cup also, after supper, saying, 'This cup is the new covenant in my blood. Do this, as often as you drink it, in remembrance of me.' For as often as you eat this bread and drink the cup, you proclaim the Lord's death until he comes" (1 Cor 11:23b–26)—the Lord's death for the salvation of the world, the Lord's death that was his culminating act of faithful obedience to God and loving servanthood to humankind, the Lord's death that calls forth our *own* faithful obedience to God and loving servanthood to humankind, the Lord's death that opened the way to *eternal* life for all who are united to him in *this* life, at this table, in ministry to those in need, in faith that Jesus Christ is the way and the truth and the life, God's own Son, our Lord and Savior. Every time we receive the Lord's Supper, we are taking part in a grand testimonial dinner, joining our voices and our actions in our own place and time to the great chorus of witnesses from the past, and those who are yet to come, that God's will is righteousness, that God's ways are mercy, that God's truth is justice, that God's purpose is salvation, that God is the God of life, which not even the powers of death, not even death on a cross, can defeat. The evidence of that profound and joyful truth is found in this meal itself—not a memorial dinner, because you can't have a *memorial* for someone who is *alive* and *present* in our *midst*—Jesus Christ, who is still at work in the world and acting through us to bring peace and wholeness and forgiveness to all people.

Come, take and eat, satisfy your deepest hunger. Come, receive and drink, quench your driest thirst. Come, enjoy the hospitality of the *living*

Lord Jesus Christ, and find him present here, at this very table, embracing us into his family, welcoming us into the kingdom of God, nourishing us for our work of loving service, compassionate forgiveness, awakening faith, to which he commissions us anew each time we give testimony to him by eating and drinking from his hand. At this table, divisions end, prejudice loses its power, fear is overcome, hope is renewed, faith leads to life. Each time we eat this bread and drink the cup, we testify that the God who delivered Israel from bondage to slavery through the waters of the sea has delivered *us* from bondage to sin and death through the sacrifice of Jesus on the cross and has joined *our* lives to *his* life in the waters of baptism. Come, for all is ready. Our host, the living Lord Jesus Christ, is here.

Good Friday
April 22, 2011
Spanish Springs Presbyterian Church, Sparks, Nevada
JOHN 18:1—19:42, WITH ISAIAH 52:13—53:12 AND
HEBREWS 4:14-16; 5:7-10

A Reading for Three Voices

AFTER JESUS HAD SPOKEN these words, he went out with his disciples across the Kidron valley to a place where there was a garden, which he and his disciples entered. (John 18:1)

> *In the days of his flesh, Jesus offered up prayers and supplications, with loud cries and tears, to the one who was able to save him from death, and he was heard because of his reverent submission. Although he was a Son, he learned obedience through what he suffered; and having been made perfect, he became the source of eternal salvation for all who obey him, having been designated by God a high priest according to the order of Melchizedek.* (Heb 5:7-10)

Now Judas, who betrayed him, also knew the place, because Jesus often met there with his disciples. So Judas brought a detachment of soldiers together with police from the chief priests and the Pharisees, and they came there with lanterns and torches and weapons. Then Jesus, knowing all that was to happen to him, came forward and asked them, "Whom are you looking for?" They answered, "Jesus of Nazareth." Jesus replied, "I am he." Judas, who betrayed him, was standing with them. When Jesus said to them, "I am he," they stepped back and fell to the ground. Again he asked them, "Whom are you looking for?" And they said, "Jesus of Nazareth." Jesus answered, "I told you that I am he. So if you are looking for me, let these men go." This was to fulfill the word that he had spoken, "I did not lose a single one of those whom you gave me." Then Simon Peter, who had a sword, drew it, struck the high priest's slave, and cut off his right ear. The slave's name was Malchus. Jesus said to Peter, "Put your sword back into its sheath. Am I not to drink the cup that the Father has given me?" (John 18:2–11).

> By a perversion of justice he was taken away.
> Who could have imagined his future? (Isa 53:8a)

So the soldiers, their officer, and the Jewish police arrested Jesus and bound him. First they took him to Annas, who was the father-in-law of Caiaphas, the high priest that year. Caiaphas was the one who had advised the Jews that it was better to have one person die for the people (John 18:12–14).

> Surely he has borne our infirmities
> and carried our diseases;
> yet we accounted him stricken,
> struck down by God, and afflicted. (Isa 53:4)

Simon Peter and another disciple followed Jesus. Since that disciple was known to the high priest, he went with Jesus into the courtyard of the high priest, but Peter was standing outside at the gate. So the other disciple, who was known to the high priest, went out, spoke to the woman who guarded the gate, and brought Peter in. The woman said to Peter, "You are not also one of this man's disciples, are you?" He said, "I am not." Now the slaves and the police had made a charcoal fire because it was cold, and they were standing around it and warming themselves. Peter also was standing with them and warming himself.

Then the high priest questioned Jesus about his disciples and about his teaching. Jesus answered, "I have spoken openly to the world; I have always taught in synagogues and in the temple, where the Jews come together. I have said nothing in secret. Why do you ask me? Ask those who heard what I said to them; they know what I said." When he had said this, one of the police standing nearby struck Jesus on the face, saying, "Is that how you answer the high priest?" Jesus answered, "If I have spoken wrongly, testify to the wrong. But if I have spoken rightly, why do you strike me?" Then Annas sent him bound to Caiaphas the high priest.

Now Simon Peter was standing and warming himself. They asked him, "You are not also one of his disciples, are you?" He denied it and said, "I am not." One of the slaves of the high priest, a relative of the man whose ear Peter had cut off, asked, "Did I not see you in the garden with him?" Again Peter denied it, and at that moment the cock crowed (John 18:15–27).

> See, my servant shall prosper;
>> he shall be exalted and lifted up,
>> and he shall be very high. (Isa 52:13)

Then they took Jesus from Caiaphas to Pilate's headquarters. It was early in the morning. They themselves did not enter the headquarters, so as to avoid ritual defilement and to be able to eat the Passover. So Pilate went out to them and said, "What accusation do you bring against this man?" They answered, "If this man were not a criminal, we would not have handed him over to you." Pilate said to them, "Take him yourselves and judge him according to your law." The Jews replied, "We are not permitted to put anyone to death." (This was to fulfill what Jesus had said when he indicated the kind of death he was to die.) (John 18:28–32)

> Who has believed what we have heard?
>> And to whom has the arm of the Lord been revealed?
> For he grew up before him like a young plant,
>> and like a root out of dry ground;
> he had no form or majesty that we should look at him,
>> nothing in his appearance that we should desire him. (Isa 53:1–2)

Then Pilate entered the headquarters again, summoned Jesus, and asked him, "Are you the King of the Jews?" Jesus answered, "Do you ask this on your own, or did others tell you about me?" Pilate replied, "I am not a Jew, am I? Your own nation and the chief priests have handed you over to me. What have you done?" Jesus answered, "My kingdom is not from this world. If my kingdom were from this world, my followers would be fighting to keep me from being handed over to the Jews. But as it is, my kingdom is not from here" (John 18:33–36).

> Just as there were many who were astonished at him
>> —so marred was his appearance, beyond human semblance,
>> and his form beyond that of mortals—
> so shall he startle many nations;
>> kings shall shut their mouths because of him;
> for that which had not been told them they shall see,
>> and that which they had not heard they shall contemplate. (Isa 52:14–15)

Pilate asked him, "So you are a king?" Jesus answered, "You say that I am a king. For this I was born, and for this I came into the world, to testify to the truth. Everyone who belongs to the truth listens to my voice." Pilate asked him, "What is truth?"

After he had said this, he went out to the Jews again and told them, "I find no case against him. But you have a custom that I release someone for you at the Passover. Do you want me to release for you the King of the Jews?" They shouted in reply, "Not this man, but Barabbas!" Now Barabbas was a bandit (John 18:37–40).

> He was despised and rejected by others;
> > a man of suffering and acquainted with infirmity;
> and as one from whom others hide their faces
> > he was despised, and we held him of no account. (Isa 53:3)

Then Pilate took Jesus and had him flogged. And the soldiers wove a crown of thorns and put it on his head, and they dressed him in a purple robe. They kept coming up to him, saying, "Hail, King of the Jews!" and striking him on the face. Pilate went out again and said to them, "Look, I am bringing him out to you to let you know that I find no case against him" (John 19:1–4).

> All we like sheep have gone astray;
> > we have all turned to our own way,
> and the LORD has laid on him
> > the iniquity of us all. (Isa 53:6)

So Jesus came out, wearing the crown of thorns and the purple robe. Pilate said to them, "Here is the man!" When the chief priests and the police saw him, they shouted, "Crucify him! Crucify him!" Pilate said to them, "Take him yourselves and crucify him; I find no case against him." The Jews answered, "We have a law, and according to that law he ought to die because he has claimed to be the Son of God" (John 19:5–7).

> He was oppressed, and he was afflicted,
> > yet he did not open his mouth;
> like a lamb that is led to the slaughter,
> > and like a sheep that before its shearers is silent,
> > > so he did not open his mouth. (Isa 53:7)

Now when Pilate heard this, he was more afraid than ever. He entered his headquarters again and asked Jesus, "Where are you from?" But Jesus gave him no answer. Pilate therefore said to him, "Do you refuse to speak to me? Do you not know that I have power to release you, and power to crucify you?" Jesus answered him, "You would have no power over me unless it had been given you from above; therefore the one who handed me over to you is guilty of a greater sin." From then on Pilate tried to release him, but the Jews cried out, "If you release this man, you are no friend of the emperor. Everyone who claims to be a king sets himself against the emperor."

When Pilate heard these words, he brought Jesus outside and sat on the judge's bench at a place called The Stone Pavement, or in Hebrew Gabbatha. Now it was the day of Preparation for the Passover; and it was about noon. He said to the Jews, "Here is your King!" They cried out, "Away with him! Away with him! Crucify him!" Pilate asked them, "Shall I crucify your king?" The chief priests answered, "We have no king but the emperor." Then he handed him over to them to be crucified (John 19:8–16a).

> But he was wounded for our transgressions,
> > crushed for our iniquities;
> upon him was the punishment that made us whole,
> > and by his bruises we are healed. (Isa 53:5)

So they took Jesus; and carrying the cross by himself, he went out to what is called The Place of the Skull, which in Hebrew is called Golgotha. There they crucified him, and with him two others, one on either side, with Jesus between them. Pilate also had an inscription written and put on the cross. It read, "Jesus of Nazareth, the King of the Jews." Many of the Jews read this inscription, because the place where Jesus was crucified was near the city; and it was written in Hebrew, in Latin, and in Greek. Then the chief priests of the Jews said to Pilate, "Do not write, 'The King of the Jews,' but, 'This man said, I am the King of the Jews.'" Pilate answered, "What I have written I have written." When the soldiers had crucified Jesus, they took his clothes and divided them into four parts, one for each soldier. They also took his tunic; now the tunic was seamless, woven in one piece from the top. So they said to one another, "Let us not tear it, but cast lots for it to see who will get it." This was to fulfill what the scripture says, "They divided my clothes among themselves, and for my clothing they cast lots." And that is what the soldiers did.

Meanwhile, standing near the cross of Jesus were his mother, and his mother's sister, Mary the wife of Clopas, and Mary Magdalene. When Jesus saw his mother and the disciple whom he loved standing beside her, he said to his mother, "Woman, here is your son." Then he said to the disciple, "Here is your mother." And from that hour the disciple took her into his own home.

After this, when Jesus knew that all was now finished, he said (in order to fulfill the scripture), "I am thirsty." A jar full of sour wine was standing there. So they put a sponge full of the wine on a branch of hyssop and held it to his mouth (John 19:16b–29).

> For he was cut off from the land of the living,
>   stricken for the transgression of my people. (Isa 53:8b)

When Jesus had received the wine, he said, "It is finished." Then he bowed his head and gave up his spirit.

Since it was the day of Preparation, the Jews did not want the bodies left on the cross during the sabbath, especially because that sabbath was a day of great solemnity. So they asked Pilate to have the legs of the crucified men broken and the bodies removed. Then the soldiers came and broke the legs of the first and of the other who had been crucified with him. But when they came to Jesus and saw that he was already dead, they did not break his legs. Instead, one of the soldiers pierced his side with a spear, and at once blood and water came out. (He who saw this has testified so that you also may believe. His testimony is true, and he knows that he tells the truth.) These things occurred so that the scripture might be fulfilled, "None of his bones shall be broken." And again another passage of scripture says, "They will look on the one whom they have pierced" (John 19:30–37).

> *Since, then, we have a great high priest who has passed through the heavens, Jesus, the Son of God, let us hold fast to our confession. For we do not have a high priest who is unable to sympathize with our weaknesses, but we have one who in every respect has been tested as we are, yet without sin. Let us therefore approach the throne of grace with boldness, so that we may receive mercy and find grace to help in time of need.* (Heb 4:14–16)

After these things, Joseph of Arimathea, who was a disciple of Jesus, though a secret one because of his fear of the Jews, asked Pilate to let him take away the body of Jesus. Pilate gave him permission; so he came and removed his body. Nicodemus, who had at first come to Jesus by night, also came, bringing a mixture of myrrh and aloes, weighing about a hundred pounds (John 19:38–39).

> They made his grave with the wicked
>> and his tomb with the rich,
> although he had done no violence,
>> and there was no deceit in his mouth. (Isa 53:9)

They took the body of Jesus and wrapped it with the spices in linen cloths, according to the burial custom of the Jews. Now there was a garden in the place where he was crucified, and in the garden there was a new tomb in which no one had ever been laid. And so, because it was the Jewish day of Preparation, and the tomb was nearby, they laid Jesus there (John 19:40–42).

The Resurrection of the Lord
Spanish Springs Presbyterian Church, Sparks, Nevada
March 23, 2008
ACTS 10:34–43
COLOSSIANS 3:1–4
MATTHEW 28:1–10

"Already Raised"

IN MY FIRST PASTORATE, I served a church in the Dallas area. I was an associate pastor at Grace Presbyterian Church in Plano, Texas. Just a few months before I began ministering there, the congregation completed building a large new sanctuary. Up until then, the church had worshiped in its small fellowship hall. As one of the few congregations in that fast-growing suburb to have an actual sanctuary, we received a lot of requests for weddings, frequently from people who normally attended much more fundamentalist churches that didn't yet *have* sanctuaries. They thought that *our* worship space, with its dramatic upswept ceiling and stained glass, would make a nice backdrop for pictures of their wedding service—not the very best reason to get married somewhere. A lot of these people from other denominations and non-denominations would otherwise have had no interest in being involved in a Presbyterian church whose theology, in many cases, they would have judged to be deficient.

On one of those occasions, the prospective groom looked around the sanctuary and noticed the stained glass window in the east wall—a window that depicted a butterfly. The butterfly had been chosen, sometime before I arrived, as the *symbol* of that congregation, depicting its motto, "Celebrating New Life in Christ." In fact, the butterfly and the motto were colorfully printed on the front of the order of worship each week. *This* young man came from a church background where, apparently, symbolism was minimal (some of these churches didn't even have a *cross* in their worship space). Referring to the butterfly, he said, with a bit of a laugh that contained more than a trace of contempt, "So are Presbyterians 'nature-worshipers,' or what?" I explained to him that the butterfly is a centuries-old symbol of the resurrection—of new, transformed life springing forth from the tomb-like cocoon. He remained unimpressed, I'm afraid, as he mentally classified us with the druids or the pantheists.

The resurrection, of course, is the central event that gives meaning to the Christian faith. God's raising to life again the body of Jesus who had died on the cross is the decisive vindication of all that Jesus said and did, certifying Christ as the Son of God, the Messiah, Lord of all and Savior of the world. As an earth-bound caterpillar disappears into the dull cocoon, and then emerges transformed into a beautiful being no longer confined to the earth, we are reminded of Christ's burial in the tomb, and emergence in a body no longer restricted by map or calendar, but raised to power and glory and eternal life. And in his resurrection, he promises, we, too, who are united to him, are transformed, have the gift of eternal life.

A lot of people, including a lot of churchgoing Christians, are accustomed to think of the resurrection as all having to do with what happens to us when we *die*, when, at whatever age we have attained, our body gives out and our heart stops beating and our brain quits thinking. Rather naturally, on the basis of what they have heard some churchgoers pray and some ministers preach, many folk come to regard Christianity as a sort of insurance policy. Living a life of obedience to Christ is often considered to be a price paid to get into a place called "heaven." But the Bible gives little support to the notion that heaven is a *location*, or that we can reach a *bargain* with God, trading our "goodness" in *this* life as a claim on life after *death*.

Consider the first words of our epistle reading this morning: "So if you have been raised with Christ . . ." (Col 3:1a). The letter we know as Colossians was surely not addressed to *corpses*, but to *living, breathing people* in a church in Asia Minor. Even the theologically conservative New International Version of the Bible translates that phrase, "Since, then, you *have been* raised with Christ . . ." (3:1a NIV). Both translations make the same point: being *raised* is something that has *already* happened to the Colossian Christians. Being *raised* is something that has already happened to the person who has been baptized and become a follower of Christ. The *resurrection* has to do with our relationship with God through Christ, and thus our relationship with *others* through Christ.

Eternal life describes what we experience when the risen and living Lord Jesus Christ is alive in us. The proof of the resurrection of Christ was *not* that the *tomb* was *empty*. There could conceivably have been *other* reasons for *that*, including some that first occurred to the disciples who feared that someone had stolen the body. The disciples became convinced of the resurrection not because there was no body in the tomb that had been sealed and guarded since Friday afternoon, but because on Sunday *evening* and *afterward*, they recognized Christ present at table with them, as Peter testified, eating and drinking—and not as someone who had just been unconscious for a while, but who bore the marks of the nails and, in John's account, even the incision made by the sword thrust into his side. Christ had died. But Christ was alive again. And the risen and living Christ was a real presence in fellowship with them, drawing them into fellowship with each *other*, encouraging them, instructing them, forgiving them, loving them, and, when the Holy Spirit came upon them, living *within* them.

"So if you *have* been raised with Christ," says Colossians, clearly indicating that being raised with Christ is something that happens *this* side of the grave, "seek the things that are above, where Christ is, seated at the right hand of God. Set your mind on things that are *above*, not on things that are on *earth*, for you *have* died, and your life is hidden with Christ in God" (3:1–3). We have been *changed* from what we *were*. The *old* is *gone*, the *new* has taken its *place*, as we are transformed by our relationship with Christ, as our relationships with others are transformed—enlarged, deepened, broadened, made less self-centered—by our relationship with Christ. Earthbound, plodding habits are changed to freedom from all that weighs down the spirit.

"Set your minds on things that are above, not on things that are on earth" (3:2). Some people assume this requires turning their backs on the world. The young man who came to inspect the sanctuary in Texas apparently thought that Christ had nothing in common with physical things, not even nature. But "setting our minds on things that are above" does not mean *repudiating* this world or regarding it as having no spiritual *significance*. The very reason that God raised Jesus was because he had been faithful in ministering *in* the world, had been obedient in carrying out God's purpose by feeding hungry people, healing sick people, welcoming estranged people, forgiving sinful people, *engaging* the world, not cutting himself *off* from it. Nor are *we* to turn *our* backs on the world as we stand gazing *skyward*, but to bring Christ into every earthly and human relationship, let him touch every earthly and human need, transforming us and redeeming creation, infusing the world with the habits of heaven. To *die* with Christ and be *raised* with him must happen precisely in *this* world if it is to have any relevance to God's announced purpose of *redeeming* this world. Dying with Christ *releases* us from allegiance to the world's pretensions, the world's values, the world's preoccupations, but allegiance to the risen Christ, being raised *with* him, having him *alive* in us, reorients us exactly back to *caring* for the world, intensely, as the resurrection transforms us from being prideful, self-consumed individuals into a merciful, self-giving community of faith, mindful of God's intentions as *Jesus* was mindful of God's intentions, being generous as *Jesus* was generous, being forgiving as *Jesus* was forgiving, free from the world's judgments as *Jesus* was free from the world's judgments. Is this world, then, its limits and its flaws, our final destiny? No. But, as it was for *Jesus*, it is for *us* the realm in which faithfulness must be lived. And that can *only* happen when, like *Christ*, we have *died* to *its* ways, and have found, in the *cross*, the *only* way to genuine *life*.

The transformation that overtakes us will likely not be the spectacular conversion that makes the Christian talk shows. Being raised to new life with Christ may well be something like what happened to Peter, might be as simple as answering the question of "Who shall eat at our table?" Like many Jews of his time, Peter had assumed that living *right* required *exclusion*, involved cutting oneself off, had to do with reputation. He was prevailed upon to show the grace of the God of Israel to Cornelius, a Roman, a Gentile, a non-Jew, by baptizing him and his entire household. *Before* the resurrection, Peter would never have *thought* of doing such a thing. And even *now*, the impulse came upon him not as a general dictum, but by way of his actual contact with Cornelius, a Roman, a Gentile, a non-Jew, a relationship person-to-person, as *Jesus* so often ministered. And not only did Peter baptize this Gentile household (remarkable as that was, it could still have been a rather official, impersonal sort of act). Peter actually stayed with the family for several days, meaning that he sat at their table, meaning that he ate their food, meaning that he no longer felt bound by the exclusions of the Jewish law by which he had so long measured his purity and his righteousness and his preparation for heaven, but that now he was being transformed into seeing the world, and other human beings, through God's eyes: "I truly understand," said he, "that God shows no partiality, but in every nation anyone who fears him and does what is right is acceptable to him" (Acts

10:34–35). Understanding that God shows no favoritism—not to a *race*, not to a *gender*, not to a *nation*, not even to a *religion*—was a transformation of Peter that was being achieved, could *only* be achieved, by Christ alive and at work within him. The old Peter had died, and a new Peter had been raised with Christ—a person strong and faithful enough boldly to break forth from the darkness of the cocoon he had spun from pride and self-righteousness and prejudice and fear into the glorious brightness of the resurrection.

Are your ways the ways of heaven? Are your hopes the will of God? Do you find your bliss in forgiving others, being generous toward others, healing others, loving others, and not just *some* others but *all* others? If not, come out of your tomb. The Lord is risen! And anyone who *believes* that has *already* been raised with Christ.

Second Sunday of Easter
May 1, 2011
Spanish Springs Presbyterian Church, Sparks, Nevada
ACTS 2:14a, 22–32
1 PETER 1:3–9
JOHN 20:19–31

"The Rest of the Story"

ALL AROUND THE WORLD, Christian churches *last* Sunday experienced their largest worship attendance of the year. All around the world, Christian churches *this* Sunday are experiencing perhaps their *smallest* worship attendance of the year. The resulting emotional letdown of ministers alone could explain why the Sunday after Easter is sometimes referred to as "Low Sunday." More officially, the name refers to the contrast with the high feast of Easter Day, theologically the most important event on the Christian calendar when, historically, even as here, brass ensembles and the "Hallelujah Chorus" and many other traditions celebrate the special significance of the annual commemoration of the resurrection. Unfortunately, the typical precipitous decline in worship attendance suggests that a *lot* of people think there isn't really anything else left to *say*, or *hear*; as far as *they* are concerned, the story that began in a lowly stable in Bethlehem was completed in an empty tomb near Jerusalem.

In fact, only *Mark's* Gospel ends *there*. The *other* three Gospels have more story to tell (and even some early readers of *Mark* found its abrupt ending, with the discovery of the empty tomb, ambiguous in itself, unsatisfying, and so they added more verses to relate how Jesus, risen from the dead, actually appeared to his disciples). The Gospel of *John* testifies that Jesus, having been raised from the dead, "did many other signs" in the presence of his disciples (John 20:30).

Of all the stories that John apparently *could* have recounted, he selected only a *few*, one of which is the episode in which Thomas, who had earlier refused to believe his friends' account of how Jesus had appeared to them in Thomas's absence on the evening after the tomb was discovered to be empty, came immediately to believe when he himself saw and heard Jesus a week later. On that *first* Sunday night, it seems that Jesus suddenly and miraculously appeared in the midst of the disciples, addressed them with a common Jewish greeting, and verified that it was indeed he himself by showing them his hands and his side, where he had been nailed to the cross and pierced by a spear. "Jesus said to them again, 'Peace be with you. As the Father has sent me, so I send you.' When he had said this, he breathed on them and said to them, 'Receive the Holy Spirit. If you forgive the sins of any, they are forgiven them; if you retain the sins of any, they are retained'" (20:21–23).

Thomas wasn't there when that happened, and, when he arrived at the house where they were all staying and was told such an extraordinary tale, he declared that he would not believe it unless he could see for himself the marks of the nails and even touch them, and the wound in Jesus' side. The *next* Sunday, when the disciples were again gathered in the house, this time with *Thomas* present as well, Jesus again appeared miraculously among them, not entering through any of the doors, which were shut and, presumably, locked again, as before, and once more he greeted them with the familiar Jewish salutation. Jesus invited Thomas to touch the wounds, and to believe. Thomas immediately confessed his belief in Jesus as Lord and God, perhaps without even *doing* what he had *insisted* would be *necessary* for him to believe that Jesus had been raised from the dead. "Jesus said to him, 'Have you believed because you have seen me? Blessed are those who have not seen and yet have come to believe'" (20:29).

There have always been people whose interest in Jesus ends with their concern about themselves—specifically, what will happen to them when they die. And their interest is satisfied, more or less, with the news that the tomb was found to be empty—they have hope that *theirs* will therefore be empty, *too*. And, with that hope renewed, whatever else the Bible has to say isn't particularly important. The pews might as well gather dust until *next* Christmas and Easter. But as special as the *Gospels* are, and as critical as the story of Jesus' earthly life, death, and resurrection is, *much* of the New Testament has to do, one way or the other, with what happened *after* Jesus was raised from the dead and verified God's miraculous deed by appearing to the disciples in his resurrection body. And what we read from John today was not merely a *postscript* to the *conclusion* of the story. It was, as far as the early church was concerned (and, I believe, is too little credited by those who think that what we do the *other* Sundays of the year isn't worth their attention), merely the marvelous *starting* point. Jesus didn't just pop in that night to impress his friends with his new disappearing act. He confirmed that the same one who died on the cross was the one who had been raised from the tomb. The same one who had said and done such wondrous things to reveal the heart and mind of God now lived again, and eternally, in the closest union imaginable with the Father. He spoke the words, "Peace be with you" (20:19), to his disciples not as a *bromide* or a *platitude* nor even a *promise*, but as a *fact* centered in and dependent upon his living presence among them. He commissioned them to leave the locked house that they had made into their own tomb after the crucifixion, and go out into the world to do the same things that God had commissioned *him* to do: "'As the father has sent me, so I send you'" (20:21b). And he bestowed on them the power that they would need to do so: "When he had said this, he breathed on them and said to them, 'Receive the Holy Spirit'" (20:22). And then, most remarkable of all these remarkable things, he authorized them together—the verb is plural, not singular, suggesting not just as individuals, but as the whole community of believers—to continue and extend his ministry: "'If you forgive the sins of any, they are forgiven them; if you retain the sins of any, they are retained'" (John 20:23). And so, John shows, Jesus launched the church and its mission.

To celebrate the resurrection is not merely to rejoice over the possibility or even the promise of one's personal survival after death in some form or other. To celebrate the resurrection is also to celebrate the beginning of the church's mission in the world. Though many of us try to wring a private benefit from the gospel, none of the Gospels, and certainly not the book of Acts or the letters of Paul or the Revelation to John nor any of the other writings in the New Testament, supports the individualism that too many preachers preach and too many lay people profess. The resurrection life that Jesus wrested from the grave, he shared with his disciples by breathing the Holy Spirit upon them, giving them new and eternal life that equipped and emboldened them, as the church, to make judgments and perform deeds with the same authority that Christ himself had done during his earthly ministry. And, as *Jesus* overcame such barriers as locked doors and sealed tombs, so his *church* was now authorized, *expected* even, to break down whatever excludes or imprisons and to break open whatever stinks of death. And they would do it possessing and manifesting the peace that filled Christ himself—confidence in the face of opposition, serenity in the face of oppression, wholeness in the face of all the disintegrating forces arrayed against the will of God. For now they knew, indeed, that Christ *was* and *is* the resurrection and the life, and that he is emphatically the life of his church. By its works of love, the community of faith reveals God to the world, continuing Jesus' ministry of love for the world, summoning it to believe that Christ is indeed the Son of God, bringing it out of the shadows of sin, which is blindness to the revelation of God in Jesus Christ.

The Christians in the early church knew that the resurrection was not the *end* of the story. The first couple of generations of Christians did not yet have the Gospels, did not all know the stories about a virgin birth, had not heard all of the parables, were not all aware of the healings and exorcisms and feedings. They had been won to Christianity by the preaching of the resurrection, and by the proclamation of forgiveness, but not simply as the report of a historical event, but as the explanation of a present experience. They understood *themselves* to be *already raised* with *Christ*. For them, death was not something in the *future* and resurrection a promise relevant only *beyond* the *grave*. They had *already* died to unbelief and were *already* living in triumphant joy. *Already*, they had experienced a new birth and possessed a living hope. *Already*, they were living *beyond* the discovery of the empty tomb, in a landscape that featured one wondrous revelation after another. The resurrection had been only the *beginning* of what life was now all about. Every day they were experiencing in new and exciting ways what the Gospels would later point toward. They knew what it meant to have new life in Christ, recognizing themselves to be blessed, believing, though they had not been there to see for themselves the nail marks in the hands and the wound in the side.

Too many people think of the New Testament as a history lesson and of Easter as something that they should know *about*, and having *heard* the story and received some *assurance* from it, go on about life much as they *always* have, truth for them being nothing greater than what can be touched and measured, expectations for them being governed by what they have already experienced and understood, relevance for them being whatever might benefit them personally, but not much more than that. And so the bulk of the New Testament—the story of the spread of the gospel, letters addressing the problems and possibilities of communities of believers living as resurrected people in a world that stubbornly resists being raised to new life—is largely unexplored territory. And the popular assumption is that the discovery of the empty tomb is all there is to the story. And, so, pews are not as full on the Sundays *after* Easter, and people who give themselves and their resources to the church's mission remain an *oddity*, a strange *exception* in a world that holds grudges, that stockpiles weapons, that hoards wealth, that would rather not be bothered to change its habits of cruelty and selfishness and revenge—not that it doesn't *claim* to want an *alternative*, but refuses to believe that there *is* any such when it has only hearsay upon which to rely. But into that sad and cynical environment, God in Jesus Christ, through the gift of the Holy Spirit, has injected a seed of new life, believers in the resurrection who have the authority of the Resurrected One himself to forgive as completely, to heal as effectively, to feed as generously, to open locked doors and dispel fear and offer peace as Jesus *himself* did and, *through them, does*. And that new life is in and through his church, whenever and wherever it is faithful to declare, "My Lord and my God!"

The story of the resurrection only *began* with the discovery that Sunday morning long ago that the tomb into which the body of the crucified Jesus, dead as dead could be, was placed, was *empty*, the linen wrappings that testified to death just lying there, no longer needed. So, today, the truth of the resurrection, its reality and its meaning, only *begin*s in the worship service on Easter. What it is really all about lies beyond words written on a page, beyond a doctrine expressed in creed. It unfolds on all the other Sundays, and indeed all the other 364 days of the church's year, and its truth is proclaimed in the deeds of mercy and compassion and generosity and courage worked by the community of faith contemporary in every age since that first band of disciples was breathed upon by the risen Christ and received the Holy Spirit and was granted the authority to forgive sins. You and I are the very ones who are blessed not to have seen and yet who have come to believe. *We* are the *rest* of the story.

Third Sunday of Easter
First Presbyterian Church, Dodge City, Kansas
April 25, 1993
ACTS 2:14a, 36–41
1 PETER 1:17–23
LUKE 24:13–35

"Love Walks on Wounded Feet"

CAN YOU IMAGINE HOW those two disciples felt, walking along the road from Jerusalem, going back home after the worst three days of their lives? As disciples of Jesus, they must have been following him for some period of time, listening to his teachings, observing his compassionate care for folk who were ill and despised, hearing his words of forgiveness to the sin-ridden and the disreputable. By some miracle of faith implanted in their breast, they had dared to hope that Jesus was the Messiah, even though he had not come among them astride a magnificent horse nor at the head of a great army. Perhaps the two disciples had *been* in that parade only a few days before, when people gathered to welcome Jesus up from Jericho to the holy city with shouts of "Hosanna!" Undoubtedly, they had been with him in the temple and had accompanied him through the streets. He was hailed by so many people, it would not have been an unreasonable notion that the crowd might proclaim him Israel's new king, and enthrone him by a consensus of the popular will. Things seemed to be working so beautifully toward the end.

And then it had all fallen apart so very quickly. Jesus had been arrested and put on trial, secretly and without what we would call "due process." He was hauled before the procurator who dragged him before the mob, and when offered the choice between Jesus the teacher and healer and forgiver and Barabbas the murderer and robber and insurrectionist, the mob chose Barabbas and rejected Jesus and said, "Let him be crucified!" (Matt 27:23) And that is what had happened—just like that, he whom the two disciples had *hoped* was the one to *redeem Israel* was *executed* like a *criminal*. As they trudged back home, grieved and discouraged and perplexed, they talked with each other about all the things that had happened the past few days, wondering, perhaps, whether they dare ever hope again. They were quite defeated people.

There really was nothing very promising to walk home *to*, so it is likely that their pace was slow, and, by and by, they were joined or overtaken by another who listened for a while and then inquired about their disheartening conversation. They came to a halt and turned with sad expression toward the stranger, asking if he did not know the things that had happened to Jesus—really, a rather remarkable thing to ask of a stranger, when admission to the *wrong* person of having been a companion of Jesus would have been dangerous indeed. They went on to summarize the suffering and death of Jesus and the discovery that very morning of the empty tomb. "Then [the stranger] said to them, 'Oh, how foolish you are, and how slow of heart to believe all that the prophets have declared! Was it not necessary that the Messiah should suffer these things and then enter into his glory?' Then beginning with Moses and all the prophets, he interpreted to them the things about himself in all the scriptures" (Luke 24:25–27).

The reader of Luke knows all along that the stranger is Jesus himself. Up until he suffered the *scourging* and the *mocking* and the *cross*, the two disciples had been quite *willing* to entertain the possibility that God's *righteousness* and God's *power* and God's *love* were walking *alongside* them in the earthly person of the engaging teacher and healer and forgiver. But just as something had prevented them from recognizing the *crucified* Jesus as the genuine Messiah, something prevented the two disciples from recognizing the *risen* Jesus as the one who was walking with them now.

It seems to have been a supernatural disability—it was not just that the stranger didn't *look* like Jesus. What had changed the minds of these two disciples about *Jesus* being the *Messiah*? It was the thought of him on the *cross*—nails in his hands and his feet, blood dripping from his brow and welts crusting his back, and a criminal hanging on the cross to his right and a criminal hanging on the cross to his left, and Jesus crying out, "Father, into your hands I commend my spirit" (23:46), and then dying. Those *same* wounded feet now bore the *risen Christ* alongside the pensive pair, and the stranger started to speak to them about how it could not be *otherwise* that God's love must be worked in the world.

Love walks on wounded feet. One of the questions that I always ask of couples whom I am counseling before marriage is, "Have you ever had an argument?" I have some reticence about marrying any couple who answer that question with a firm *no*, for the ability to work through disagreements, for a relationship to absorb the hurt and pain of feeling injured in an argument and to practice redeeming whatever strain that has placed on the relationship so that the couple's love *emerges* from that experience stronger, deeper, more committed and more caring and more accepting—more *Christ*-like—gives some indication of the *durability* of that love and the *growth* potential of that love through many years of married life ahead and despite *any* couple's share of sorrows and disappointments. (Please don't interpret me as saying that it's not true love without an argument!—in fact, I have finally ended up marrying one or two couples who swore that they had never had a disagreement, and to the best of my knowledge, their love for one another is real and their marriages are strong and they *still* haven't had an argument.)

Love walks on wounded feet. *Hatred* may, as well, and *cynicism*. The bruisings of life have the potential of either making us more *sensitive* to others and *appreciative* of their tender uniqueness, or *hardening* us to others entirely; they cannot leave us the same as we were. They may be our entry point into deeper understanding of God's ways with the human spirit, if we allow them, or they may move us to curse the day we were born. But those who love deeply and stubbornly are those who understand what it means to be rejected, abandoned, despised, but who by the grace of God are not embittered but are made whole. Just as they were walking back from Jerusalem and its ugly Golgotha to Emmaus and its bleak hopelessness, the two disciples felt closer to *defeat* than *redemption*. The wounds of Calvary looked to them very much more like God's *curse* than God's *anointing*, more like God's *failure* than God's *plan*. How could God be with a *criminal*? How could God love a man on a *cross*? How could *Jesus* have been the one to redeem Israel?

Love walks on wounded feet. On November 14, 1940, a German bombing raid on an English industrial area north and west of London resulted in the destruction not only of *military* targets, but *civilian*, not only *manufacturing* installations, but centers of *community life*. Among the towns targeted was Coventry, and among the buildings left in ruins was the Anglican cathedral. Ironically, according to my dictionary, for almost three hundred years *prior* to the bombing, since the days when the town was a center of Roundhead sympathies during the English civil war, the name "Coventry" had been synonymous in England with banishment or exclusion from society—ostracism, rejection, abandonment. Shortly *after* the bombing raid, someone made a cross out of the remains of the timbers that had supported the roof of the cathedral and set the cross in the blackened chancel and wrote on the cross the words, "Father, forgive."

Love walks on wounded feet. A child grows into adolescence and moves out of the house and for the first time begins to be involved in drugs and promiscuity, and awakens from a binge one morning to discover that the party is over—the money is spent and the charity agencies are closed. The child decides to go back home to plead for forgiveness knowing that none is deserved, but an anxious parent who never quit loving but increased in love with every distressing report of the child's irresponsibility, seeing from the window the child walking hesitantly toward the door, runs out of the house with arms open and with kisses to bestow. Or one spouse is unfaithful to the devoted other spouse, despite all the sacrifices small and great of many years of marriage, and goes out to spend lavishly on a new lover, or paramour, rather, so that there is never enough time to do things around the home anymore, never enough money to purchase little niceties for the family anymore. And one day the *faithful* one, having become aware of the infidelity, has finally had *enough* worry and hurt, and forsaking any concern about pride and shame, goes searching for the wayward one, and finding the one who deserves no mercy, says, nevertheless, "It is time to come home to those who love you best."

Love walks on wounded feet. The Savior of the world listened quietly as he walked alongside two people who were downcast and devoid of hope, attending to their recounting of his own crucifixion and the despair even of reports that his tomb had been found empty. Still bearing the marks of the nails, he taught them how their own scriptures bore witness that the Messiah must suffer, and when they invited the Christ whom they did not recognize into their house for dinner and "he was at table with them, he took bread, blessed and broke it, and gave it to them," as he had done on the night before his arrest and his scourging and his crucifixion and as he had doubtless done on many occasions previously, and "their eyes were opened, and they recognized him" (24:30–31).

Love walks on wounded feet. Peter, the "Rock," had slept through Jesus' hour of fear and had run from Jesus' trial and had hidden himself from Jesus' cross, but then Jesus had appeared to him after the resurrection. And it is to this *same* Peter, whose slumber and denial and disloyalty must have hurt Jesus to the quick, that these words of scripture are attributed: "You know that you were ransomed from the futile ways inherited from your ancestors, not with perishable things like silver or gold, but with the precious blood of Christ, like that of a lamb without defect or blemish" (1 Pet 1:18-19). "Therefore let the entire house of Israel know with certainty that God has made him both Lord and Messiah, this Jesus whom you crucified" (Acts 2:36)—and whom *he, Peter,* once abandoned, but whom *also* God's love had redeemed from faithlessness and fear and shame.

Surely, the two disciples assumed, God's love would have protected the Messiah from *any* harm, certainly from any humiliation such as the *cross*. But, then, what victory could there have been over the grave? What vindication could there have been over the world's hatred? What vanquishing could there have been of sin and evil? What value would we be able to give to hope? Like faith itself, love is not made strong in times of harmony and pleasure. Love is not remarkable when it requires no sacrifice to find its depth. Love remains a question mark until its loyalty is tested, until its purity is tried. It is the wounded ones—still bearing the marks of the nails, or still remembering the grief of thinking that all hope was dead in God's *abandonment* of the good and the righteous and the true, but then having experienced the power of the resurrection and the joy of genuine hope—*they* are the ones who most understand, and best embody, love.

And so God, cut to the core of the great divine heart on Good Friday by human hatred and prodigality and infidelity and disloyalty, loved us so much that he raised up Jesus from the dead so that we might know the measure of his forgiveness, and have salvation to eternal life. "Oh, how foolish you are," said Jesus to the two disciples, "and how slow of heart to believe all that the prophets have declared! Was it not necessary that the Messiah should suffer these things and then enter into his glory?" (Luke 24:25-26). For love walks on wounded feet.

Fourth Sunday of Easter
April 21, 2002
Spanish Springs Presbyterian Church, Sparks, Nevada
ACTS 2:42–47
1 PETER 2:19–25
JOHN 10:1–10

"The Open Door"

EVERY NOW AND THEN, I have occasion to go in and eat at the Nugget here in Sparks. I usually park in the big open lot west of the hotel, because it is so much easier to get in and out of than the parking garage. I don't at all mind the walk, which takes me past the sculpture of a shepherd (Basque, I am sure) picking up a lamb, and a dog at his heels, there at the corner of Nugget Avenue and Fourteenth Street. It always reminds me of my early childhood in Utah, when, driving through the mountains east of Salt Lake City en route to Wyoming or Colorado, we would invariably see a sheepherder's wagon off away on the side of a hill, and we knew to expect soon thereafter that we would need to come to a stop on the highway as sheep were being herded down it or across it by the sheepherder and his dogs. One of the biggest changes I've noticed between those days back in the fifties and my recent trips across Utah since we moved to Sparks a few years ago is the *decline* in the number of such wagons, and the virtual *disappearance* of the flocks from the hillsides and roadways.

Today's youth don't have many opportunities to see sheepherders at work in modern Western culture. But Mr. Ascuaga, the owner of the Nugget, has provided us with an engaging reminder of the tender bond that linked the human caretaker and the gentle beast, an animal not known for its intelligence in making good choices for *itself*, a creature that is liable to follow its appetite right over a cliff, an innocent whose bleating awkwardness makes it an easy target for predators. And, as such, he has also provided us with a picture of the watchful affection that the image of shepherd is meant to convey at so many places in the Bible—an image that has passed from our daily experience in twenty-first-century America but was so commonly visible in first-century Palestine. The greatest heroes of the Old Testament were shepherds—Moses, who tended the flocks of his father-in-law, Jethro, and David, the little son of Jesse who grew up to fulfill God's choice to be king of Israel, shepherd of God's specially chosen flock—and, in the New Testament, Jesus himself, who described his own ministry and his followers in terms of shepherd and sheep, and remained faithful to *his* task where Moses hesitated and David stumbled.

Like a shepherd, Jesus regarded himself as responsible for the welfare and safekeeping of those who recognized his voice of love and care and authority and dependability. In a very real sense, he himself was the door by which those who responded to his voice entered into the enclosure where the flock was kept safe from the dangers of the night, and he himself was the door by which those who were entrusted to his care came back out into the world, as well as the one who watched over them as they grazed, to make sure that they remained safe from harm. Anyone who did not enter the sheepfold by way of the gate, but climbed over the wall, was obviously there only to do mischief—to steal and kill and destroy. Anyone who claimed a *different* way into the sheepfold, a *different* way to safety, a *different* way back out into the goodness of what the world had to offer, was bound to lead them astray, at best, and determined to *scatter* the flock and *destroy* the sheep, at worst. Half of the tenth chapter of John is devoted to Jesus' words on the subject.

Just who these people were who played such an illegitimate and destructive role, we can only surmise from the rest of the Gospel. But we have a strong hint. Jesus' words in chapter 10 follow immediately the incident in chapter 9 in which Jesus, one sabbath day, restored sight to a man born blind and forced to beg for a living. The Pharisees—the self-appointed guardians of the law—were furious at what Jesus had done, and tried to get the man who had been cured to *denounce* Jesus as a *sinner* for working such a merciful miracle on the sabbath for someone whom the *good* people thought was justly deserving of blindness. They were *sure* that the blind man was a sinner, or his parents were, and so it was *blasphemy* to *cure* him, whether on the *sabbath* or *not*. When Jesus heard that they had thrown the man out of the synagogue, he sought him out and declared that it was the self-righteous Pharisees *themselves* who were *spiritually* blind. They *saw*, but they didn't *comprehend*. They listened to Jesus' words in order to try to trap him in some heretical statement, but they never heard the *gracious* words of God's saving love. The man, who could only hear, not see, when Jesus first approached him, responded to the words of Jesus' voice by saying, "'Lord, I believe.' And he worshiped him" (John 10:38). And it was to the *Pharisees*—the ones who had judged the man's blindness as having to do with sin, and had been critical of Jesus' broad and urgent message that constituted a judgment upon *spiritual* blindness—that Jesus went on to say that he was not only the *shepherd* of those who hear and respond to his voice, but the gate into the fold, the way to salvation. *He* is the door. Not, in other words, the law. Not, in other words, denial of forgiveness. Not, in other words, any claim of privilege as guardians of purity, but only by answering Christ's call, which means recognizing our common failings, our shared waywardness, our mutual sinfulness, and the need for *all* of us to repent and seek the living water that flows from Jesus Christ, God's fountain of forgiveness. And Jesus' words about his being the gate through which the sheep enter, about his being a good shepherd who will lay down his life for his sheep, are the last teachings that Jesus gave in public.

You don't brand sheep. And in the days before they began tagging their ears, on the hills and in the pastures of Utah and Nevada and elsewhere, the identity of the flock was known by which sheepherder they followed. Just so, the identity of *Jesus'* flock is determined by the *shepherd's* relationship to the *sheep* and *their* relationship to the *shepherd*. The flock that gathers around Jesus—the community of faithful people who hear and respond to his voice—receive their identity through Jesus' gift of his own life for them. To be a member of *Jesus'* flock is to know oneself as being among those for whom Jesus was willing to die. Who the *church* is cannot be separated from who *Jesus* is. Who *Jesus* is determines, for those who hear and answer his voice, what the *flock* is like—what it does, how it manifests itself to the world. Jesus manifested *his identity* to the world through his unlimited care, his merciful love, his willing sacrifice. That means that the identity of the *flock*—the clear expression of the one to whom the flock *belongs*—will be found in those *same* characteristics of care and love and sacrifice, unlimited, merciful, willing and not coerced. It will be a testimony to *life*, as Jesus came to *give* life, and God *vindicated* his life by raising him from the dead to life eternal.

But the Pharisees tried to destroy life and to destroy the community to whom Jesus *imparted* life, by driving out one of whom they disapproved, one whom they had judged to be a sinner, one whom they decided no person of God may love and forgive. In essence, they assumed for *themselves* the role of the door, usurping the identity of Jesus, which had been ordained by God, and shutting the door firmly even against one who had heard and recognized Jesus' voice, one of Jesus' own flock, known as such not because he was perfect in every way, but because he believed in Jesus and worshiped him. Later, even many in the early *church* tried to close the door against some who heard and recognized Jesus' voice as the voice of *their* shepherd, but who happened to be *Gentiles*; Pharisaic zeal for purity had infected some Christians and rendered them spiritually blind, so that their identity was no longer based on the character of the Shepherd. Jesus is the door, and Jesus is an *open* door, the entryway into the community of believers who receive their identity from him, and a door that is never closed to anyone. "When he was abused, he did not return abuse; when he suffered, he did not threaten; but he entrusted himself to the one who judges justly. He himself bore our sins in his body on the cross, so that, free from sins, we might live for righteousness" (1 Pet 2:23-24). Our righteousness comes through *him*, not through our own credentials of law-keeping, certainly not through any belief that we have no *need* for repentance. It is by his wounds that we are healed, not by our own doing. And to the degree that anyone thinks his or her own goodness and righteousness are the door into God's kingdom, they are going astray like sheep. *Jesus Christ* is the shepherd and guardian of our souls.

The believers in the very first weeks and months and years of the church were daily experiencing, learning and teaching, what it meant that Jesus himself was the entryway into the sheepfold, into the community of Christ's own. So many attitudes had to be changed. So many ideologies had to be set aside. So many truisms had to be unlearned so that the believers could find their identity in Christ and be known accurately by the world as his sheep. Their identity was made *un*true within, and *mis*represented without, any time there emerged in the church a spirit that was not compassionate, that was not loving, that was not forgiving, that was selfish, that was exclusionist, that was coercive. They recognized their identity not just in being Jesus' *sheep*, but in being Jesus' *flock*—not, that is, as so many individuals, each claiming his or her own place, but as the group which was called together in a common fold. "All who believed were together and had all things in common" (Acts 2:44). Together, "they devoted themselves to the apostles' teaching and fellowship, to the breaking of bread and the prayers" (2:42). Together, they witnessed the awe-producing wonders and signs that were done by the apostles. Together, they recognized a common destiny, even selling their possessions and goods and distributing the proceeds to all, as any had need. Together, day by day, they spent much time in the temple and broke bread in their homes and ate their food with glad and generous hearts, praising God and gaining the good will of the people who saw what they were doing. "And day by day the Lord added to their number those who were being saved" (2:47b)—those, in other words, who heard and recognized Jesus' voice through the teaching and ministry of the apostles and the other believers and found the doorway open, not closed, into the church and the life of gracious love and acceptance and sharing and caring that they found there, and that *they*, then, freely offered to *others*. A spirit of generosity, a spirit of welcome, a spirit of awe, a spirit of oneness—long before doctrine was defined, long before polity was adopted, long before any observer could have charged the church with hypocrisy of any sort, the flock that found its identity in Jesus the Good Shepherd demonstrated its identity to the world with an open door, who was Jesus himself. The test for admission to the fold was simply the response of the beggar whose blindness had been removed—"Lord, I believe" (John 9:38), and he worshiped Jesus—even in the midst of those who made a profession of closing doors to just such people—"'You were born entirely in sins, and are you trying to teach *us*?' And they drove him out" (9:34).

Jesus, the gate of the sheep, is the open door, never closed to those who respond to his voice. The church, whose only *true* identity is in *him*, must be characterized by the same traits as the Shepherd. That does not mean to be without standards, but to remember that those standards are all about profound care and love and sacrifice, genuine generosity and forgiveness and hospitality. That does not mean to be undiscriminating, but to remember that what we are to *shun* is the voice of those who would scatter, divide, destroy any or all of the flock. That does not mean that any and all roads lead to salvation, but it *does* mean that we are to give witness that *our* salvation is in Jesus Christ *alone*, *his* life and *his* death and *his* resurrection, *not* in *our* knowledge, *not* in *our* successes, *not* in *our* righteousness.

Once upon a time, a blind beggar who had nothing to commend himself to God or to humankind was touched by the merciful love of Jesus Christ that reached beyond any human assessment of his sinfulness or his worthiness and discovered that the door that he had been told all his life was *closed* to him was in fact *wide open*. And those who made a habit of closing doors to others suddenly found that they had shut themselves *out* of the fold, found that they had excluded themselves from the flock by their own attitudes, by their own actions, by their own claims of deciding who was in and who was out. Jesus Christ is the door, none other, and the door is open to all who hear his voice. "'Very truly, I tell you, I am the gate for the sheep. All who came before me are thieves and bandits; but the sheep did not listen to *them*. I am the gate. Whoever enters by me will be saved, and will come in and go out and find pasture. The thief comes only to steal and kill and destroy. *I* came that they may have *life*, and have it *abundantly*'" (10:7–10). "All who believed were together and had all things in common; they would sell their possessions and goods and distribute the proceeds to all, as any had need. Day by day, as they spent much time together in the temple, they broke bread at home and ate their food with glad and generous hearts, praising God and having the good will of all the people. And day by day the Lord added to their number those who were being saved" (Acts 2:44–47).

Fifth Sunday of Easter
First Presbyterian Church, Dodge City, Kansas
May 9, 1993
ACTS 7:55-60
1 PETER 2:2-10
JOHN 14:1-14

"The Way of Forgiveness"

THIS MORNING'S READING FROM Acts recounts one of the great injustices of history, close behind the injustice of Jesus' crucifixion. Yes, Stephen's sermon was provocative, rather like Jesus' speech at the synagogue in Nazareth, threatening the established order, alarming those who had grown comfortable in the thought that God was confined to a building made of stone and that the kingdom was only a remote possibility. But though provocative, and certainly undiplomatic, Stephen's words were true—the people of Israel *had* proved themselves to be a stiff-necked people, piously sacrificing to God in the temple and then oppressing widows and orphans in the streets, who had written a history of persecuting their prophets who called for justice and equity, and killing those who announced the coming of the Righteous One. In the case of the Righteous One himself, Jesus, the residents of Nazareth tried to throw him headlong over a cliff, but he escaped the mob. Stephen, however, will always be remembered as the first Christian martyr, stoned to death as a young man named Saul watched approvingly. And as Jesus, the preacher of forgiveness, having finally fallen into the hands of the authorities at Jerusalem, looked down from the cross upon those responsible for his torture and execution, and prayed, "'Father, forgive them; for they do not know what they are doing'" (Luke 23:34), so *Stephen* cried out above the shouts of insult and hatred and the thud of rocks upon his flesh, "'Lord, do not hold this sin against them.' When he had said this, he died" (Acts

7:60b). The followers of Jesus, Luke seems to be saying, not only *live* like Jesus, but even *die* like Jesus, praying for God's mercy upon those who have done them wrong.

First Peter was written to give hope and encouragement to Christians in northern Asia Minor as they faced persecution for their faith. Whether they had heard about the death of a disciple named Stephen, we do not know, but surely they had heard reports of the remarkable things Jesus had said while he hung from the cross. These Christians were mainly Gentiles, for whom the notion of a savior executed by the authority of the law would have been a great scandal indeed—a stumbling block of major proportions. But in our own time and place, as well, the cross— the reminder of God's Son having been ridiculed, spat upon, cursed even, and tortured and executed between two criminals—is an affront to some, particularly when they learn that *they* are to follow obediently the way of the cross *themselves*. Humility and meekness, willingness to bear unjustified reproach and acquiesce even to punishment based upon false reports, is hardly the standard of character that most of us honor or the measure of virtue that most of us teach. And forgiveness of those who wrong us is certainly not the practice that we all follow. But in *God's* estimation, that is *deep courage* and *high valor*.

We sometimes suppose that Jesus was a man who was misunderstood by the authorities; else, how could they have put such a good man to death? Surely, Pilate and the Sanhedrin were in grave error about Jesus, letting themselves give credit to whispered gossip that he planned to tear down the temple and overthrow the government. Actually, Pilate and the Sanhedrin perceived much more deeply than *most* of the people in the *streets* the significance of Jesus. The truth is that Jesus wasn't crucified because of false rumors, any more than Stephen was stoned because he was preaching lies. Jesus was crucified, and Stephen was stoned to death, because those in authority could not bear to hear the truth about themselves and about God. Jesus and Stephen were killed because they dared to declare before people who considered themselves to be "good," even "righteous," that their sacred values were upside down and their pious behavior was self-serving and their holy legalism was idolatry and their divine worship ignored the reality of the living God. And many of the good Gentiles of Asia Minor stumbled at the gospel the Christians proclaimed and decided it was best to silence such disturbers of the status quo, just as many of the good Jews of Palestine had stumbled at the truth of Jesus' teachings and had stumbled at the truth of Stephen's preaching.

Almost any minister can list instances in which the truth proclaimed by Jesus Christ and passed on by his apostles has been a stumbling block for individuals—even for the minister her- or himself, if the minister is honest about it. And of those teachings and qualities of Jesus that people find difficult to model, and which perhaps constitute a stumbling block even to professing faith in Christ, the *most* difficult, in my pastoral experience, is forgiveness. "You mean I have to forgive . . . ?" Fill in the blank, anywhere from Judas Iscariot to Adolph Hitler to Al-Qaeda to an ex-spouse to the drunk driver who killed one's child. "You mean I have to forgive?" The status quo has become familiar and comfortable—the person's world has been arranged to accommodate or even revolve around hatred and resentment over old wounds. And the would-be follower of Christ shakes his or her head and mutters, "But I just can't do that." Some people genuinely *want* to be like Christ, to forgive generously and completely, but cannot seem to, despite years of trying. Others proudly wear their *refusal* to forgive as a badge of honor, presuming it to be a mark of character—"I don't care what the Bible says, I'm certainly not about to forgive so-and-so for whatever."

"I just hope he suffers half as much as he made my Jimmy suffer," the camera sometimes catches the words of a victim's parent or spouse outside the courtroom. "I just hope that whoever is responsible for this burns in the hottest corner of hell," a British commander said a few years ago, looking at the aftermath of the carnage inflicted upon a defenseless town in Bosnia. Too often, the inability to *forgive* infects entire populations, even when the original bloody wrong dates back generations or centuries, so that reason takes flight and *revenge* becomes life's motive—that is what happened in Yugoslavia, apparently; that is what happened in Armenia; that is what happened on both sides of the endless conflicts in Northern Ireland and is happening in the Holy Land. Forgiveness in such cases must be monumentally difficult. But for *most* of us who say, "I don't care what the Bible says," or "I just can't bring myself to forgive no matter how hard I try," we are responding to a hurt or insult *far* less consequential than manslaughter or genocide.

The effect of harboring and nurturing deep hatred over some past wrong is as devastating to our soul as if *we* had murdered God's messenger of forgiveness. The pain of the stones bruising his flesh and crushing his bones was surely Satan's temptation to Stephen to die with bitterness in his heart and curses on his lips, but, visited by the Holy Spirit, Stephen lifted up his eyes and saw the glory of God and Jesus standing at the right hand of God, and instead of yielding to the bitterness and curses, he prayed, "'Lord Jesus, receive my spirit. . . . Lord, do not hold this sin against them.' When he had said this, he died" (7:59b, 60b). That is how the followers of *Christ* receive blows and insults, even those that threaten death. Stephen's words were not words of fear, but of trust; his prayer was not one of reproach, but of gentleness; his petition was not a sign of suicidal indifference or weakness of character, but a mark of spiritual discipline and profound courage.

That is a hard teaching, a stumbling block for many, especially those who experience persecution at the hands of stubborn unbelievers or at the hands of self-righteous believers. And yet, if Jesus *is* our way, our truth, and our life, then *his* way of *forgiveness* must be *our* way, as well. And the church, of all places, must be the institution in which forgiveness is practiced most vigorously. But do you know that there are still Presbyterians who, thirty-some years after the fact, will not forgive their denomination and its leaders for providing money for the defense of Angela Davis, but continue to punish the church by casting insinuation and withholding their offering? Do you know that there are people in congregations who remain bitter over some hurt or insult committed thirty, forty, fifty years ago, and purposely transmit gossip and withhold their attendance? Do you know that in many churches there are people who call themselves by the name of Christ, but who refuse even to speak to each other because of matters as momentous as the choice of the color of carpet in the church parlor? O Christians, it is past time to let such bitterness go and to cauterize the wound! How can anyone honestly be a child of the God who promises forgiveness of sin and has forgiven even *our* great sins, or be an ambassador of the Christ who taught forgiveness without limit and forgave even those who crucified him and those who abandoned him in his hour of need, while cultivating the noxious weeds of bitter resentment in the soul? How long shall Christians whip the body of Christ for something that the church or someone in it has done with which they disagree? How long shall we withhold our Christian love and fellowship from a brother or sister who once said or did something, something mildly insensitive or even something deeply hurtful? How long shall we weight our soul with the dull lead of resentment and infect our spirit with the lethal germs of hatred? The time it takes even to ask the question is too long. Yet while the stones are *striking* us, yet while the nails are being driven into our *hands* and our *feet*, should not the words of forgiveness be spoken from our lips and the emotion of love be flowing from our heart?

If our desire is to be *God's* people—to live up to our calling as "a chosen race, a royal priesthood, a holy nation" (1 Pet 2:9),—those of us who have heard the words and seen the works of Christ must acknowledge that he is our only way to our destination. And *he* spoke words of peace and hope and forgiveness, and if his *words* are not enough to convince us of the truth that he is the way, that we must be peacemakers, that we must be hopeful, that we must forgive, then surely we must be convinced by his *works* of peace and hope and forgiveness. He forgave even those who rejected him, who ridiculed him, who tortured him, who crucified him. And the trusting words and merciful works of Stephen, the first Christian martyr, prove Jesus' promise that "the one who believes in me will also do the works that I do and, in fact, will do greater works than these, because I am going to the Father" (John 14:12).

Is forgiveness a stumbling block for you?—something that you can scarcely believe is expected of you, something that you cannot seem to bring yourself to do? Jesus said, "I will do whatever you ask in my name, so that the Father may be glorified in the Son" (14:13). Have you prayed in Jesus' name, asking God to forgive, and to help *you* forgive? The testimony of Acts reminds us modern practitioners of polite, civil, legally-protected, and well-respected Christianity that once there were followers of Christ who joyfully parted with their possessions, their family, their friends, even life itself, some of them, in order to remain faithful, and who counted Jesus' command to *forgive* as more important than pride or reputation. We must permit the prayer of forgiveness to become the pattern of a forgiving life; it is possible to bring the most powerful passions of self-preservation and hatred under the sovereign rule of the spirit; it is possible, gazing into heaven and seeing the glory of God, and Jesus standing at the right hand of God, to resist the impulse to vengeance, and to purge the soul of bitterness. Jesus is the very picture, the very essence, of God. He who forgave so freely and so quickly said, "I am the way, and the truth, and the life" (14:6). "Very truly, I tell you, the one who believes in me will also do the works that I do and, in fact, will do greater works than these, because I am going to the Father" (14:12). What great works of forgiveness is Jesus calling *you* to do?

Sixth Sunday of Easter
Spanish Springs Presbyterian Church, Sparks, Nevada
April 17, 2008
ACTS 17:22-31
1 PETER 3:13-22
JOHN 14:15-21

"... Who Made the World and Everything in It"

A SPECIES, MAJESTIC AND noble, edges close to extinction as the ice floes on which it makes its home and from which it hunts for food melt, leaving the Arctic Ocean a vast expanse of open water incapable any longer of supporting the polar bear. Densely populated coastlands in Bangladesh and island nations in the Pacific and Southeast Asia disappear under a rising sea level that inundates croplands and makes more fierce the human competition for food and living space. Weather patterns change, and rising temperatures tip the balance toward even worse drought, meaning more famine in Africa, already reeling from political upheaval related to scarcity. The cumulative effects of human economic activity wrap the planet in a brownish-gray haze while politicians first *deny* the problem, then say there's no evidence of *human* causes, then say that *other* nations must change *their* polluting ways before *we* change *ours*. Government scientists are muzzled or fired for trying to do their job of sounding the alarm, and when the attention of voters and consumers finally is awakened to the danger, the very corporations and whole industries which over the decades have spent many millions of dollars to prevent, soften, or ignore environmental regulations suddenly market themselves as saviors of the environment. And a large segment of the Christian church which has previously *denied* that the condition of the air and the water and the soil is *any* concern of the *believer*, recently makes headlines with its proclamation that it has decided God is now, after all, interested in the future of the planet that he created.

While, for decades, Presbyterians and other mainline churches have sought to call the followers of Christ to responsible stewardship of the earth, some have ridiculed us and other environmentally minded people of faith as being worshipers of nature—a charge not only *derogatory*, but *defamatory*. For how can *anyone* read the first two chapters of Genesis, the opening words of the Bible, and conclude that the world can be fouled with impunity? How can anyone read the opening words of the twenty-fourth psalm and conclude that any person or group of persons can claim to do with the earth as they wish and it not be anybody else's business? How can anyone read the Old Testament prophecies about sin devastating nature, or all nature joining in glorifying God, and think that preservation of lakes and mountains and forests is a sentimental pastime of atheists and secularists? How can anyone read Jesus' declaration of God's care even for the birds of the air and the lilies of the field and conclude that they are of no account? How can anyone learn that the *poor* are being disproportionately affected by pollution and global warming and not remember God's repeated insistence in scripture that the chief duty of governments and rulers and leaders is to care for the destitute and relieve the burdens of the oppressed?

Bald self-interest *should* be enough for people to be *concerned* enough about the environment to insist on a change of policy and embrace a change of habit. But *Christians*, of *all* people, should know that there is an even *better* reason than self-interest! That reason is the will of God, both written in the workings of nature itself and testified to in the words of holy scripture. And whether the climate change that is threatening species and devastating the poor is caused *totally* by hydrocarbon emissions or only made *worse* by hydrocarbon emissions, our attention to God's priorities surely obligates every Christian to respond to the crisis by *reducing* hydrocarbon emissions.

Wherever disdain for the environment and the people who are concerned about the environment comes from among some groups of Christians, such disdain does *not* come from the *Bible*, and it does *not* come from the *orthodox faith*. Many centuries ago, when Christianity was first spreading beyond Palestine into the parts of the Roman Empire that were steeped in Greek culture and Greek thought, the faith that arose from a Jewish sect who proclaimed that the Jewish prophecies had been fulfilled by a Jewish teacher from a Jewish village in the Jewish homeland found itself competing with the assertions and perspectives of Greek philosophy. And Greek philosophy was much centered around the conviction that the *world*, and all things *material*, even the *human body*, is inferior, crude, something to be regarded with contempt, something, indeed, from which to be *free*. It led, on one hand, to claims that whatever one does with one's body is morally irrelevant, and, on the other, to teachings that one should only pursue and be interested in things of the spirit, *ignoring* the needs of the flesh and other physical concerns.

When Paul the apostle stood in front of the Areopagus in Athens and spoke to the crowd gathered there for philosophical chitchat, he was addressing people whose interest in the well-being of the world—that is, air, soil, water, and the creatures dependent upon these things—was virtually nil. And yet, they were extremely religious, if one could judge by the gods enshrined in the statues and temples that filled the city. Their thoughtways were certainly alien to those of the Jews, who could not conceive of a spirit being separate from a physical body. The Jews reacted to the pagans who surrounded them by insisting that it was *God* who brought into being the waters and the land and the plants and the animals. Searching for a point of intellectual contact, Paul the Christian apostle said,

> The God who made the world and everything in it, he who is Lord of heaven and earth, does not live in shrines made by human hands, nor is he served by human hands, as though he needed anything, since he himself gives to all mortals life and breath and all things. From one ancestor he made all nations to inhabit the whole earth, and he allotted the times of their existence and the boundaries of the places where they would live, so that they would search for God and perhaps grope for him and find him—though indeed he is not far from each one of us. For "In him we live and move and have our being"; as even some of your own poets have said. (Acts 17:24-28)

Those of us who are in the Wednesday night adult class this spring learned this week about the Gnostics—a category of Christians who believed that salvation comes from supernatural knowledge rather than a faith that sees our salvation in Jesus' death on the cross. Imbued with the Greek dualism between spirit and matter, the Gnostics rejected the notion that God could truly have been in the flesh, or indeed that God would have had any active role in creating the world of material things or have any concern for it after it *was* created. That, apparently, is why some of Paul's audience "scoffed" (17:32) when he spoke of the resurrection of the dead; *they* thought that the goal of life was to be *free* of the body and its needs. Surely no divine being could promise resurrection! Surely no son of a divine being, after death, would appear again in bodily form! *Paul*, though, was saying that our bodies are important enough to *God* that they will be raised up from the *grave*—something that would have offended the Gnostics, for sure. The church judged their belief to be wrong, and rejected it as heresy. So, for instance, the Apostles' Creed affirms the creation of the earth by the God who is also at home in heaven, and affirms Jesus' physical birth, Jesus' physical suffering, Jesus' physical death, *and* the resurrection of the body.

God created the world, the Bible testifies, and said *yes* to it, called it good in each of its parts. If *God* judged the world to be *good*, should *we* not treat it *well*?—as the very place in which God is known and the very place in which God works salvation and the very place in which he is Lord, as well as in heaven? Paul encountered a culture that was "extremely religious" (17:22) and yet cared *nothing* for fellow human beings, really, because they had no sympathy for their physical condition, and cared nothing for the earth upon which their physical welfare depended, and ultimately were only interested in their own salvation, which they defined as separation from this world and everything in it. Isn't it interesting that John's Gospel, which uses many gnostic terms and images to deliver a very anti-gnostic message, says specifically that "God so loved *the world*"—not just the heavenly spiritual realm—"that he gave his only Son, so that *everyone* who believes in him"—not just people who have the right knowledge about the superiority of the spirit and the yuckiness of matter—"may not perish but have eternal life. Indeed, God did not send the Son into the world to condemn the world, but in order that the world might be saved through him" (John 3:16–17)? Not just a few elite *spirits*, but the *world*—the Greek word is "cosmos," certainly not a word that is restricted in meaning to human beings or *some* of them.

The world's fate and human salvation are wrapped up together in the New Testament. Does that not mean that people who believe that Jesus the Christ is the Son of God sent into the world to bring salvation to all creation bear responsibility for the well-being of the world as a whole and in each of its parts?—God's creation that even many *Christians* have participated in scarring, polluting, devegetating, poisoning, and now warming to the point of intensifying devastating storms, extending drought, melting polar and glacial ice, and inundating fields and villages, all to the detriment of the very people we are supposed to be caring for most especially? And for *what?*—largely ease and convenience, largely amusement and pleasure, largely increasing profit and competitive advantage. The *Bible* says, "The earth is the Lord's" (Ps 24:1). Surely the people of God must not treat it with contempt. Surely the people of God must cherish it. Surely the people of God must acknowledge that they will be judged for how they have or have not cared for it.

There are still Gnostics around today, or at least people who have much the same attitude. It was discouraging to hear a former church member once refer in conversation to "tree huggers" in a way that, in her mind, showed anyone who has concern for the environment is something other than a true "Christian." Well, she eventually decided that *we* weren't true Christians. First Peter advises, "Keep your conscience clear, so that, when you are maligned, those who abuse you for your good conduct in Christ may be put to shame" (1 Pet 4:16b). It is time clearly to acknowledge, as our confessions proclaim, that stewardship of the earth is a matter of good conduct in Christ, who cares about the well-being of the poor, who cares about the well-being of future generations, who taught that everything that exists comes ultimately from a loving and generous God, even the birds of the air and the lilies of the field, and that greed corrodes not only the individual soul but injures others, too—indeed, all of creation. It is time clearly to declare, as our confessions proclaim, that caring for the environment is too important to leave to people whose primary concern is getting votes or increasing stock prices. It is time clearly to insist, as our theology spells out, that the health of the environment is a concern of the God who recognizes no national boundaries and favors no single race and blesses no economic system, but judges them all according to their effect upon the most vulnerable and the least influential. It is time, *past* time, clearly to give witness, as the Bible does from beginning to end, that the one true God is the God who created us, our bodies as well as our souls, and created the whole world around us for our home and for the home of *all* creatures, great and small, rich and poor, American, European, African, Asian, Pacific Islander, and who must wonder, daily, whether we really believe it.

Ascension of the Lord
May 1, 2008
Spanish Springs Presbyterian Church, Sparks, Nevada
ACTS 1:1–11
EPHESIANS 1:15–23
LUKE 24:44–53

"Powerful Witnesses"

HAVE YOU EVER TAKEN your Bible and compared the endings of the four Gospels in our New Testament? It is an interesting exercise that helps us understand the special purpose that each of the evangelists had in mind when he wrote *his* version of the good news. Alone of the four Gospels, Luke *ends* where it *began*—in the temple at Jerusalem—which is probably no coincidence. Filled with faith, the disciples are praising and blessing God in the temple—something which, at the beginning of the Gospel, Zechariah, the temple priest and father of John the Baptist, could not do, for he was made mute for his unbelief. But the entire final chapter of Luke is richly suggestive of what Luke wanted us to understand about Jesus—that he was raised from the dead (the chapter begins with the women's discovery of the empty tomb); that his suffering and death fulfilled the scriptures (Jesus explained this to two disciples along the road to Emmaus, and then in his appearance to the eleven); that the disciples were *witnesses* to Christ's fulfillment of the scriptures; that the followers of Jesus are to proclaim repentance and forgiveness of sins to all nations; that Jesus clothes his followers with power to perform their task; and that God in Jesus Christ blesses those whom he sends out into the world. "Lifting up his hands, he blessed them. While he was blessing them, he withdrew from them and was carried up into heaven. And they worshiped him, and returned to Jerusalem with great joy; and they were continually in the temple blessing God" (Luke 24:50b–53). Saving, sending, and blessing—this is the work of God in Jesus Christ that Luke seems to want us especially to appreciate. From that theological platform, Luke then launches into the Acts of the Apostles, his account of how the followers of Jesus obeyed the instructions of their Lord and carried the gospel to every corner of the world.

The task continues today. A few years ago, I had the experience of meeting and hearing a Presbyterian missionary to Colombia by the name of Alice Winters. I was especially interested in what she had to say, because about thirty years ago, my father and I were in Colombia on business and had the opportunity of meeting the moderator of the General Assembly of the Presbyterian Church in Colombia. What Reverend Winters and, before her, the moderator, described closed, for me, the two-thousand-year gap between Christ's directions to his *first* disciples and where *we* stand as Christ's disciples today. It is no secret that the mainline church in Western Europe and English-speaking North America has lost much of its fervor. We have basically sound theology and we have orderly government, but where is our zeal? We read about the disciples worshiping Christ and returning to Jerusalem with great joy and going continually to the temple to bless God, and we can hardly recognize these people as our spiritual ancestors, or ourselves as their spiritual offspring. We go to church board meetings and committee meetings and want to do the business and leave, and so many times the name of Jesus Christ is not even *spoken* in our deliberations and the principles of *faith* are not even *acknowledged*. Many modern church members have no contact with their brothers and sisters in the congregation except for one hour on Sunday mornings, and *some*, apparently, find *that* to be too much. Praising God together in song is not an *optional* activity in scripture, but it seems to be *becoming* optional in many sanctuaries. Most of us are not only reluctant to speak of our faith to *strangers*, but even to fellow congregation members. Evangelism has become a job for the professional minister, we say, because she or he can do it better—or is it simply because we don't think that it should be expected of us? If sermons get too specific, we complain that the preacher is meddling in our personal affairs or crossing the line into politics. If someone asks us to pray out loud, we get flustered. If a team of Jehovah's Witnesses comes to our door, we can't answer their bizarre claims. And then we wonder why the mainline church is declining in membership and influence—why it is unable to hold the middle-aged and to attract the young.

This missionary who spoke to a group of which I was a part—and the same sort of story could be told by hundreds of other missionaries working in developing places—described Christians slogging through ankle- and knee-deep mud to bring their first fruits to the Lord, as the Bible says, singing and praying and listening to the Word read and preached through the whole night and cherishing the opportunity to receive the Lord's Supper. Joyful, these same people who live under the threat of political oppression and drug-lord assassination and deadly disease and rampant inflation; hopeful, these same people who can raise barely enough to survive; faithful, these same people who face every temptation to live only for themselves and only for the moment. Praise God for the Presbyterian Church in Colombia. Clearly, the power of the Holy Spirit is wonderfully at work as these believers share the gospel and enjoy the fellowship that is theirs in Jesus Christ. Clearly, Christ is head of the church in Colombia, and the church is Christ's body, and together they form a unity, so that Christ is manifesting his power and presence as Messiah in and through the church, and so is bringing to fulfillment the divine purpose of salvation, of uniting all things in him and presenting them to God the Father. What powerful witnesses these Colombian Presbyterians are! They are reminiscent of the *first* disciples, who, at the departure of Christ from their midst, were *not* dejected or down-cast, somber or restrained, but joyful and expectant. They did not look wistfully back to Galilee and to the life they knew before the threat of persecution and shunning by family and friends, but looked forward eagerly to the gift of the Holy Spirit. In the hope of power from on high, they joyfully blessed God in the temple. And when the Holy Spirit came at Pentecost, they were not disappointed. They went out, as Jesus had commanded, and they did amazing things. Grateful for what God had done for them, obedient to the Lord's command, they responded faithfully and joyfully in worship and in mission.

The first Christians, according to the scriptures, gave witness to their faith by telling of Christ's present power in and through the church. People came to belief in Jesus Christ not by hearing the doctrine of the virgin birth or learning the teachings of the Sermon on the Mount or reading about the miracles that Jesus did once upon a time, but by the miracles that were happening presently in and through the church— miracles of generosity, of healing, of forgiveness, of walls being torn down and bridges erected, of minds opened and hearts warmed. The church grew by attraction to what the Spirit was doing in and through the community of the faithful. It was dynamic—literally, endowed with power, as the resurrected Lord had promised—the same immeasurable power that God used to raise Jesus from the dead. Cynicism could not stand against such a power. Doubt and despair had no place. Phrases like "common sense tells us" or "we've never done it that way before" or "we tried that once and it didn't work" or "you'll never get people to agree to that"—phrases which may well be the unforgivable sin, blasphemy against the Holy Spirit—had not yet defeated people's expectations and destroyed their hopes. Creation was new again, and the horizons were unlimited, and the church confidently *proclaimed* the gospel in *word* and *demonstrated* the gospel in *deed*, and the church *grew* until it won over an emperor and his empire. These people dared to *act* upon their belief, attested in the story of the ascension, that Jesus Christ is the Lord and Master of *all* things, and they discovered that their belief was confirmed and substantiated by one experience after another. The power that Jesus promised was not just a theological proposition. It was the principal fact in their daily experience. And, precious as the stories of Jesus' earthly ministry became to them as they grew in faith, they never longed for the old days *before* the ascension, but woke each new day to the excitement of anticipation that the Holy Spirit was about to make something miraculous happen in their lives and in the lives of fellow believers and in their life together in the church. History entered a new era of mercy and compassion and sharing. The church became the most influential instrument for change that the world has ever known.

Ascension Day is the celebration not of Christ's going *away* to *abandon* the church, but of Christ's going *up* so that the church may be *empowered*, and that the followers of Christ in every age may take up the commission to be witnesses to the crucifixion and the resurrection, to look forward in expectancy to the new miracles that the Holy Spirit will work through their mouths and hands and feet, through their worship and prayer and study, through their ballots and bank accounts and perhaps, on occasion, even their picket lines. In Colombia and many other places of poverty and vulnerability, that experience of Ascension Day is as current as today's headline and as fresh as today's offering. Understanding and celebrating and proclaiming the ascension fuels a zeal that kindles faithful outreach.

Have I been too hard on the contemporary mainline church, of which we American Presbyterians are a part? Of course, not all is gloom. Miracles are happening *daily*, many of them written about in *Presbyterians*

Today, our denominational magazine. Some of them are happening here in our own congregation. The truth of the ascension has the power to transform the way we approach our daily vocations and avocations. The truth of the ascension has the power to transform our relationships with other people—including people who look and sound different from us. The truth of the ascension has the power to transform our relationship to our possessions. The truth of the ascension has the power to transform our view of our household and of the world.

Can our celebration of the truth of the ascension *tonight* create a more conscious dependence upon God and allegiance to Christ and expectation of the Holy Spirit? Much of this will only be known in retrospect. But it is really not our business to gauge each other's spiritual temperature, anyway. The point is for each one of us and all of us together as the church to worship God joyfully and be powerful witnesses to the lordship of Jesus Christ to the ends of the earth. Thank God that he is raising up powerful witnesses in the Presbyterian Church in Colombia. Thank God that he is raising up powerful witnesses in Spanish Springs Presbyterian Church in Sparks, Nevada.

Seventh Sunday of Easter
Spanish Springs Presbyterian Church, Sparks, Nevada
May 4, 2008
ACTS 1:6–14
1 PETER 4:12–14; 5:6–11
JOHN 17:1–11

"Nobody Said It Was Going to Be Easy"

> I have made your name known to those whom you gave me from the world. They were yours, and you gave them to me, and they have kept your word. Now they know that everything you have given me is from you; for the words that you gave to me I have given to them, and they have received them and know in truth that I came from you; and they have believed that you sent me. I am asking on their behalf; I am not asking on behalf of the world, but on behalf of those whom you gave me, because they are yours. All mine are yours, and yours are mine; and I have been glorified in them. And now I am no longer in the world, but they are in the world, and I am coming to you. Holy Father, protect them in your name that you have given me, so that they may be one, as we are one. (John 17:6–11)

THOSE WORDS THAT *JESUS* addressed to God in prayer on the night before the *crucifixion, John* passed on to the Christians *he* knew sixty or more years *later*. On the night before the crucifixion, they were important as a prayer for the unity and safety of disciples who would soon feel abandoned and fearful and confused, and *themselves* perhaps be the target of the Jewish priests and elders, in the wake of Jesus' arrest and execution. In the midst of persecution and contention in the early Christian church more than half a century after Good Friday, it was important to Jesus' followers who might wonder what it was they had gotten themselves into when they became members of his church to know that Jesus had foreseen their plight and had taken it up with God the very night before he died.

For the *original* disciples to hear Jesus' prayer, for his *later* followers to hear Jesus' prayer, was to be reminded of what being a follower of Jesus was really all about: "Father, the hour has come; glorify your Son so that the Son may glorify you, since you have given him authority over all people, to give eternal life to all whom you have given him. And this is eternal life, that they may know you, the only true God, and Jesus Christ whom you have sent" (17:1b–3). And, by their "knowing" God, and himself, Jesus did *not* mean simply that the disciples and his later followers would have *heard* about himself and the Father, would not simply have facts and quotations filed in their memory and poised on the tip of their tongue, but would have a deepening *participation* in God and in Christ. The goal is eternal life, which is a relationship with God that is only possible through *faith* in Jesus Christ. The purpose of Christ's coming was to reveal the God whom no one has ever seen. To "know" God is to accept the revelation of God in Christ and to be transformed by it. To "know" God is to accept the mission of being a sign of God's presence in the world. And therefore, for Christ's first disciples and his later followers to "know" God is to trigger the world's reaction against them, as the world reacted against Christ himself, who was the revelation of God.

Jesus prayed that God would protect his disciples who now had the task of carrying on the ministry that Jesus was relinquishing on the eve of his death, and safeguard them in the face of the dangers they would encounter in a world that was a realm of untruth and of opposition and resistance to the light of the Word that Jesus brought. And Jesus prayed that, even as they encountered the world's opposition, God would unite Jesus' disciples as one. *John* wanted *later* followers of Jesus who were *still* facing a world that was a realm of untruth and of opposition and resistance to the light of the Word that Jesus brought, that Jesus had prayed *also* for God to safeguard *them* and for God to keep *them* united.

That situation may seem like a far different time and place from our own involvement today in Christ's church. But if we think so, it only shows how far we have come in accommodating ourselves and Christ's church to the world that is still basically hostile to the gospel. I rather suppose that there are people here today who attend worship and other church functions, who have even joined the church, expecting a haven of peaceful retreat from the problems of the world and the troubles of humankind—the sort of church experience that seems to be promoted by Precious Moments knickknacks and Thomas Kinkade paintings. I don't suppose that any of us has ever seen a figurine of Christ feeding the hungry or forgiving a prostitute, or a painting of Christ eating with a trembling drug addict or embracing a withered AIDS victim. That sort of thing is not so charming to look at. I'm still a little bruised by the woman in another church who shook her head and chided me on her way out of the sanctuary for not having delivered a "nice Mother's Day sermon" rather than preaching on the power of the Holy Spirit to equip us to continue Christ's ministry. *That* Mother's Day, like *this* Mother's Day coming up, happened *also* to be *Pentecost*. I refrained from telling her that I could think of not one passage of scripture that shows us a mother behaving the way that greeting cards suggest our mothers should be remembered (including Mary, whom the neighbors surely would have gossiped about for having given birth less than nine months after her marriage).

The Bible does not envision, and the Christians of the New Testament did not experience, a church where one could check one's cares in the narthex or buy an hour of tranquility in exchange for a few dollars in the offering plate. The *Bible* is more *honest* than that. And the New Testament *church* was more honest than that. The peace that Jesus promised *his* disciples—peace not as the *world* gives peace, but as *Jesus* gives peace—was peace branded with the cross on which he died—a fate that many of his disciples, and many Christians in the time of John's Gospel, *shared*. To be a Christian, to be a member of Christ's church, was to be a *disciple*, not a *customer*; to be a *participant*, not an *audience*; to advocate an *alternative* to the world's priorities and values and manners, not to *succumb* to them. And that meant that, to be a Christian *was*, still *is*, a dangerous activity for which Jesus prayed God's protection.

Our Wednesday night class recently has been studying some of the writings of a North African theologian named Tertullian. He lived from the mid-second century through the first quarter of the third century, a period during which the Christian church was still illegal in the Roman Empire and still subject to persecution. Considered one of the theological giants of the ancient church, he was keenly aware of the hazard of living in a predominantly non-Christian culture. One of his most famous writings was on the subject of idolatry—not just how Christians should avoid *worshiping* idols, but how Christians must refrain from engaging in the business of making or selling wooden or metal figures of pagan gods, even though they themselves knew that they were not real.[1] By *engaging* in such business, they were promoting untruth, facilitating, in effect, the work of the devil. But Tertullian's writings call our attention to the larger question of just how cozy Christians should become with the means and goals of the culture around them, and its standards of success. As the Christian movement grew more mature, was it also losing its effectiveness as a prophetic witness and an evangelical voice? In order to gain *acceptance*, was it drifting *away* from the crucified and risen Christ? By being so *friendly* with the world, was it forgetting its assignment and losing the power to *transform* the world? Was it *saving* its *life* at the cost of *losing* its *soul*? Was being a Christian becoming too *easy*?

The mission of the church is to be a sign of God's presence in the world. Surely that involves a lot more than being a building of a certain shape at a particular street address. John's Gospel witnesses to a point in the history of the infant church when a vision of the world as it might be and the experience of one actual community of faith came together. It may seem strange to us to think that a congregation should have been considered blessed when it was conscious of being under the threat of persecution and struggling just to survive. A little more accommodation to the world, perhaps, and things would have been a whole lot easier. But, fortified by knowing that Jesus had *foreseen* their difficulties, had prayed for their safety *and* their unity in the midst of all kinds of forces of disintegration, they remained *faithful* to him, which is the *only* true and legitimate measure of *any* church's success.

Not far distant in time or circumstance, a letter written in the name of the apostle Peter—one of those very disciples for whom Jesus had prayed that final night at dinner—reached a group of Christian churches in Asia Minor, what is now Turkey, that was facing persecution for their faith. Whereas *John's Gospel* was written for Christians who were mainly *Jewish* in background, and who probably felt persecuted largely by orthodox, Torah-thumping Jews, *1 Peter* was written for *Gentile* Christians who had broken away from paganism and whose relatives and friends still sacrificed to the Roman gods and expected *them* to be good citizens by doing the *same*. Perhaps some of those same relatives and friends were turning them in to the authorities and seeing them arrested for not "going with the flow" by bowing to images of the Emperor Domitian and honoring him as a god. Very likely, the people addressed in 1 Peter had

---

1. See Tertullian, *On Idolatry*.

never heard of John's Gospel, and perhaps had not heard that Jesus had prayed for his followers who would face just such abuses as *they* were experiencing. But the *encouragement* was the *same*: "Beloved, do not be surprised at the fiery ordeal that is taking place among you to test you, as though something strange were happening to you. But rejoice insofar as you are sharing Christ's sufferings, so that you may also be glad and shout for joy when his glory is revealed. If you are reviled for the name of Christ, you are blessed, because the spirit of glory, which is the Spirit of God, is resting on you" (1 Pet 4:12–14). Is that the sort of blessing that most of us are expecting in *our* church experience?—to be reviled for the name of Christ (that is, being known as "Christian")? How did the church ever survive and grow, proclaiming such a message, declaring such a truth? Faith in Jesus Christ must have been stronger than a desire for nice music, nice prayers, and a nice sermon.

To be reconciled to *God* involves us in a life that is *un*reconciled with the ways of the *world*. Indeed, it is strange when Christians are *not* persecuted, if they are being faithful! The new life of the Christian should be at *odds* with the *old* life and a *rebuke* to *any* life not centered in God. As one commentator on 1 Peter puts it: "For Christians to be so safely conformed to the world and its course of living that they run into no trouble at all may [indicate] that they have denatured their way of life of its radical, world-judging and world-changing spirit."[2] In such case, Christ has been made a *footnote* to one's life instead of its radical *center*.

The faithful Christian does not *escape* suffering, but is assured of God's presence *in* suffering. Suffering for being faithful to Jesus Christ, for being identified as a Christian, takes on a profound meaning that sets it in the context of eternity—it means to be a companion of Christ, though always recognizing that Christ enters into *our* ordeal much more profoundly than we can enter into *his*. And *that* is to have our *suffering* transformed into *joy*, our *ordeal* transfigured into *glory*.

The real issue of Christian living, the real issue of the life of a Christian congregation, is faithfulness to Jesus Christ. There is no other standard by which we can be measured, and there is no other way to eternal life. And Jesus Christ said to his disciples, that same night when he prayed for their protection from harm and for their being kept together in unity, "The one who believes in me will also do the works that I do and, in fact, will do greater works than these" (John 14:12). But nobody said it was going to be easy.

---

2. Homrighausen, "First Epistle of Peter: Exposition," 143.

Appendix

THE WEEK OF PRAYER for Christian Unity is an annual eight-day ecumenical observance from January 18 through January 25, commemorating Christ's prayer that his church should be one. Featuring scripture passages selected by an international committee representing a broad range of Christian traditions, worship materials are provided through the Graymoor Ecumenical & Interreligious Institute. For the 1993 local observance in Dodge City, Kansas, where Dr. Taylor was pastor of the First Presbyterian Church, he was chosen to present the sermon for that year's interdenominational worship service held at the neighboring Roman Catholic church.

Week of Prayer for Christian Unity
Sacred Heart Catholic Church, Dodge City, Kansas
January 19, 1993
PSALM 133
GALATIANS 5:13–26
MATTHEW 18:1–7

"Bearing the Fruit of the Spirit"

The theme of this year's Week of Prayer for Christian Unity—"Bearing the Fruit of the Spirit"—is taken from Paul's letter to the Galatian Christians. When we read Paul's letters in the scriptures, we are inspired, we are uplifted, we are instructed, we are edified, we are encouraged, and, many times, we are frustrated—frustrated because we cannot be completely certain exactly what issues of faith and living Paul was writing about. We have only one half of the pastoral conversation between the apostle and these churches that he founded, and it is always hazardous to guess the questions he was answering or reconstruct the crisis he was hoping to resolve or diagnose the disorder he was trying to heal. In the case of the Galatians, some scholars suggest that Christians of Jewish background had raised a dispute about the necessity of circumcision among the Gentile Christians; others speculate that the real problem was false teachers who had encouraged a strain of irresponsible abandon among some of the congregations. It would be helpful to know the precise nature of the disagreement that Paul addressed, but that is beyond our ability. What is clear is that the specific issue which plagued the churches of Galatia was one that prompted Paul to write about the nature and proper exercise of Christian *freedom*, and what he said on the subject is still of inestimable value to Christians today.

"Freedom," like "love," is a word that means different things to different people. To a young child, "freedom" may mean the ability to stay up late when an indulgent babysitter is on duty rather than the child's parents. To a people long under oppressive rule, "freedom" may be the ability to place a simple telephone call without wondering whether the conversation will be monitored. It seems that some of the Galatian Christians assumed that "freedom" meant the right to follow one's own desires, whatever their source, and to scandalize others, whatever the result. Beautiful on the lips of prophets and apostles, the word had become ugly in the arrogant practice of Galatian church members, and the situation must have sickened Paul to the very core of his being. His own life had once been a straitjacket of rules, a prison built out of prejudice and pride, and now he knew the sweet taste and the true meaning of liberty, and he could not abide the thought that anyone should remain shackled in the chains of his or her own selfish desires or others' judgmental legalism. But neither could he permit anyone to blaspheme the Lord Jesus Christ by riding roughshod over ethical sensitivities, nor permit every sort of dishonorable behavior in the name of Christianity. Beyond the specific issue—whether it be the legalists demanding circumcision or the libertines debasing Christianity into a license for wicked immorality—Paul was alarmed at the ease with which the communities of faith in Galatia were succumbing to the satanic ways of competition and criticism, biting and devouring one another in the name of Christ. "You were called to freedom, brothers and sisters; only do not use your freedom as an opportunity for self-indulgence, but through *love* become slaves to one another" (Gal 5:13).

Slaves to one another? What sort of freedom is this? "'You shall love your neighbor as yourself'" (5:14b)—you must, Paul said to the Galatians, be creatively self-invested in each other's lives, not quarreling and dividing and presuming a monopoly on the truth, so that you are threatening to consume one another. "Live by the Spirit, I say, and do not gratify the desires of the flesh. . . . [And] the fruit of the Spirit is love, joy, peace, patience, kindness, generosity, faithfulness, gentleness, and self-control. . . . If we live by the Spirit, let us also be guided by the Spirit. Let us not become conceited, competing against one another, envying one another" (5:16, 22, 25–26). When the Spirit is present in a person's life, it leaves its indelible tracks in the way of love, gentleness, and self-control. Any other behavior—such as the enmity and strife and jealousy and anger and dissension that characterized the Galatian factions—was evidence enough for Paul that the Galatian Christians were anything but free, still slaves to the yearnings of the flesh, still ruled by ego and self-promotion, their spirits still imprisoned behind bars of pride and self-interest and pettiness, regardless the precise practices or accusations involved in their dispute.

In the heat of battle over principles, it is easy for minor details to take on gigantic proportions and make us slaves of self-interest. And ancient wrongs involving generations long dead are quickly resurrected as justification for today's hatreds. The whole complex of issues involved in the Middle East shows just how far pride can disengage reason when it comes to social relations. And some wonder whether pride has not disengaged reason on *both* sides of the Iraq crisis. Just as tragically as in political matters, pride, strife, jealousy, anger, factions, envy have left an embarrassing history in the church of Jesus Christ. Beyond his real concern for the Galatian Christians themselves, Paul must have wondered what sort of advertisement they were offering for Christianity—what sort of damage they were doing to the reputation of Jesus Christ and the Holy Spirit among nonbelievers in their neighborhood. Had the gospel been given to the Gentiles only to have Jesus Christ defamed by the bickering of his own followers, by their fleshly concerns of personal privilege and prideful self-assertion? Was this the sort of behavior that one could expect from the visitation of the Holy Spirit—hatred, contention, immorality? Perhaps the picture of Christianity in the sixteenth century and the face of Christianity today would be different had Paul still been alive to write such a letter as Galatians to the churches in Rome and Geneva and Canterbury.

You and I, by whatever other name we may call ourselves—Catholic, Presbyterian, United Methodist, Orthodox, Lutheran, Baptist, Episcopalian—have been directed first to call ourselves by the name "Christian." And that means to believe that Jesus Christ was and is the Son of God, speaking and acting with the authority of God, and that Jesus Christ has sent among those who believe in him and love him and genuinely seek to follow him the Holy Spirit of God to give every Christian the breath of eternal life. The words of Paul are as true for Christians in Dodge City, Kansas, today as they were for Christians in Galatia almost two thousand years ago: "Those who belong to Christ Jesus have *crucified* the flesh with its passions and desires. If we live by the Spirit, let us also be *guided* by the Spirit. Let us not become conceited, competing against one another, envying one another" (5:24–26). And the soul's penalty for acting in any way among ourselves that dishonors our Lord is the same today as it was when Jesus said: "If any of you put a stumbling block before one of these little ones who believe in me, it would be better for you if a great millstone were fastened around your neck and you were drowned in the depth of the sea" (Matt 18:6). "Truly I tell you, unless you change and become like children"—weak, flexible, innocent, guileless,—"you will never enter the kingdom of heaven" (18:3).

Ten centuries ago, issues considered to be of great theological import caused the one church of Jesus Christ to fall into dissension and division. *Five* centuries ago, the fragments multiplied. And the process continues today. Many of the old disagreements now seem so arcane as to be imperceptible to the twentieth-century mind. And yet the ancient distrust remains in many quarters, and pride and jealousy and even hatred have had long centuries to boil and fester. But the words of the apostle remind us today, as they first reminded Asian Christians in Paul's own time, that such characteristics can*not* be the fruit of the *Spirit*, but can only be the embarrassing works of the flesh. Stale legalisms have no place in the fresh air of the gospel. Selfish pagan passions of old are still to be recognized as selfish pagan passions having nothing to do with our freedom in Christ. We have erected great monuments to how our traditions have become self-perpetuating and self-justifying in our churchly capitals of Rome and Athens and Nashville and Louisville and a hundred other cities. It is time to bury old feuds with the generations that produced them. It is time to answer our Lord's prayer for unity among those who would follow him. It is time to cast aside division over nonessentials and recognize that *pride* has divided us much more deeply than beliefs. It is time to acknowledge by our attitudes and our words and our behavior that there remains *one* kingdom of God, and *one* Lord Jesus Christ and *one* Holy Spirit. And it is time to give witness that the fruit of the Spirit is love, joy, peace, patience, kindness, generosity, faithfulness, gentleness, and self-control. If we are truly of the *Spirit*, all people will know us by these traits, and we will be free of the *past* to be an honor to the Lord Jesus Christ *today*.

List of Sources Cited

Bonhoeffer, Dietrich. *The Cost of Discipleship*. Rev. ed. Translated by R. H. Fuller. New York: Collier, 1963.

Boring, M. Eugene. "The Gospel of Matthew." In *The New Interpreter's Bible*, vol. 8, edited by Leander E. Keck, 89–505. 12 vols. Nashville: Abingdon, 1995.

Brueggemann, Walter. *Genesis*. Interpretation. Atlanta: John Knox, 1982.

Buttrick, George A. "The Gospel according to St. Matthew, Exposition." In *The Interpreter's Bible*, vol. 7, edited by Nolan B. Harmon, 231–625. 12 vols. New York: Abingdon, 1951.

Chiusano, Mary. "The Way of Sorrow." In *Unite Our Hearts*, edited by Barbara Bridge, 28–31. Portland: Oregon Catholic Press, 2021.

Hilary of Poitiers. *On the Trinity*. In *Nicene and Post-Nicene Fathers*, vol. 9, edited by Philip Schaff and Henry Wace. Peabody, MA: Hendrickson, 2004.

Homrighausen, Elmer G. "The First Epistle of Peter: Exposition." In *The Interpreter's Bible*, vol. 12, edited by Nolan B. Harmon, 77–159. 12 vols. Nashville: Abingdon, 1957.

Kilpatrick, G. D. "The Book of Isaiah, Exposition." In *The Interpreter's Bible*, vol. 5, edited by Nolan B. Harmon, 165–773. 12 vols. New York: Abingdon, 1956.

Nouwen, Henri. *The Wounded Healer*. New York: Doubleday, 1972.

Olearius, Johannes. "Comfort, Comfort You My People." Translated by Catherine Winkworth (alt.). Hymn #3 in *The Presbyterian Hymnal*. Louisville: Westminster John Knox, 1990.

Rauschenbusch, Walter. *A Theology for the Social Gospel*. New York: Macmillan, 1917.

Tertullian. *The Apology*. In *Ante-Nicene Fathers*, vol. 3, edited by Alexander Roberts and James Donaldson. Peabody, MA: Hendrickson, 2004.

———. *On Idolatry*. In *Ante-Nicene Fathers*, vol. 3, edited by Alexander Roberts and James Donaldson. Peabody, MA: Hendrickson, 2004.

www.ingramcontent.com/pod-product-compliance
Lightning Source LLC
Chambersburg PA
CBHW060607230426
43670CB00011B/2010